# The Jennifer Tree:
## A Memoir of Grief and Love

## Julie Beadle

*Cover illustration: Adam Snowball*
*Cover design: Adam Snowball*
*Author Photo: Alina Hromko*

**ISBN: 978-1-927974-38-4**

© *2023, Julie Beadle*

All rights reserved. No part of this publication may be reproduced or transmitted in any form by any means, electronic or mechanical, including photocopying or scanning, recording, or any information storage and retrieval system, without permission in writing from the author of this book.

## Acknowledgements

I have been working on *The Jennifer Tree* for ten years. So many people have helped me on this journey.

I want to thank my writing groups: Prose and Cons as well as Just Write Orillia (under the expert and gentle guidance of Stephen Davids) for their critiques, friendship and emotional support during the writing of this book.

Later in the process I met Beverly Pearl. She has been instrumental in editing and publishing this memoir. Talented, insightful, kind, professional–I would have been unable to complete my story without her.

My aunt, Carol Waldock, has been editing what I write for years. She was in the book business for most of her working life so her expert advice and her love have always been appreciated.

And, of course, thanks to my lovely daughter Megan Beadle who has held my hand, cried with me, spurred me on always saying, "Dig deeper Mom. Don't be afraid to share your truth." She also did substantial edits and wrote the forward to the book. She is a wonderful writer in her own right.

Meg's husband, Adam Snowball is responsible for the book cover illustration and design of which I am so proud. It's almost as if Jennifer's soul is staring out of her blue eyes on the cover. Adam, thank you.

To my kids, their partners, and our grandchildren thanks for always encouraging me to share our story of grief and loss. What a wonderful, supportive, close family I have. It is your love that has allowed us to go on together.

Most of all thank you to my husband Rob. Without you in my life there would be no stories. You are endlessly supportive and always there for all of us. Your courage in allowing me to reveal so much to so many is admirable.

# Forward

*By Megan Beadle*

June 4, 2023

At first, when my mother asked me to help her edit the memoir she was writing about the loss of my sister, about the struggles in my mother's marriage, I considered saying no. It was too personal. How could I, her daughter—the daughter who lived—help develop and structure a book which I was so close to? A memoir by the woman who brought me into the world? Writing about the family I was a part of and a grief that I shared, albeit in a different way? I didn't think I was the woman for the job or that I could be partial or professional. I was worried it could be harmful for our relationship, this part-editor, part-counsellor, part-other-daughter role I did not know how to inhabit comfortably.

But she was struggling, and she was asking for help. She needed me. And, I had made a promise.

What my family does not know: my sister made me swear, unequivocally, three days before her death, that I wouldn't let us fall apart once she was gone.

We were in a bathroom together. She was sitting on the toilet seat, and I was standing holding her frail body as we both cried, my tears falling into her short tufts of brown hair. She remained upbeat and optimistic with everyone except, on rare occasions, with me, though I'm sure her husband saw this side of her too. Our pact: sisters never ever lie to each other. I was there for her final confession, as I had been for all her previous ones—whispered during sleepover parties, while holding hands and walking our cottage beach, over gab sessions between best sister-friends.

"I'm dying. Soon, Meggie," she said. "I thought maybe there was a miracle left for me, but there isn't, and

*Forward*

I'm okay with that, but I don't have much time." Not *I'm accidentally pregnant*, or *he was a jerk, anyway*, or *your hair looked better blonde*. These were the sorts of truths I'd come to expect.

You can find a million ways to deny the obvious when you want to. Chemo and radiation were to blame for her deteriorating health and weight. The doctors couldn't know for sure how much time she might have left. She was doing better than the specialists thought she would. She was fighting hard. She was in such high spirits.

We let everyone else hold onto hope for just a little while longer. She knew, I knew—she was never going to reach 38. My big sister was dying from 'the big C', cancer. Lung Cancer. She had never smoked a day in her life—was obsessed with dancing and health foods. Nonetheless, she wasn't going to survive.

It seemed impossible, a world where I existed but my gregarious older sister did not. It had seemed impossible when she'd developed lung cancer. Lung cancer is growing in young women who have no genetic markers for it, no history of substance-use to blame, who have never smoked. My sister was among them. After going to the emergency room with a vicious cough and what she thought might be pneumonia, she was shocked to discover there was a tumour the size of a baseball in her chest. Stage four cancer had already metastasized, spread like fungus up the trunk of a long-limbed tree, to her spine and brain and bones.

"You can mourn me later, Megs," she said. "But first you have to be strong and make sure our family is okay. Okay? Make sure Mom is okay. If Mom and Dad are alright, as long as they still have each other, everyone else will get through this. Don't let everything fall apart."

My older sister always had this unwavering belief in my ability to do anything. I couldn't admit how daunted,

## Forward

how completely insufficient I felt, in the face of her faith in me. This same belief, this idea my sister had that I could do anything, though encouraging, was also so expansive that I felt lost.

"I'll try," I said, having no idea what that promise would entail or how I would manage to follow through without her.

"Now my baby girl won't have me...", she trailed off. My niece, her 11-year-old daughter, Kaia.

"I'll be there," I said. "Always. I'll be the best damn aunt in the entire world. Her dad will be there. She's got a great dad. She has her uncles—and her grandparents. She will be smothered in love."

She nodded.

Faced with her impending mortality, my brave Jenny was still thinking about everyone else—so like my sister.

***

It was Valentine's Day, 1969. My parents met on a long-distance bus ride and fell instantly in love. Six months later they got hitched and moved to Africa. And over the years, on to Ivory Coast, Egypt, Jamaica, the Philippines, France, Ethiopia, Bangladesh—my father became a diplomat involved in aid work, my mother a teacher and librarian. They spread their optimism and passion in the hopes of making the world just a little bit better.

They had the sort of epic love story that becomes a daunting ideal. Like the title of Osa Johnson's world travel memoir, my mother would joke that she had *Married Adventure*. "Adventure," she'd say, "is your father's middle name." Through nine postings and four children, their love flourished. Their passion for world travel only dimmed in comparison to their love for each other and their children. They treated moving like they were ordering takeout from an exotic restaurant —"perhaps Egyptian this time around? Or maybe Thai?"

They held hands wherever they walked, could be found making out in dark corners, "necking" my mother would call it—fighting loudly and making up loudly, talking and consulting each other. There was a compassionate domestic soundtrack constantly humming in the background, best friends chatting about their day, the news, philosophy, their deepest thoughts.

I remember being at a dinner party in our home in Addis Ababa as a teenager, resentful of my invisibility to the other adults there and my parent's insistence I attend. With nothing better to do, I watched the two of them interact. They were talking to different groups of people, even across the room from each other. It was as if the connection between them was tangible and electric; they pivoted around each other's axes. Every fifteen minutes they would check in: my dad would wink, my mom would smile coyly. And then, they'd do something incredible. They would stare at each other and talk telepathically.

Dad: "I'll go talk to the Ambassador of Norway about the Clean Air Project, if you go entertain Jerry." Mom: "Got it. I'll tell him the story about the exploding cat so he'll stop thinking about his divorce."

Dad: "I love you."

Mom: "Love you, too."

I know because I questioned them, separately, before they ever had a chance to debrief about their tacit exchange. It was as if they had spoken aloud.

"How?!" I demanded an answer from my father. "After so many years together," Dad said, "it's just something we can do."

I watched the other adult couples curiously. None of them seemed to be x-men.

## *Forward*

Periodically, my parents would come back together. My dad would squeeze my mom's bum and my mom would give my dad a peck, and their quick exchange would create an aura of happiness. Then they'd part ways again. When they sat down to dinner, they'd play footsie under the table.

I came to the conclusion that it was magic. And rare magic, at that. It gave me faith that they could handle anything.

Until my sister died.

Death changes the people affected by it drastically. My family was no different. Together, and alone, we traversed a world of mourning.

Each one of us was struggling with grief. I was trying to be strong, but I was a complete mess. I had recently quit my job and ended my own eight-year relationship. I was deeply depressed, lost and unemployed. I had no idea how to help my siblings, my parents, my niece, and my sister's widow. Without my sister's sage advice, I didn't know how to help myself.

My brothers were overwhelmed and hurting. Jenny had been Dan's co-pilot on every adolescent adventure. Jen had been like a second mom to Andrew, old enough with seventeen years difference between them to help him navigate the world. Her own daughter, Kaia, fondly referring to Andrew as her *bruncle*, also known as a brother-slash-uncle.

My niece, Kaia, seemed the most resilient of us all, leaning on her incredible stepfather as they navigated the waters of her impending teenage years without a mom. But it had been just Mother and daughter, the two of them, for so long. Jenny's absence became a constant presence, her lack an ache in the hearts of Kaia and her stepfather, Michel, as they established their new two-member family. Michel requested full custody of Kaia, admitting to our

## Forward

family that he couldn't handle losing both his wife and his daughter. He had suffered enough heartbreak.

For Kaia, Michel was a saviour, but the agony would always mar her and leave her feeling different from her peers. "I have all of you raising me. I'll be okay," she'd say. That strength. It is impossible not to see that she is becoming a young woman all her own, but with a soul and heart so like my sister.

Michel, the love of my sister's life, still managed to navigate fatherhood with grace in the wake of widowhood. A deeply private man about his emotions with anyone who wasn't my sister, his tears, and the shrine he kept of her were clues, the tip of the iceberg, but his loss and grief were unimaginable.

My father's constant optimism, the echo of my sister's, was nowhere to be found. He sobbed, crying out in agony, while he slept. During the day he'd hide at the bottom of a bottle of wine, drinking himself into a stupor. He wished it had been him, that he could have changed places with her, spared her.

And my mother, my larger-than-life mother, could hardly function. She was angry at the world and in constant pain. She wrote about her past, about Africa, hiding there and checking out of her own life. Floundering herself, she had no patience for my father. I watched as my parents became strangers to each other, as the love that had been their touchstone all their lives began to crumble.

I had heard the stats about divorce after a child's death, read the articles on the controversy surrounding it. The fairy-tale that was my parents love story, however, had seemed unbreakable. As I watched them fight and push each other further and further away, I could no longer deny that they were struggling.

When my parents refused to get counselling for their grief or their marriage, I did the only thing I knew how to

## *Forward*

do: Tasked with keeping my family together, I encouraged my mother to not only write about Africa, but also her experiences with grief, her personal story, her past. Together, what we crafted was a reminder of how my parents had fallen madly in love. About their adventures together, and then about their daughter's death and their struggle with her loss. My mother's narrative was my father's story too, and it was fragmented into before, during and after Jenny.

\*\*\*

There are some things you should never know about your parents, and yet, there I was, dissecting an excruciatingly detailed account of their raucous lovemaking ensconced between scenes of passionate fights and raw, unbearable pain, as I edited the manuscript.

Occasionally, I felt like a bully, urging my mother to shine a light into the darkness, to lay her daughter's faults out for the world to see in raw honesty. Their relationship was, at times, strained. And I wonder if Jenny—the woman who would painstakingly cover every single zit and pimple, straighten or curl every wayward hair, put on a face of perfection before even her husband could see her—could ever forgive me for exhuming her ghost with her flaws drawn up so vividly. Her life was not easy: a first marriage to an alcoholic, an accidental pregnancy, a long stretch as a single mom with chronic illness. Despite all of it, she lived an incredible life focused on helping others.

To ignore these imperfections about Jenny would paint an incomplete picture of a real, beautifully complex person. It's brutal honesty that makes her pop off the page and come alive, pulls the reader into her aura of charisma until they are desperately in love and deeply distraught over her death, as we were. We have laid her bones bare. But I think Jenny would be okay with us exposing her life,

## Forward

her secrets, and fears and faults, if we are able to touch others in need of healing.

And so, each and every day, together, my mother and I worked on a book about Jenny. We resurrected her life in rich detail on the page. It was not easy on our relationship, this mother/daughter/editor relationship: I pushed and pulled, I knew too much, we argued, we remembered difficult memories, we fought, we sobbed and hugged when we discovered the words that fit. It was something akin to the regular editorial process, but even more invasive and personal. The author is, after all, my mother. Where my sister was so like my father (so much so, that they oftentimes drove each other crazy, which left my mother perplexed). I am very much my mother's daughter. I sometimes hear her thoughts before she types them. We speak the same way, our hands pulling words from the air, with passionate and wild gesticulations. We know each other outside the stories at the core of the family we are a part of, know the details that seemed irrelevant, or the colourful tidbit that didn't fit quite right, or the living breathing aspects of the woman Jenny was that are not possible to capture in print.

More than anything, the writing process was cathartic. I have watched my mom remember who she was before she had Jenny, before she was a mother. For so long, motherhood dominated her understanding of her own life's purpose; but who she is now, the fiery backbone of our family, is something so much more than one facet. She cannot be encompassed. This book became her therapy—as she wrote, she healed. And I was able to help, to be there, the way I promised Jenny I would be.

My parents have started to reach for each other's hands on their daily walk again. Though I will let the memoir tell you about their journey, individually they have fallen in love anew with the people they are now becoming—

reconstituted in the wake of losing a child. Even in the shadow of their loss, they made it to their 50$^{th}$ wedding anniversary.

I am so thankful for the redemptive qualities of writing and narrative. It is a gift the women in our family have always shared with each other. I remember Jenny crafting a children's book for me, with painstakingly detailed illustrations of the elves at the North Pole, as a Christmas present. I was three; she was 14. We were living in Jamaica. I hear her reading *The Hunchback of Notre Dame* out loud to me in Paris while I was sick on New Year's Eve of Y2K. I am lying on a bed in our Canadian home, as she tells me anecdotes of her experiences with boys and love and life. All of a sudden, we are in her place in Dhaka, Bangladesh, Jenny's fingers tracing the words on the page as her five-year-old daughter sounds them out. Then, an older Kaia and I are reading my sister's poetry to each other, on my parent's flower-patterned couch, as tears stream down our faces. This book we are creating feels right somehow; so much of our lives revolved around the stories we told each other and the ones that kept us rooted as we travelled.

The women in our family unite over words—talking, sharing, writing, telling—a legacy we pass down from mother to daughter. Jenny was an exceptional poet, though her prose is left in diaries and journals on our bookshelves, like pressed flowers, pockets of love and consciousness between pages.

I hope Jenny would be proud of how far my mother and I have come. But my sister asked me to keep my family together, not to let us fall apart. Sometimes I feel like I'm failing: there is a new depth of sadness that lives within us, that eats at us and demands to be acknowledged. There are days when we fall apart. We are now more expansive people; we have explored new

*Forward*

depths of ourselves we never knew existed. Her loss will continue to be felt every single day. It doesn't get easier the way people say it will, but it becomes possible to continue on, as each of us, her family, become more resilient, as we grow stronger and closer as a whole. Yes, we keep going. But we will always miss her.

Kaia will be without her mother, I will be without my sister, and my mother and father will be without her daughter.

But as the fabric of our lives weave together in print, my sister dances through the pages. And as the story unfolds, the person coming back to life—vivacious, adventurous, courageous and once again whole and in love—is my mother.

I am so incredibly proud of my mother for going on this journey. She has left a legacy, a narrative that others can not only used to feel empathy and healing, but an imprint of my sister that will live on in the world, so others might also be inspired by her light.

So like my sister, to help us find our way even after she's gone.

Love,

**Megan Beadle**

# Prologue
## The Jennifer Tree (2013)

We dug a hole.

It was early spring, when we got the terrible news and decided to plant her tree.

"Let's get a red maple," Jen pleaded. "They're so lovely in the fall and would add a splash of colour to our yard."

"A red maple?" asked the expert at the nursery. "Sometimes they don't live through their first winter. What about an evergreen?"

But Jen's heart was set on a red maple. "It'll live," she said to him, ferocity in her eyes.

Together we gently eased our new tree into the earth so that the root system would settle in and thrive. We added more soil, fertilized, watered and picked weeds away from the base.

But now it's fall. I look out the large, picture window. In the middle of our muddy yard stands our newly planted, 11-foot tree. Its dried-bone, skeletal branches shiver and tremble, seemingly dead, buffeted by the wind, just like my frail Jenny. Raindrops are sliding down the glass creating tracks and racing with each other for the finish line at the bottom, the end of their journey. The sky is grey—an absence of colour—a shroud.

On November 6th, the day our child, my Jennifer, dies, the tree gives up its last scarlet leaf and naked, approaches the future.

The birds and their songs have disappeared. Our feeders hang suspended, two feet from our window, on shepherds' hooks. One is sky-blue, the other emerald green. They provide the only artificial slash of hope in a sea of death.

I miss the tiny canary yellow finches as they flit from feeder to feeder—the patterned black and white on blue of

## *Prologue*

the jays as they squawk and scream their strength and superiority. Even the flocks of blue-black starlings bullying and frightening the other birds away would be a welcome sign of life. The winter birds will arrive soon with the first snow—the chickadees with their black caps, the upside-down grey, black and white nuthatches, even the occasional brilliant red cardinal will visit our feeders, passing through ...

This is the November of nothingness.

Someday the birds will come back, but I don't yet know if Jen's tree will be around to watch them. My Jenny will not be.

I try to picture the tree in summer, in full bloom, with birds dancing in between the bright green leaves. I hope the Jennifer tree will survive the winter. It seems unlikely.

# Chapter One
## The Beginning of the End (2013)

I know she is gone. I do. The scent of her 'Blue Water' perfume lingers in our living room. I can still feel her long, warm, piano fingers as she reaches out and grasps my hand. In my mind we sit cuddled together on the couch. "I love you, Mom," Jen says, as she rests her light brown wig in the crook of my shoulder.

"Love you too, sweetie," I answer.

My throat constricts and aches with longing.

I have a casket to choose, a burial to attend, a memorial to plan: the to-do list of impossibly painful tasks left after a loved one's death is endless. I can't seem to catch my breath. The cells in my body have shifted and realigned, my universe has exploded, never to be put back together in quite the same way. I am crippled by a new wave of torture each time something triggers a memory of my beautiful daughter. I try to busy myself in the kitchen, but am hit by a barrage of mental snapshots of Jen at every stage of her life as they flash before me: a baby, naked, wide open blue eyes, looking at me adoringly as her stocky legs kick with delight in her crib, taking her first toddling steps with abandon, arms outstretched to her father—at six, dancing, whirling across the stage dressed in a diaphanous, white tutu with pink ballet slippers on her long, slim feet—at her high school graduation, tall, straight, sophisticated, chin held high as she gracefully sails across the stage to claim her diploma.

I propel myself towards the sink searching for something to do, to hold on to. Still, I picture her, in her gold, Indian sari, hair curled and flowing around her shoulders, marrying Mo despite my objections. I see her holding her new baby girl, Kaia, crying with joy and wonder. And then, there she is, devastated and heartbroken in the aftermath of a marriage to a man who chooses

## Chapter One

drugs and alcohol over her and his baby daughter. I see her later marrying Michel, the love of her life, walking down the staircase on her father's arm, dressed in a strapless white, silk gown, her hair piled high on her head, looking like a fairy princess—so happy. I try to stop it from coming, to focus on the tactile feel of the soapy water while I wash the dishes. It doesn't work. I cannot block the visions of Jen's suffering from lung cancer, pain etched across her features as she tries in vain to defeat the inoperable tumours within her frail lungs, bones, and brain. They come unbidden. There she is ringing the bell in the cancer ward that signifies the end of her chemo therapy—a smile of achievement on her uplifted face while tears stream down her cheeks. In one hand, she clutches a huge bouquet of gladiolas, her favourite flower, posing for the clicks of the cameras of the many people that adore her. The last vision of my daughter wakes me up at night in agony. My baby lies dead in a cold hospital room at thirty-seven. Her lifeless blue eyes are wide open when I touch her, hold her long, slender fingers in my hand for the last time. There is no sign that her formidable spirit is still there. Her body is but a shell and her soul has gone somewhere else. I wonder where she is. I feel alone, without her for the first time.

Those last months of her life after the prognosis of stage four lung cancer are jumbled in my memory. "Six months to live," they'd said, and they'd been right. Desperate with hope and fear, our family and loved ones moved as if at the bottom of the ocean. And now here we all are, drowning.

Without warning, anger erupts like a volcano from the top of my head. I slam a porcelain plate against the stack in the sink, propelling the dish under the buoyant water with violent force. It shatters. I clutch the piece that I still

## Chapter One

hold, wrapping my fingers tightly around the rough jagged edges until I bleed. I visualize hot lava pouring out of my skull. Even my skin feels hot and angry.

Everything I love, everything I believe in, is lost. The realization that anyone in my world—the people I love so much it hurts—could simply vanish, die suddenly, without warning, in a matter of months-minutes—is now glaringly obvious. My three remaining children, my grandchildren, my husband of forty-four years, my mom, my siblings, my best friends—my little world, and everyone in it—is vulnerable. The grief and fear rise up, like twin monitor lizards, breath smelling of rotting flesh, to devour my emotions and dreams.

Nothing feels sacred anymore. Faith and spirituality always played a major role in my life. Prayer and belief in God are replaced by hatred for an impotent divine power. I find it impossible to believe in a deity that strikes down a lovely young woman in the prime of her life—a gentle, spiritual soul who prayed more than I thought was healthy. My husband used to tease Jen; "You must be half-way to heaven already. Could you stop praying, come down to earth and deal with the mess in your room?" I find myself wondering if he remembers his words to our teenage daughter.

I feel arrogant. We have lost our vibrant girl, but we are not alone in this grief. Rob, my husband, and I aren't strangers to death, hunger, loss, and despair. Could I have been more empathetic, more caring for others who have experienced personal tragedies? I have walked the streets of Dar es Salaam, Cairo, Addis, Abubu, Manila, Abidjan and Dhaka, worked in Third World countries much of my life, and am not without compassion. But personal grief is something entirely new to me.

## Chapter One

In all the years living and working overseas my kids have been healthy. Our family dodged elephantiasis, hepatitis, bilharzia, sleeping sickness, rabies, and TB. The list is endless. We circled around catastrophe. We knew friends who had succumbed to the perils of the countries we called home. I thanked God every day for how lucky we were. Not now.

I leave the kitchen in search of a band-aid to stop the blood flowing from the gash on my palm, and pass a door to the open living room where my husband paces and talks to himself. He doesn't look up at me as I pause to watch.

What of my marriage? Rob, my best friend, my husband of forty-four years, has come away from our daughter's death a changed being. Gone are the days of extreme optimism, that 'we-can-do-anything' attitude. He spends his days cooped up in the house, listless and lost in thought; outgoing as he usually is, he no longer wants to see anyone. Being retired there is no job to fall back on, no alternative place to occupy the space of his grief. He's hiding in too much sleep and at the bottom of too many bottles of wine. He weeps while he dreams. I cannot help and it breaks my heart. Occasionally the darkness lifts for both of us at the same time. His mischievous grin and the dimple on his left cheek reappear. Then I see my daughter, Jen, again, in the attitude and indentation on my husband's face, and I am newly destroyed.

I wonder, after all our wonderful years, will we stay together? The pain is unbearable; we seem to bounce off each other. When one person is strong, the other brings everything down. What a relief it would be, to be with someone who has no idea—someone who could look at me without regret and agony. No one at all might be a solution. Alone, maybe, just perhaps, I could begin to deal with this loss.

## Chapter One

Henceforth, I will always think of my world in terms of before and after Jennifer's death. The world as Rob and I knew it has tilted on its axis. Before, we lived a lucky, enamoured life where, even though we took extreme risks, everything worked out. We both saw such sorrow and suffering, and although we were deeply affected, it never touched us at such a personal level. Now the planets of our existence have realigned. We are no longer the parents of our charismatic, intelligent, and sympathetic oldest child. We thought that she would be with us for our entire lives, by our side as we grew old. Now we need to re-evaluate our identity, our future.

I want to hit rewind and return to a world that was golden and full of passion and promise. I want to hide in that place. To forget.

I rifle through the closet in the bathroom searching for the band-aids, leaving a smear of red on the stark white cupboard door. I have no choice but to continue bleeding. I still have my family, my friends, but I've lost myself. I need to go on for them even though I would rather curl up and disappear, forget what has happened to my child. I must fight for my life, although I find it hard to believe I will ever be happy again.

I hope the past has the power to inform the present. I have a compulsion to tell the world how positive life was before, how dreams can come true and how Rob and I started the story of all of us. In remembering, perhaps I can escape to a world before Jenny. From our old story, our new story may evolve. Perhaps I will find my way. The least I can do is try. Maybe, if I can remember who I was before becoming a mother, what our love was like then, I can save my marriage. Save myself.

I walk out of the bathroom and into our computer room. I look through old pictures until I find the one I'm

*Chapter One*

looking for: a picture of a nineteen-year-old me in a red beret and a beaming, handsome young man with sideburns, his arm around me, in front of the Château Frontenac in Quebec City.

## Chapter Two

### When Julie Met Rob (1969)

"Marry me!"

It was Valentine's day, 1969, and Brian Greenwood was down on one knee proposing to me in front of Glendon College, in Toronto, as I waited by the bus, to go on a reading-week trip to Quebec City for Winter Carnival. He clutched a large, sparkling, diamond ring between his index finger and thumb. He held it up in front of my face for my inspection. His dark brown eyes shone brighter than the diamond, full of love, promise, and anticipation.

'Oh God! Oh God! Oh God!' I thought. Marry him? Did Brian just say marry? How had I not seen this coming? We'd been dating for four years. Our families were best friends—inseparable. What was wrong with me? Why not say yes? Four years before I'd been smitten with him, as was every other girl in my high school. I was in grade ten. He was in grade twelve. He was halfback on the football team, Eaton's rep, and had his own band. He played the sax, just like my dad, and oh could he sing and dance.

Brian had not been an easy catch. I was a teenage nothing, a mere speck on his horizon. But I was not stupid. I'd been watching teenage boys operate. Guys hated being idolized and fawned over. They loved a challenge and I went out of my way to provide one. I flirted outrageously, then ignored. I played every game.

I quizzed my friends. "Pretend you don't care," Doug my next-door neighbour advised. "You're really young but kind of pretty. Dress up in something sexy and follow Brian's band. Stand near the stage and dance. He'll notice, trust me."

## Chapter Two

Before I knew it, Brian and I had become a couple. I was the envy of the entire female population of West Hill High. Now, four years later, this wonderful and handsome man with his brown eyes and tousled, curly hair, this man who loved me and could provide me with a secure, suburban life, was asking me to marry him.

"Please get up," I whispered to Brian "The whole college is looking at us."

Brian staggered to his feet looking hurt, embarrassed and annoyed. "Couldn't you just have said yes?" He asked.

"I'm only 18, Brian. I just started university. You know my dream. I want to go to Africa and teach after I graduate. That's not exactly what you have in mind for our future, is it?"

"Not that again. I love you, but Africa has to be a no. That's just some crazy idea you've gotten into your pretty little head. You're young and naive. You'll change your mind. I'll have my teaching degree soon and a real job. You can quit school, and we can start a family."

Family, house with a white picket fence, no more university, no Africa. What on earth had I gotten myself into? My hands started to sweat. My face was red and hot. "Look, don't be mad. Everyone is listening and staring at us. Just let me have this week in Quebec, alone, to think about it. Okay, I've got to go now, or I'll miss my bus." I gave Brian a quick hug and ran through the refuge of the accordion bus doors.

I collapsed into the only available seat I could find, right behind the bus driver but by the window, and gazed down at Brian, hand outstretched to me, holding the red ring box. There were tears in his eyes. He drooped like a dejected puppy. Snow was falling and there were specks of white all over his black wool coat. None of that

## Chapter Two

detracted from the fact that he was such a perfect, masculine guy. Had I just made the worst mistake of my life? Would he ever forgive me my initial rejection? I felt the guilt in my gut multiply.

I placed the palm of my hand against the cold glass of the window as the bus began to move. Brian ran alongside, waving and blowing kisses. I should have said yes, I thought as tears escaped from my eyes. My throat ached as I desperately tried to get control of my emotions.

Why was I so weird? It was my stupid grade five teacher's fault. "Hey kiddo, one day you can go to Africa and see for yourself!" He'd promised me. What kind of teacher says that to a ten-year-old child? I remember lingering in that magical classroom, staring at Mr. Little's world globe. His descriptions of fierce lions, rolling desert dunes, dense rain forests, and exotic tribal people had captivated the imagination of the impressionable child that I had been. I decided that one day I was going to live a life of adventure.

Although Mr. Little had never strayed outside Ontario, his words took root in my soul. These were the words that were about to change the course of my entire life. This was why I was probably not going to be able to accept a loving, gentle, smart and handsome young man as my husband.

In the middle of my reverie, I felt a body flop down in the aisle seat next to me. Oh, just what I need, I thought. The scent of cold, fresh air mixed with 'Old Spice' deodorant filled my space.

"That was close," said a very deep voice. "I would have hated to miss this trip. I've never been to Quebec City, have you?" the young man next to me asked as he glanced at my tear and mascara-streaked face. "Are you okay?

## Chapter Two

"I'll be fine." I found myself wishing he would just disappear, or at the very least, not talk or ask questions.

"Right. Well, I'm Rob," He gave me a cheeky smile and looked at me with concerned, baby blues. I couldn't help but notice the adorable dimple in his right cheek.

"I'm Julie," I answered abruptly, trying not to encourage any more conversation. I turned away and glanced out the window at the grey sky and swirling snow.

"Julie, this would be much more of an adventure if we were riding my motorcycle," he sighed.

"Motorcycle? Who rides a motorcycle in February?" I asked, intrigued.

"I do. I guess I'm just a little crazy."

"Maybe," I said, "but I'm probably crazier. As soon as I graduate, I'm going to Africa to live and work." I held my breath. Brian would suggest a one-week, all-inclusive resort in the Caribbean as an alternative, a location where malaria wasn't a problem. My parents would forbid it. My friends would laugh at me, and ask if I really dreamed of being abducted by Somali pirates.

"Can I come too?" What a pick-up line, I thought. I wondered if this Rob person was joking or making fun of me, but a second glance at his face indicated that he was serious. "And then we can go Asia, the Middle East, maybe South America or Europe."

"You don't think I'm nuts?" I asked, amazed.

"I guess you're different… but crazy? Never! Our ancestors got it wrong, though. An entire planet and they settle in Canada. Bonkers. It's freaking cold here. And I've always wanted to travel the world. Africa seems like an awesome place to start. My motorcycle will fit right in."

Maybe Africa wasn't the only reason I was going to have to say no to Brian.

## Chapter Three
### Love Bus (1969)

I remember nothing and everything about that bus trip to Quebec City; I did not notice who else was in the other seats, what the weather was like, which route we took or the beauty of the white wonderland outside. About Rob, I remember everything. I should have been sad, confused, worried about whether to accept Brian's marriage proposal. Instead, I became completely absorbed by another human being—mesmerized, hypnotized—intellectually, physically and emotionally involved with Rob.

How could this happen? I wondered. My boundaries began to melt, and I could feel myself shifting, blurring at the edges, moving into a softer, more flexible version of whom I used to be. My senses were electrified and the current bounced off me and towards Rob. Did he notice any of this? I had no idea. He was pleasant, friendly, and talkative, but perhaps that was the way he acted with everyone. Whether he was attracted to me was a mystery.

Rob seemed a rare bird, or maybe I had just led a very sheltered life.

"Have you thought about how you're going to get to Africa?" he asked. "Which country do you want to go to? Africa's a big place. Have you read Ivan Illich? He maintains that westerners shouldn't interfere in the development of Third World countries. But Tanzania, now that would be a great choice. Julius Nyerere is in power, and he believes in African socialism. He's actively welcoming westerners to fill in the employment gaps."

I began to realize this guy was really informed about things I'd never even contemplated. He spoke about

## Chapter Three

going to Expo 67 and riding his motorcycle to New York City to cover the Nixon/Humphrey presidential campaign, as well as the Columbia student protests for the Glendon College student newspaper. As a student council rep, Rob was concerned with affordable housing, student rights and unequal distribution of wealth in western nations. He ranted about how Canada's native population were treated as second-class citizens.

Holy cow! It was like attending a lecture on life. I was fascinated. Rob reached out and touched my arm just to make a point, just a butterfly touch, nothing really, but my whole body responded. A tingling jolt, a tremor shot through me. It was everything I could do to sit still in my seat and not reach out and stroke the light brown hair on his forearms. Crazy, just crazy!

I felt ashamed of my response to this almost-stranger. How was it that I could be so drawn to someone I'd just met? What was I going to do? How could I explain this to Brian, to our friends and family? By the halfway point in our journey I knew two things so clearly that there was no longer any doubt about what I had to do when I returned home: I knew that I was not, nor had I ever been, in love with Brian, and I knew that I could not spend the rest of my life with him.

So many things just didn't add up. Although I thought that someday I might want children, I certainly wasn't ready yet. I had fought hard to go to university. My father had advised me to skip a step and go directly into Teacher's College. After much discussion, I won that battle. I was looking forward to becoming bilingual and studying international issues.

I dreamed of changing the world. Brian loved the world just the way it was. Visions of folk festivals, tie-dyed shirts, peace symbols and flowers in my hair danced

## Chapter Three

through my head. Brian dreamed of buying a bungalow on the outskirts of metro Toronto. The music of my generation shaped my wants and needs; Bob Dylan, Jimmy Hendricks, Judy Collins, Joni Mitchell, Janice Joplin, Joan Baez, Neil Young and Leonard Cohen were my guides and role models. Brian loved the big band sound and swing dancing; Frank Sinatra, Nat King Cole, and Paul Anka were his idols.

I almost think Brian, who was four years older than me, was a throwback to a previous generation. He loved his big, blue Oldsmobile and longed for a quiet family life devoid of adventure and trauma. The word 'straitlaced' came to mind. He was not a talker and I loved to talk. His idea of an exciting evening out was going to Swiss Chalet to eat chicken and fries. The mention of my favourite food, curry, turned him green.

Rob and I talked non-stop. I was already toying with the idea that here was someone I could spend the rest of my life with. It was the middle of the night and almost everyone else on the bus was sound asleep. Normally, by this point in meeting a guy, I would have been playing coy games. In this case, I couldn't bat my eyelashes and play hard to get. We had connected at a level that precluded games. He would have seen right through me. I found myself being completely honest. I had no choice. Both of us should have been exhausted after an all-night bus trip. I felt more awake and alive than I had ever been.

We arrived in Quebec City at dawn on February 15th,1969. Maybe the fact that most of the trip had taken place on Valentine's Day had something to do with what I was experiencing—some kind of hypnotic magic had taken hold of my usually rational mind. Maybe all the stuff about cupid and arrows held a grain of truth. I could only hope I would regain my sanity.

## Chapter Three

The sky was robin's egg blue, the air crystal clear—colder than I ever dreamed possible. "Is that all you have to wear?" Rob asked, looking concerned. I was dressed in a stylish, unlined brown leather coat, a short skirt, nylon stockings and a flimsy, white silk blouse. Perched on my head was a Parisian-style, red beret. At least I had boots on my feet and black, dollar store gloves on my hands. "Here," he said, handing me a very long, striped red and white woollen scarf. He wound it around my neck five times. "My Mom knitted this for me. Kapuskasing, where I'm from, is always this cold in winter. I gather you've never experienced this kind of temperature."

"I'm used to Toronto. It's never this cold. Thanks for the scarf," I said as our group stumbled out of the bus and were confronted by a small, suburban bungalow on the outskirts of Quebec City. In the basement there were two large rooms, one for girls and one for boys. In each room the owners had placed wall-to-wall bunk beds with less than a foot between them. To get out of bed, we would have to climb over the end. I found myself hoping that I'd be on the bottom because it was unclear how anyone could get out of a top bunk—pole vault, perhaps. There were 40 people in our group, and we had to share one bathroom. What a disaster!

In the next minute, another aspect of Rob's character was revealed. "This is ridiculous!" he said in a deep, assertive tone. Everyone turned to look at him as he took over. "What were the organizers of this trip thinking? Who can we talk to about this? We can't all stay here. This has to be illegal. What if there's a fire?"

The owner of the home came forward, head bent, wringing his hands. *"Desole,"* he murmured. "But no choice. No spare rooms in Quebec City. This is Carnival." The man had a point, so we reluctantly unpacked and

## Chapter Three

crammed our belongings onto our allocated bunks. At least I was assigned a bottom bunk. Best to attempt to be positive, I thought.

Not wanting to waste a second of time we all put on as many layers of clothing as we could manage and fell out into the snow and minus 30-degree temperature.

I looked around, but my new friend, Rob, was nowhere to be seen. My friend, Shirley, and I headed out to join the crowds and see Quebec City.

## Chapter Four
### Paradise (2014)

We're in Cuba for the first time. My sister called in early January, two months after Jen died. I must have sounded desperate, barely able to hold a conversation without breaking down. "Come with Dave and me to Cayo Coco for seven days. You and Rob will love it there—sun, sand, an all-inclusive hotel on a beautiful beach. It's just what you need. Get away from the cold and grey of winter. I'm worried about you guys. Please come."

We agree. Both of us have been finding it hard to get out of bed, to brush our teeth, to continue to pretend we are okay as a couple.

All we do is cry and avoid one another. We've also both been sick—just colds and the flu, but annoying nonetheless. Maybe Cuba will help. God knows, we need to get through this, if not together, then at least each of us separately. Survival is the only option.

The hotel in Cayo Coco is like nothing I've ever experienced. It doesn't feel like the real world. The weather is reminiscent of half of our lives spent in the tropics. I'm sitting on a pristine balcony, three floors up, looking out at the turquoise ocean. Bird songs fill the air and the wind plays in the leaves, a lullaby of sound. The familiar scent of frangipani flowers lulls me into a calmer place. I should feel comforted. To an extent, I do.

Memories of Jen are everywhere in Cuba, though she has never been here—a place so much like the Ivory Coast, Egypt, Jamaica, or the Philippines where my little girl grew up. I can see my daughter as a baby in Abidjan dancing on the white sand wearing a little, rose, cotton dress with white sandals on her feet. Her blonde, curly hair sticks out from the sides of a flowered sun bonnet.

## Chapter Four

The waves in West Africa were huge, and Jen was terrified of the ocean at that young age. She loved the pool, though, and learned to swim at three years of age.

Later, in Jamaica, when she was a young teenager, the ocean became an integral part of her being. She learned to dive in Kingston, and before we knew it, was swimming with stingrays and stroking their mottled, reptilian skin. The ocean was her haven of peace.

In Manila, Jen was with us for her last year of high school. She was so lovely. I worried about sending my pretty, naive daughter off to a Canadian university—a third culture kid—innocent, protected, unsophisticated, and so close to her family. How would she cope, on her own, in a place that she barely knew? Would she be scared and lonely? Would she have trouble with culture shock?

The ocean was a long way from where she'd be living in Canada—a cold and foreign place to someone like my Jen. Before she left the Philippines for university, she spent months after her graduation from high school on the island of Mindoro. She lived in a beach hut, first of all learning to be a dive instructor, and later taking tourists diving.

She told the story of how she had to rescue a Japanese tourist twice her size. He was impetuous, put on too many weights, and sank like a stone. On the way down he landed on a wall of sea urchins and got impaled by their spines. He panicked and began to flail and flap, fighting to ascend too quickly. Jenny manoeuvred him slowly to the surface, against his will—proud of her accomplishment.

The vibrant colours here in tropical Cuba are indescribable. The heat, the dance, the rhythm, the bright sun would have lifted my daughter's soul. She wanted to live and teach in this realm. The cold, white winters of

## Chapter Four

Canada killed her spirit, made her grow pale and thin. "Too cold, too white, too dead," she declared.

Jen at 32, her six-year-old daughter Kaia and second husband Michel, followed us to Dhaka, Bangladesh. They taught at the Korean school and were happy. They took trips to the mangrove swamps of the Sundarbans to stalk Bengal tigers, and to the Chittagong Hill Tracts to mix with indigenous people. They swam in the ocean at Cox's Bazaar and snorkelled in Thailand—all of these things my beautiful daughter got to do.

Jen designed a simple water filter, with used plastic Coke bottles, water hyacinths and beach sand. She donated it to a local Non Governmental Organization (NGO). It's being used in the kitchens of rural Bangladeshis to this day. She visited hospitals and volunteered in places that terrified me. HIV, TB, cholera, and hepatitis C were rampant in Bangladesh.

I pleaded with her to be careful, but of course, I was ignored. Ironic that she succumbed to none of the obvious threats to her health but got lung cancer later, in Canada, before she could use her new teaching degree and get herself and her family back to the tropics.

Cuba is killing me. My daughter should be enjoying this experience instead of Rob and me. The gentle, kind Cubans, dancing day and night, laid back, laughing souls, ocean bound, form a perfect reflection of Jen's values. The maid leaves huge, red hibiscus flowers on the bedspread every day.

I remember such flowers tucked behind Jen's ear as she sat holding her baby sister, Meg, in Jamaica, and again holding baby brother Andrew at a beachfront bungalow on the island of Mindoro in the Philippines. In both cases, her crazy, curly, red-blonde hair formed a crown around her head.

## Chapter Four

I snap back to the present and stare at the hibiscus flower in our bedroom in Cuba. The bloom is like my daughter. It only lives a short time—one day. By nightfall, it shrivels up and dies, once so vibrant and alive—gone too soon.

# Chapter Five
### Toilet Trauma (1969)

"Ooh," said Shirley. "Quebec is such a romantic city. Don't you wish Brian was here? I saw the whole proposal thing—you must be over the moon."

I shrugged. "Let's just go see this beautiful city and hit as many sites as we can. Later we can go to the Pierre Trudeau rally by the Château Frontenac." Though I said nothing to Shirley, my attendance at the event had an ulterior motive: I suspected Rob might be there.

Quebec was so charming, quaint and old that I almost forgot how cold I was, and Pierre Trudeau—oh my—what a charismatic, incredible man. His idea of making French the second official language of Canada particularly impressed me—my dream of a bilingual country could come true under his leadership. My struggle to learn French at Glendon was worth it.

As Shirley and I stood listening and shivering the crowds kept getting bigger. People were pushing and cheering. Crushed on all sides by excited Trudeau fans, my friend and I got separated, lifted off our feet and swept up in the current of humanity.

"That was terrifying," said Shirley when we eventually escaped the crowd and found each other. "Let's get out of here and find a restaurant for coffee and a warm-up."

Even if Rob happened to be watching Trudeau, we would never spot him—too many people—so I agreed. As we walked away, I glanced back at the Château Frontenac standing at the top of the cliff in upper town far above the frozen river below. The spires, turrets, archways, thick limestone walls and huge windows reminded me of the

*21*

## Chapter Five

fairyland Disney castle at the beginning of the program, 'World of Disney' on TV.

Despite thoughts of Brian and Rob, it was easy to enjoy myself in Quebec. The city was like nothing I'd ever seen. Narrow, ancient streets, a fortified wall surrounding the upper town, crowds of happy people speaking French, old majestic buildings, snow castles, ice sculptures, and the jolly, giant snowman—*Bonhomme Carnival*, created a scene that drew me in. I forgot everything but my surroundings. Smells of *croissants, crêpes, boeuf bourguignon* and onion soup wafted through the air. What a sensual banquet. The feeling of having stepped back in time thrilled me.

Over all these wonderful and new experiences, I kept hoping to meet up with Rob, but my thoughts kept turning back to Brian, waiting hopefully and patiently at home for an acceptance to his proposal. He was such a nice guy and also my best friend, but if I were truly honest with myself, how could I be so mentally and physically drawn to someone I'd just met if I really loved Brian. We weren't even engaged, and already I wanted more than Brian could ever give me.

Pulling Rob's scarf more tightly around me to ward off the cold, I reminded myself that I had to find a way to say no to Brian. He would be shocked, and my family and friends would not understand, but the deed had to be done. Whether Rob and I eventually got together had nothing to do with my feelings for Brian. I couldn't spend the rest of my life married to someone I didn't love.

At the end of the day, Shirley and I stumbled back to our humble living quarters, frozen and exhausted. We crashed on our bunks, but not before I wandered around the bungalow looking for Rob. He was obviously still out

## Chapter Five

enjoying himself. Guess he wasn't as interested in me as I was in him. Damn! Where was he?

At two o'clock in the morning I woke to a sickening stench. Shirley slipped over the end of the top bunk looking as white as a sheet. "What is that awful smell?" she gasped, gagging and holding one hand over her mouth. All the girls in the room were pouring out of their bunk beds with similar reactions. One poor girl was retching into a garbage can in the corner of the room.

I had large, pink, spongy rollers in my hair and was dressed in navy blue flannelette pyjamas covered with red Scotty dogs—not exactly the height of fashion. I could hear the boys in the next room groaning and swearing. Girls and boys began to mingle and commiserate. I looked up and there was Rob.

If there had ever been any doubt about my future with this guy, given my current hideous appearance, the jury was now in. He would never look at me again. So much for romance. Bye, bye love. Brian's proposal was looking like the only one I was likely to get for some time. Rob, of course, walked right over to me. By that point the green shade of my skin was clashing badly with the pink, blue, and red of my outfit. Rob looked relaxed and completely normal in light blue cotton pyjamas that matched his eyes. The scent of Old Spice and fresh air wafted around him and helped to settle my stomach. I suppressed the desire to bury my face against his shoulder and breath in deeply.

Rob grinned at me. "Love the look. Grab your coat and suitcase. You might want to get dressed and ditch those hair things. Oh, and bring the blankets off your bunk. The toilet has backed up and there's raw sewage everywhere. I have no idea where the owners are, but we can't stay here." I loved the way this young man was taking charge.

## Chapter Five

I did exactly as I was told and Shirley followed. "Who is that gorgeous guy?" she whispered as Rob shot out ahead of us.

"Rob," I answered. "I met him on the bus. We were both late getting on so he and I got the last two seats at the front."

"Lucky you," Shirley said. "You've already got Brian. You have to introduce me to Rob. I'm coming with you."

It was approaching minus forty that night. My nostrils were freezing together, and it was hard to breathe. At the same time, a lovely shade of rose framed the horizon and the air sparkled with the cold.

We splintered off into smaller groups and tried to figure out what to do next. By the time we were organized the sun was up. Rob, his friend Don, Shirley and I set off for the old city. "Don't worry," Rob said. "There has to be somewhere we can stay."

"I thought the owner of that hellhole told us there was nothing else available," Shirley said.

Rob looked annoyed. "We can't just sit here. I'm not about to live with the sewage backup even if most of our group chooses to. With the number of people relying on one toilet it's bound to happen again. Let's go."

We stopped at each and every hotel, B & B and inn until finally someone took pity on us and rented us a small room. It was a basic hotel halfway down *Rue de Remparts*, in the lower town, close to the river and all the activity of Carnival. There was one double bed in the room, so Shirley and I took that. The guys agreed to sleep on the floor. At least we had the blankets we'd carried from the previous place, and later in the day we could buy a thin slab of foam from Kresges for the boys to lie on.

Just as we were getting settled, I had a new and terrible thought. Here I was with this great guy, and no money to

## Chapter Five

pay for the hotel room. Now what? "Um, Rob," I stammered. "I just realized that I only brought enough money on this trip to buy my food. I can't afford to stay here."

Rob laughed. "Off you go then." I must have looked absolutely dismayed because he quickly put his arm around my shoulder and said, "Just kidding. You don't have to worry about paying. My parents gave me money for Christmas to buy clothes and I just happened to have brought the entire amount with me. Who needs more than one pair of blue jeans anyway? This is, after all, an emergency. Mom and Dad would certainly understand. No problem."

All I could think of was, "I love this guy."

"Julie," Rob said, looking only at me, "Let's blow this pop stand." He held up a large, silver flask. "There's cherry brandy in here. That should keep us warm." Shirley looked hurt. Don looked hopeful—as if we'd change our minds and let him come too. I should have felt some sympathy for my friends and invited them along, but I accepted Rob's offer, and we headed out alone.

# Chapter Six
## Paradise Revisited (2014)

Rob and I are back in Cuba, at the same resort in Cayo Coco, just a month and a half after our first visit. It's still only about four months since our daughter died. This time we're with our oldest son, Dan, his wife, Kim, and our two grandsons, Ben (three), and Max (six months). Max was born in late October just before Jen died in early November. Kim says Jen is Max's guardian angel, and I agree. She is up there watching over him. Max's birth was the last time Dan and Kim saw Jen. We have lovely pictures of our daughter holding baby Max before he left the hospital.

Now, there's no time to grieve, thank God. I'm collecting shells on the beach. I'm at the children's centre with Ben. I'm watching him in the kiddy pool. Rob and I volunteer to look after the baby while Dan and Kim take Ben out for his first ride on a small catamaran. Max is so tiny, still nursing. What will we do if he wakes up and cries? I look at him lying there on a beach chair, sound asleep and vulnerable. His innocence, his soft baby roundness, and his rosebud mouth as he suckles in his sleep, leave me limp with gratitude and wonder.

I, who never thought I could love anyone as much as Rob, my children and my first grandchild Kaia, am in love again with these two little boys. Later, big three-year-old brother, Ben and I go to the snack bar. His new favourite food in Cuba is liquid yogourt, and he wants to drink it all the time. "Kim," I ask, a bit alarmed. "Is it okay that Ben is having three or four yogourts a day?"

"It's fine," Kim answers. "I guess if he's going to eat a lot of something yogourt's not a bad choice. It's healthy. We're on holiday."

## Chapter Six

In the evening we traipse down the long poinsettia lined path to the amphitheatre for the children's show. Ben has a crush on Maria, the children's activity leader. He looks at her with wide, adoring eyes. He's normally shy, but follows Maria's instructions and goes up on the stage to dance and sing.

I can't take my eyes off him—so handsome, so self-confident, just like his dad, our son Dan. I'm reminded of all four of our children, including Jen. I feel proud and happy. This joy, this rush of pure emotion, is an antidote to the grief that stalks me night and day. For the time being I'm able to imagine life beyond sorrow. There is and always will be love and happiness in our family.

I find myself thinking of my lovely granddaughter Kaia, Jen's only child. I wish she were with us on this trip, but she's now a teenager and in school. When I sat nursing my own babies, all four of them, I could never have imagined loving any other children as much. Now it seems that love is endless and expands to grandchildren as well.

# Chapter Seven
## New Mothers (2014)

How can I have held my first-born baby, my child, watched her grow, graduate, get married and have a daughter of her own, and now be expected to let her go? Will I ever learn to say goodbye? A light in my life has gone out, a light I expected would shine to the end of my days, an ongoing sunrise of love and hope. My role of mother to a child I loved more than life has disappeared. Who am I now? Rob and I waited a long time to have our first baby—seven years. I remember the day our daughter was born like it happened yesterday. August 10th, 1976, Ottawa—the hottest day imaginable. On that day I became a mother first, foremost, always and forever. 'Till death do us part' should have meant that someday I would die, and my daughter would have to say goodbye to me—tough but normal.

Oh my God—motherhood! Is there one woman in the universe who really understands what it's like to hold her new baby in her arms for the first time? I, at least, was totally unprepared for the emotions that surged through my body. Before I gave birth, I had the world all figured out. "Nursing—God who does that?" I asked Rob. "Those La Leche Leaguers—horrors! They come off like nursing is some kind of religion. Not for me. I'm gonna have this baby, stay at home a reasonable three months and then straight back to the job I love. Bottles, disposable diapers, baby outfits, crib, carriage—check—ready!"

Neither Rob nor I had any notion of what the future held. How could we have been so stupid? Did we not have successful mothers and fathers in our lives—friends who had babies? Why did we not ask questions, observe what

## Chapter Seven

others had already been through? The moment our baby was born nothing else mattered.

Those first hours are like a movie playing in the present: I put my newborn to my breast and cry, overwhelmed. Rob leans over us, reaches out and strokes our child's soft, round cheek with his finger. Sucking noises fill the room and I feel a contentment that I have never experienced.

Rob's eyes look up at me, surprised, holding nothing back. The emotion in his face mirrors my own feelings. "Now we're a family," he says. "Weirdly, I would kill to protect this perfect little one. I had no idea. Did you? Can I hold her?"

Rob bends over and takes our newborn in his arms, supporting her head with his hand. August sunlight slants through the window, creating a circle of softness, like a halo, around the three of us. I have never felt so content, so fulfilled.

A young, red-haired nurse, with endearing freckles on her face arrives in the early evening. She smells like 'Lily of the Valley' perfume. "Time to put the baby in the nursery," she says as she takes Jen from Rob and places her in a pink bassinet with wheels, by my bedside.

My arms feel empty. "Take my little girl away?" I ask, horrified. "She was just born hours ago. My baby needs me. I have to nurse her, so my milk will come in. We need to bond!"

"Sorry," the nurse answers, her green eyes narrowing and a flush of pink appearing on her cheeks. "Doctor's orders. You just gave birth. You must be exhausted and your baby's fine. Get some rest. We'll take good care of her, I promise. Also, visiting hours are over. Time for your husband to leave," she says as she pushes the bassinet out of the room.

## Chapter Seven

"I guess I'd better get going," Rob says. "Oh, and I thought you were going to bottle-feed. What's all this stuff about nursing?" Rob asks, not waiting for an answer. "Wo! What a day. Can't believe you pulled that off. Amazing, like super woman stuff. We have a daughter. Love you guys so much. I'll be here first thing in the morning." Rob kisses me and leaves the room.

I walk to the nursery and stand, rigid, gazing through the large glass window at my daughter. Pink and blue bassinets are lined up, row after row, across the brightly lit room. Baby powder and milky smells surround me. Jenny is three rows back and screaming her lungs out, as anxious to be with me as I am to be with her.

My child—rose bud lips, dark fuzzy hair on her well-shaped head, a cute turned up nose and long slim baby fingers that are now clenched in tight fists. Her whole, tiny, perfect body is a picture of distress and anger.

I knock on the window. My red-headed nurse appears looking surprised. Up to the moment our baby was born I've been an exemplary patient, quiet and not demanding. "Please give me my baby. If you don't, I'll stand here, crying, all night and I doubt anyone wants that."

"Look, you need permission from your doctor to keep your baby with you. My shift is almost over, and I need to go home to my family. Please go back to your room."

"Call my doctor then," I demand. "Look at my baby. She's upset. She's crying. This is stupid. She's mine and I want her, now!"

"I can't possibly disturb doctor Allen. He's a busy man."

"I will make a scene. I promise. Just call, okay. Please!"

"Very well, but if I can't get him, or if he says no, you have to go back to your room. Deal?"

## Chapter Seven

"Thanks. I really appreciate your kindness, but I'm not leaving." I wonder if this young nurse has children of her own yet. Does she not understand how I feel? The call to my doctor goes through, and he agrees that I should have my baby with me day and night.

I scoop Jen up and hold her close to my heart. I smell her warm, sweet scent and brush my lips against her downy, baby hair. My breasts are sore and no mother's milk is apparent, but my baby sucks with all her tiny strength. The wailing stops. Both baby and mom are perfectly content. With my child in the circle of my arms I feel complete. I want, more than anything, to be a good mother.

Now after Jennifer's death I'm looking through her writing. I find a poem she wrote shortly after she gave birth to her daughter, Kaia. As I read, in tears, I'm so grateful that, although she died young, Jennifer had a child of her own. This is what she wrote:

*To My Baby Daughter*
*Piano fingers of life*
*Hands grasping, little miniatures of your father's*
*Imp eyes bright as a spark*
*Mind nimble and swift*
*Wrists a perfect balance between mother and father*
*Cheeks chubby and flushed with vivid curiosity, with wrinkles where dimples will be*

\*\*\*

*I am stubborn with a will of steel and loving like an ocean*
*How I long to be everything you want me to be*
*Yet I can't*
*How I thought I would be perfect by now*
*And was supposed to be*
*I thought I would be your angel, but you are mine*

## Chapter Seven

\*\*\*

*I look at your tender little bean of a body, sprightly and fair, nuzzle the soft furry down on the top of your head*

*I wonder how could anyone ever hurt such a perfect creation*

*I sniff your milky sweet scent*

*I remember your first grin (already a memory)*

*Such a beautiful being*

\*\*\*

*Yet I know the temptations of despair*

*I struggle, terrified that I will not be good enough, strong enough to hold you safe in my arms*

*To draw love from anger*

*To draw hope from misunderstanding*

*Across the miles, across oceans and countries, across life*

*I am determined and know that I will not hurt you, my angel pie*

*And yet I know I will disappoint you*

\*\*\*

*I know that I love you more fiercely than I knew possible*

*I know that you are my daughter, and I am your mother*

*This Love, this Union, will bind us for Eternity.*

# Chapter Eight
## Sea Change (1976)

My motherhood washes over me. I can't stand being physically removed from my baby. I leave Jen home with Rob and go to the grocery store. I have everything I need in my shopping cart when I look around and panic. The bright yellow and black of Loblaws grocery store jump out at me—the fluorescent lights, the noise, too many choices of cereal, strangers dashing up the isles. I break out into a cold sweat—baby separation anxiety. My breasts let down—I'm dripping milk. My shirt is soaking wet. I start to cry, abandon my full cart of groceries and flee.

Back in the car I wonder, "what was that all about?" At home, I try to explain why I have come back without any food. Rob gives me a hug, puts on his coat and heads out to finish what I started.

I pick up my four-month-old, ease down into my rocking chair and nurse her—tranquility and peace. For now, this is all I want, this is all I need.

Thoughts of returning to work, my teaching career that I have fought long and hard for, fly away, like milkweed pod seeds with their tiny umbrellas on the wind. I quit my Masters of Education. I have to force myself to leave the house without my child. At a friend's wedding I have looked forward to for years all I can think of is getting back home. I know I'm neglecting my marriage. I should go out on more date nights, spend one on one time with Rob.

When Jenny is nine months old I get a terrible breast infection. Blue veins pop out and pulsate. Angry red lines form a spiderweb pattern on my left breast which is swollen and engorged. I have to take a Tylenol before

## Chapter Eight

letting my baby suckle. Blood and milk flow together from my nipple. I ache all over. I'm freezing cold one minute, hot the next.

"Oh my God Julie," Rob says that night as he reaches over to touch me from his side of the bed. You're burning up." Out comes the thermometer. "You have a temperature of 102. Why didn't you say anything?" The three of us bundle up against the frigid, late March night and head for the emergency ward.

After two hours of waiting, wondering, a young doctor declares that I need antibiotics to kill the infection. "These particular drugs won't hurt your baby," he says, "but I suggest that you stop nursing immediately." On the way home we pick up formula and bottles. Trying to convince our stubborn, little one to take the bottle is impossible. She screws up her face, screams, pushes away with all her strength. By now both my breasts are engorged and painful.

I cheat and allow our little one to suck — biological imperative! What a relief, both physically and mentally. Jenny nurses and falls asleep. The next morning, I call la Leche League. No matter that I had no use for them before my baby was born. Now I need them.

"Keep taking the antibiotics and nurse as frequently as you can. Make sure you don't favour one breast over the other. Use different angles—lie in bed, sit in a chair. You and your little one will be just fine, but the advice the doctor gave you is nonsense. If you don't nurse your baby, you'll get sicker. Try to relax. What you are experiencing is not unusual and happens to nursing moms all the time."

My parents-in-law arrive to help out. We've told them that I'm not well but haven't explained the problem. They look worried, upset. I'm on the mend, but an emotional mess, and they pick up on my distress. "You don't have

*Chapter Eight*

breast cancer, do you?" Rob's Dad asks, forthright as ever. We explain the problem.

"Is that all?" Rob's mom says. "Just give up breastfeeding and put Jenny on the bottle. I never nursed and look how well Rob turned out."

"But I love nursing and I don't want to stop. I'm much better already," I insist.

Through all this drama, except when we try to give her a bottle, our baby has thrived. She continues to smile, roll over, play with her toys and refuse to sleep. Rob's parents are great. They take Jenny for walks in our neighbourhood, entertain her and allow me to recuperate. I find it difficult to let anyone but me look after her, but I know I need to get better for both of us.

Spring is coming. Daffodils, hyacinths, tulips pop up in our yard. The sun's rays play across the bay window at the front of our house. Shafts of light lay stripes on our red carpet in the living room. Dust mites sparkle and drift in the air and our baby stares, fascinated. She does push-ups and then proceeds to learn to crawl backwards and finally forwards. She's moving away from me—growing up.

# Chapter Nine
## Next Stop Africa (1971)

I am standing on the hot tarmac of a tiny airport in London, Ontario. My dad has his arms wrapped around me in a bear hug so tight I can barely breathe. He's crying and his body shakes. I have never seen my big, macho father cry before. In his embrace, I'm sobbing, gasping for breath. Dad releases me and I step backwards, stunned and disoriented. He puts both of his hands on my shoulders and says, "It's not too late. You can still change your mind. No one would blame you."

My little three-year-old brother Davy runs at me and throws his arms around my knees, almost knocking me over. When I regain my balance, I bend down and lift him up. He smells like baby shampoo and is warm and cuddly. His fine blonde hair feels downy soft to the touch of my lips, "Julie," he asks. "Why you cry? You sad? Let's go to zoo. That's fun."

I can't take Davy back to the zoo, not tomorrow, not for two, long years. In a few hours I will be flying far away, across the world to Africa. I will be leaving everything that is familiar and safe. Now that my dream of going to live and work in Africa is finally coming true, I want to change my mind. I can't do this. What was I thinking?

My mom steps forward and takes Davy in her arms, leaving mine empty. She hugs him and then gently lowers him to the ground. How soon he forgets me as he runs around in circles. Mom turns to me and smiles. "You'll be fine," she says. "This is an opportunity of a lifetime, something you have always wanted and carefully planned for. You're going with an organization that will take care

## Chapter Nine

of you. We'll all write every week and send audio tapes."

"But Mom, by the time I get back Davy won't even recognize me."

"Yes, he will," she answers. "Time will pass quickly, you'll see, and it will all be such a wonderful adventure. I wish that I could have done something similar when I was young."

I am trying to get control of my emotions, and it is difficult. I have to get a grip, or I'll upset my five younger siblings. I wipe my tears, put my shoulders back, look up and see Rob standing with his mom, dad, and sister, Jan. His family are more composed than mine, but they all seem sad and unsure. All, that is, except Rob. He looks excited and happy. He wears that damn grin like a badge. Walking over, he hugs me to him and strokes my hair. "Just think. This is the moment we've dreamed of, and it's finally coming true. I love you."

***

My mind circles back to that wonderful week in Quebec City and the subsequent two and a half whirlwind years Rob and I have been together since then. The old city was a wonderful place to fall in love. We were together for six full days watching canoe races on the half-frozen river and nighttime parades with the giant snowman (*Bonhomme Carnaval*) wearing his red hat and herring bone, brightly coloured scarf, while fire-works exploded over the Château Frontenac Hotel.

The cold was bone-chilling, so we drank cherry brandy out of Rob's flask and cuddled up around bowls of hot chocolate and '*café au lait*'. Rob introduced me to his version of fine dining. We ate frog legs, which were delicious, and shared '*Châteaubriand*' (beef filet with

*Chapter Nine*

sauce) at *Café D' Europe*, a quaint restaurant on a narrow street in upper town. At lunchtime the delicate, thin *crêpes* with asparagus and Swiss cheese melted in my mouth. I felt, at the time, that I had landed in some exotic, parallel universe and Rob was my guide. The sun shone and crystal snowflakes—each one an art piece, a different pattern—fell. The wind drifted the snow into waves and swirls and transported me to a new and exciting reality.

I thought the euphoria I was feeling would disappear when we returned to university—the lectures, the studying, the assignments, but the glow persisted. It was such a magical time. Rob and I spent hours combing Kensington market in Toronto looking for fine cheeses and the best *baguettes*. We drank red wine, listened to folk music and never missed an episode of Star Trek. We talked, argued and cried together. This was the man I wanted to spend the rest of my life with.

We met on Valentine's Day 1969, and we were engaged by April of the same year. There was no diamond ring this time, neither one of us had any money, but the relationship felt right. I couldn't imagine a life without Rob. I knew that my life would be filled with challenges, never secure or safe, always exciting, but that was what I dreamed of, in principle, at least.

Brian had been upset when we broke up, but it took him no time to move on. Rob and I went on a double date with Brian and his new girlfriend, Karen, in late March. It was difficult to find enough to talk about. We had so little in common with the other couple. Rob tried to discuss Pierre Elliot Trudeau and the new Canadian bilingualism policy he had instituted, but their eyes glazed over. Brian spoke of American football results. Rob had no interest in American football and wanted to know what Brian thought

## Chapter Nine

about the soccer World Cup. "What's that?" Brian asked. Karen and I just smiled vacuously and looked forward to an early end to the evening.

The life that Rob and I had been living did not change much after we were married on August 1st of the same year. We moved into a big house with five single students, two guys and three girls. All seven of us studied, went to class, partied and watched Star Trek. But my husband and I shared everything. We were able to take some of the same classes and work on assignments together. It was a great life.

Because we constituted a family once we were married, the government gave us much better grants and loans than we had been receiving. Usually, we had enough money to manage and if we ran out, we took our motorcycle and went home to my parents for dinner. In our final year at Glendon we started to apply for CUSO (Canadian University Services Overseas). Our first preference was a posting to Tanzania.

The news that we had been accepted for a two-year posting to Tanzania came in late spring. Our families, who had accepted our marriage after only six months of courtship, were not as sure about this next step in our lives. They were gracious and never outwardly negative, but we both knew they were confused, worried and unhappy about our imminent move to Dar.

Rob's father, Cecil, told me years later, "I thought with your degrees completed you would be safe. I wanted you to have good jobs, a happy family life with kids, a lovely home and enough money. When you chose to go to Africa, I believed you were making the worst mistake of your young lives. You see, I lived through the depression and have fought my entire life for financial security and a safe

## Chapter Nine

place to bring up my children. Why would you throw that all away and move to Africa? I knew my son well enough not to try to stop him, but we weren't happy. Mom and I decided that the best thing we could do would be to visit as soon as possible to make sure you were both okay."

As we boarded the flight on our way from London, Ontario to Toronto, *en-route* to Dar, I was a mess. Rob dragged me onto the plane as I cried my eyes out. "I can't do this. I've changed my mind. I'm not going," I wailed. We had a two hour stop-over in Toronto and I viewed that as the time to get off the flight and take a taxi back to my parents' home in Scarborough. Rob said little but gave no indication of relenting. I wondered what would happen if he went to Dar and I stayed behind.

Rob had arranged to meet our former house mates during the stopover in Toronto. We would take the two hours, and have a drink in the bar above the runway, looking out at all the planes taking off. I cried the whole time. Everyone was clearly embarrassed, and had no idea how to help.

Fifteen minutes before our plane was to leave for Montreal, Rob and I made a mad dash for the gate. "I'm sorry," said the flight attendant. "You're five minutes too late. We let the stand-by passengers on twenty minutes prior to the flight."

"Excuse me!" Rob said. "We're with the CUSO volunteer group heading to East Africa. We have to get on that flight."

"Look," she said not unkindly. "I understand, but it really is much too late, and you can't get on that plane. May I suggest that you go to the ticket counter, over there, and book the next flight out. That is all I can do." Surely

## Chapter Nine

this was a sign that we were making a mistake. Rob looked desperate.

"It's okay, honey," I told Rob. "Some things just aren't meant to be. Let's take some time to think about this."

"You've got to be joking. We are not going anywhere but to Africa. Come on." Rob grabbed my arm and pulled me to the counter. "You have to help us!" he said to the booking agent, a very attractive, young blonde. She looked at Rob in a way that indicated that she would love to do more than help him get on a plane. "We missed our flight, and we are about to miss our two-year posting in Africa. We have to catch the last Air Canada flight to Montreal to connect with Air Lingus before it leaves for Dublin and onward to Dar es Salaam."

I could see the agent melt. Rob put on his angelic smile and flashed his dimple. "I'll do whatever I can," she said and immediately got us on the next flight. "If there are no delays, you'll be fine because Air Lingus is late out of Chicago. You'll catch up with the group in Montreal. Have a great flight and good luck."

As we winged our way to Montreal, I cried and moaned. Rob patted, hugged and tried verbal persuasion to get me to see reason. Nothing worked. I was inconsolable, sad, and scared out of my wits. I had never been on a plane and that alone was enough to put me over the edge. The thought of Africa no longer seemed enticing. I wanted to go home!

No such luck. We re-joined our group in Montreal. Had Rob not been with me, I'm not sure what I would have done. "Why are you so upset?" he asked. "Remember you were the one who wanted this even before I did. You can't have changed your mind. You have to be okay, or I don't know what we'll do."

## Chapter Nine

"I'll try," I answered. "Before this was all a dream, a plan, and now it's really happening. I didn't know it would be so hard to say goodbye and two years seems like such a long time. I know I need to do this, or I'll never be satisfied. I'll always wonder."

# Chapter Ten
## If Only (2014)

I never imagined when we made the decision to volunteer in East Africa that it would have an impact on our future—our children yet to be born. At the time, we weren't even sure we wanted to have children. We were, after all, only 21-years old. Now I wonder how our lives would have evolved had we just been more conventional.

Had we stayed in Canada instead of moving all over the world, changing homes every three years, would our sons and daughters have been happier and healthier? Would my beautiful firstborn, Jennifer have died at 37 from lung cancer? Our own parents had given us the gift of continuity, community and belonging because they stayed in one place. Could we not have done the same for our four children?

Rob and I both have a sense of Canada that evades our offspring. We didn't move anywhere until we went away to university in our late teens. After that we chose to live uprooted lives never afraid for our family. We were trying to help the world but confident that all of us would prosper at the same time. Our children maintain they loved growing up as third culture kids. "The world is our oyster. We've had so many opportunities."

Was Jen stressed by our constant moves? Stress can cause disease. I know that our eldest was exposed to x-rays, food poisoning, vaccines against everything under the sun (except cancer) and what about pollution? There is no denying that we took her as a child to Cairo, Manila, and Abidjan—all those places have dirty air.

As a two-year-old, in Abidjan, Jen took anti TB drugs for six months because she was exposed to another

## Chapter Ten

baby with that disease. I still remember how we went to a local hospital and were led into a room with a huge x-ray machine, thirty times the size of what we are familiar with today. Who knows what damage those rays did to my daughter's lungs? Back in Canada the next summer we were informed that Jen never had TB. Her chances of getting it were negligible.

Rob and I had the same x-rays. Maybe we'll get cancer one day. The difference is that we were adults. Jen was only two and had no choice in all of this. On the spectrum of emotions, I am moving from anger to guilt. I know someone has to be held responsible for my daughter's early demise. It was more comfortable believing the fault lay with some kind of superpower. Now I wonder, was it our fault?

I want to go back, do things differently, be more careful, more caring—not allow what Rob and I wanted to get in the way of loving, nurturing and protecting our children. If only humans could see ahead, avoid mistakes and heartbreak. I would have done anything to protect my child—anything!

Sadly, it's far too late now. The harm has been done. I will always wonder whether we could have prevented this tragedy.

# Chapter Eleven
## Tiger, Tiger, What a Fright (1977)

Baby Jen, Rob and I live in a tiny white, two-bedroom, clapboard house with a wood-burning fireplace and a big bay window looking onto a street in the west end of Ottawa. It's not fancy but we're so happy. I decorate Jenny's room—buy a second-hand crib and paint it white. I choose mint green for the walls and sew cotton curtains covered with wild flowers. I find a cozy sheepskin rug to put on the shiny wood floor.

In the unfinished basement of our home there's an abandoned piece of furniture with two sides, a top and a back. I paint it the same mint green as the room and make a skirt of our curtain material to cover the front. *Voilà* - change table. I hide the diaper pail behind the fabric front. Above the crib Rob hangs a wind-up mobile with zoo animals that plays lullabies. Perfect!

Our baby loves to lie on her back, listen to music, kick her hands and feet and watch the animals as they circle above her head: tiger, lion, giraffe, zebra, rhino, hippo — round and round they go. She's a happy baby until we need her to go to sleep. That's the only time that she consistently cries.

I read Dr. Spock who tells me it is imperative to ignore the baby at bedtime—let her cry. The book promises that she will eventually fall asleep. Obviously, our daughter does not agree with the popular opinion of the time. Rob arrives home at seven—bedtime—to Jen's screaming. For night after night, we listen to her howl from seven to midnight. We can't take it anymore. Both of us are crying in frustration and sympathy. Rob caves first. "This is ridiculous," he says and picks our child up. He hands her to me to nurse.

## Chapter Eleven

She suckles and relaxes in my arms. Jen has won the battle of bedtime. After that we allow her to stay up all evening, dozing on and off in our arms. Everyone adjusts. I have more time in the day because she sleeps till 9:30 or 10:00 AM. and takes several naps throughout the afternoon.

"Rob, I'm sorry. I know you're tired after work and this can't be easy for you."

"God," says Rob. "It's far better than listening to our baby cry. I love being with her, and she's no problem as long as we don't try to make her sleep before she's ready. Obviously, she's a night person like me."

It's true. Jen is so easy. In the playpen, the Jolly Jumper, the baby swing, she amuses herself for hours. We barely know she's awake. We all go to bed at the same time and our determined little daughter seems quite happy with that scenario. I already understand how stubborn this little lady is. I'm no match for her.

Spring comes—May in all its glory—yellow daffodils, fragrant hyacinths, early tulips, lily of the valley. White and red trilliums line the bike paths and the forest floor. Birds flock to our feeders. Red cardinals, blue jays, yellow finches, upside down black and white nuthatches peck away at sunflower seeds. Bird songs mingle with the leafy scent of spring air.

Our baby is almost a year old. I put her in the baby seat behind me on my bike and phone my friend, Lydia, another new mom. "Meet me on the bike path at Richmond Road and the parkway. The Ottawa River path is clear of snow. It'll be fun. Weather's perfect—sunny and warm—a nice outing for us and our little ones."

We meet and ride happily along enjoying the day. Our babies are content and strapped safely in. A naked man with crazy, curly black hair all over his body, head and

## Chapter Eleven

long, thin limbs, jumps out in front of us. No communication between the two mothers is necessary. Lydia and I leap off our bikes holding onto the handle bars, babies in bike seats behind us. We charge towards the streaker, attacking him with our bikes. We're shouting at the top of our lungs—"Back off, or I'll kill you," I yell. Lydia just screams and screams so loud it hurts my ears.

Streaker dude is visibly terrified. I think he expected us to react with fear. He should never have messed with moms. He tucks his shrivelled penis between his legs and runs away into the bushes as fast as his spindly legs can carry him.

"Wo," says Lydia. "That was interesting. We should've been frightened. Instead, because of the babies, we were vicious mama-tigers. Amazing. I didn't know I had that in me."

"Honestly, I would have killed him," I add. "I bet he won't try anything like that any time soon. Not sure what he expected, but it wasn't what he got. Good for us. I almost feel sorry for the guy—loss of manhood and all that."

Lydia and I jump back on our bikes and speed off. Our babies don't appear to have noticed that anything unusual has transpired—just another beautiful spring day for moms and little ones to enjoy.

# Chapter Twelve
## Arrival in Dar es Salaam (1971)

"You'd think they'd never seen foreigners before," I shouted over the noise of hundreds of loud voices and airplanes landing. A sea of black faces stared at us. Our CUSO (Canadian University Services Overseas) group were shepherded across a black tarmac shimmering with heat waves, all of us pushing and shoving to break through the crowds. Sweat seeped from every pore of my body. Rob's face was beat red and his hair clung to his forehead in wet strings. His shirt was soaked.

Smells of jet fuel, body odour and dusty heat filled the air. "Guess they don't use deodorant here," I shouted without thinking. The minute the words were out of my mouth I felt terrible. Both Rob and I looked around furtively hoping I hadn't offended anyone. We needn't have worried. Everyone was speaking Swahili.

Weeds poked out of the broken concrete. There were no trees or flowers in sight, just black, cracked pavement, a low, run down, two-storey building and airplanes coming and going. The only colour came from the bright red, green, yellow, and blue patterns of palm trees, pineapples, giraffes, lions, ocean beaches and flowers printed on the kitenge cloth wrapped around most of the woman. Hopefully the real Africa was out there somewhere. "Not exactly what I'd dreamed of," I said to Rob.

Having just endured a three-day journey, which started in London, Ontario, with stopovers in Toronto, Montreal, Shannon, Dublin, Zurich, Nairobi and Mombasa, our group was so exhausted that everyone slept on the forty-five-minute bus ride into town. So much for excitement and our new life. Dirty, tired and overwhelmed, Rob and I

## Chapter Twelve

felt more like refugees than adventuresome explorers. When we reached the downtown *Twiga* (giraffe) hotel we stumbled up to the oasis of our cool, white, clean room and proceeded to sleep for the next fifteen hours.

"Mam, Sir" we heard at seven the next morning. "Bed tea."

"What's bed tea?" Rob asked as he stumbled to the door.

A lovely young woman with a huge, welcoming smile, dressed in a white starched uniform, stood in the doorway with a tea pot, two cups, milk, sugar and little yellow cakes on a tray. She entered our room and placed the morning snack on the bedside table.

"Thanks. What do we owe you?" Rob asked.

"No money sir. This just bed tea." she answered looking surprised.

After she left, we ran to the window and pulled the curtains open. We were looking up Independance Avenue to the central traffic circle in the heart of Dar es Salaam. Both of us jumped back immediately. "Wo—it's crazy bright and everything seems to be painted white. Pretty though. Look how the cars go into that round about. I wonder if they have any stop lights in town. I'm going to have to learn how to drive on the wrong side of the road," Rob said.

The roads were very wide and lined with bright yellow oleander bushes. All of the walls, around the offices, cascaded with bougainvillea flowers in shades of red, pink, and purple. Buildings were only about five stories high and white. A monument standing about 20-feet high, portraying what looked like a soldier dressed in long shorts and brandishing a rifle with a bayonet sticking out from one end, stood in the centre of the circle. Except for that reminder of warfare, the overall effect was charming.

## Chapter Twelve

When we finished our bed tea and got downstairs the heat hit us like a wall. "Holy cow," said Rob. "It's barely eight thirty in the morning. God only knows what it will feel like by noon."

Outside the hotel lobby a young man was selling beautiful *makonde* carvings made out of black ebony wood. "You buy. Be first sale today. Give me good luck. For you cheap," he called to us as we sauntered by.

Just a few yards down the sidewalk an attractive young woman, heavily made up, was sitting, legs stretched straight out, her *khanga* (wrap around *kitenge* cloth skirt) pulled tight around her hips to show off her sexual attributes. The strong, overwhelming scent of her cheap perfume filled up the space around the three of us. She looked Rob up and down seductively, gestured for him to come closer and said, "*Jambo, Habari gani*? (Hello, how are you?)"

"She can't be more than sixteen. She should be in school, not trying to pick up guys," I said.

"Who knows, she might be hungry or supporting a family. Maybe she has no choice but prostitution. You shouldn't be so judgmental," Rob shot back, looking annoyed. "This isn't Canada you know."

"Sorry!" I snapped. "Just saying. No need to put me down. This is all new and none of it is normal or easy."

"True. It's new for me too and overwhelming. Look over there: Arlechinos ice cream parlour. Let's get some. Might help us handle this heat."

"At orientation they said never to eat ice cream here. It's a medium for bacteria, often causes food poisoning—really dangerous!"

"Don't care," Rob answered. "I'm having some. The shop looks clean and there are some foreigners at the counter."

## Chapter Twelve

We sat at an indoor table, although the storefront was open to the street. I chose coconut and Rob had mango — the best ice cream I'd ever eaten.

"This must be Italian gelato," Rob commented. "I've never had anything quite like it—yum."

That day we walked for hours, taking everything in. The vibrant colours, light blue sky and bird song all along the harbour seemed almost an affront in the face of the incredible poverty we witnessed. Beggars were everywhere. The young women asking for money, with small babies lying beside them on dirty blankets, were the most heartbreaking. They looked dazed, skeletal and lost. No matter how many shillings we put into their bowls it wouldn't help for long. They'd be back tomorrow, begging again.

"Do you think they hate us?" I asked Rob. "They must resent us for having so much. I wish there was something more we could do."

Rob looked troubled but didn't answer. He just kept putting coins in begging bowls. We weren't making much money ourselves as volunteers, but we had a roof over our heads and enough to get by on. In contrast to what I saw around me, I felt rich, pampered, and guilty.

The expat community didn't help. On July 1st our CUSO volunteer group was invited to the Canadian High Commissioner's home. We dressed up as best we could. Most of us were new grads—blue jeans, sneakers and t-shirts having been our uniforms for the last few years. We were a rag tag, scruffy group compared to the glamorous gown and suit crowd we found at the palatial gardens of the official Canadian residence.

I felt like a total outsider, a waif. Rob, on the other hand, seemed to fit in well. He happily hobnobbed with The Canadian International Development Agency (CIDA) water, sanitation, and health experts. I stood by his side

## Chapter Twelve

and tried to listen to suggestions on how to solve the ills of the world, but my feet hurt, and I just wanted to go home. Royal palms lined the property and the smell of night blooming jasmine was sickly sweet. There was a gentle breeze from the ocean making the temperature almost bearable. I should have been enjoying this garden of Eden, but instead I couldn't shake the stark contrast between the poverty outside the walls and the plenty inside the garden gates.

There was a whole pig roasting on a spit beside the buffet tables. "Rob, isn't this a mostly Muslim country? Is it okay to serve pork?"

"No, pork is not the best choice. It's still oozing blood and I, for one, am not going to touch it."

I was finding it difficult to look at the pig, never mind eat it. I hadn't felt hungry since my arrival in Dar, and I'd lost some weight. Perhaps the difference in food and water was creating the constant feeling I had of slight nausea. Or maybe it was the oppressive heat and humidity wreaking havoc with my digestive system. I found myself hoping I wasn't pregnant.

Some of the CUSO volunteers were eating large quantities of everything and drinking a lot of alcohol in different forms. "Cool," said one of the agricultural experts, "they have Heineken and Canadian beer." All I could think was yuck.

I persuaded Rob to take me home. The next morning after bed tea and in the safety of our air-conditioned room I was beginning to feel better. My spirits lifted. "Did you enjoy last night?" I asked my handsome husband. Before he could answer there was a loud, dramatic knock on the door.

"Are you okay?" Sharon asked. "Almost everyone in our group is really sick. David and I are fine though."

## Chapter Twelve

"We're good too," Rob answered. "We didn't eat any pork because it seemed undercooked. Did you?"

"We're Jewish. Never touch the stuff."

We rushed up and down the halls checking on our friends. A few more people had not eaten pork, but the majority were extremely ill. I'd never witnessed food poisoning and was shocked. Already, after a night of vomiting and diarrhea, normally healthy young people looked shrunken.

"We need to get them medical attention quick," David said.

We called the CUSO director, and he arranged for the food poisoning victims to be taken to Muhumbili Hospital. Many remained there for over a week. Some were hooked up to inter-venous drips to restore their bodily fluids. Great way to start a posting.

# Chapter Thirteen
## Survival (2014)

I'm convinced that there is nothing worse than losing a child. Death, starvation, torture, all pale by comparison. Your child is your hope, your love, your destiny. Most parents would agree.

As a young mother, I nursed my kids for three years each—a total of four kids times three years—my God, that's 12 years. When those babies of mine looked up with adoration into my eyes my world was complete—such absolute joy and fulfillment. All I have ever wanted out of this life was for them to be healthy, happy, and successful.

It has been a year since our daughter died. November is a terrible time to die. The sky is black, the trees are skeletal, there is no light, and it rains all the time. For Jen though, the timing made sense. She hated winter and loved the tropics. She was always too cold in Canada, no matter how many clothes she wore. "Cold hands, warm heart," her great-grandmother used to tell her.

When Jen was three, we returned to Ottawa in late November, after a two-year posting in the Ivory Coast. Although she was born in Ottawa and spent her first year there, the only place Jen remembered was tropical, west coast Africa. I had tried to prepare her for the stark reality of a Canadian winter by sharing stories of snowflakes and snowmen, of ice skating and tobogganing.

The first time the snow fell I was so excited to introduce my first child to the magic of winter. Jen raced outside dressed in her baby blue snowsuit, her long red-blond curls escaping from the red woollen hat her grandma had knitted. She hated the mittens I put on her hands and immediately removed them to make a snowball.

## Chapter Thirteen

The second my little one touched the snow she looked up at me with huge, shocked, blue eyes.

"Cold, Mommy, cold. Wanna go home!" Jenny screamed. Her bottom lip quivered. She turned away from me in disgust and stomped up the porch stairs. I followed her into the house and made us both a cup of hot cocoa with marshmallows. "You said snow was fun. It's ouchy," Jen whimpered.

For the rest of that winter my child refused to play outside. She persisted in walking around with bare feet on the cold wooden floor of our home. The moment I put extra clothes on her for warmth, she tore them off. We spent most of that winter reading picture books that featured beaches, shovels, pails and swimming, while sitting by a roaring fire in our cozy living room. Her favourite plea was, "Take me back to Africa. I miss my beach. I wanna make sand castles, Mommy."

When I was a little kid, ten or so, I used to play silly games with my girlfriends. We would sit in a circle, join hands, breathe deeply and predict our future. After careful consideration, I believed that I would have one beautiful daughter, and then I would die young.

I remember those prophesies. It wasn't until I'd had my fourth child that I began to relax. Obviously, I was incorrect. I was going to follow family tradition and live untill one hundred and one like my grandma and her mother before her. Relief relaxed me into believing that my youthful predictions were ridiculous. Now I wonder if I was channelling the destiny of my first child, Jennifer. Did I have some future indication of what she would deal with—dying at 37, having had one incredible daughter?

I would have traded places with her, but I wasn't given that choice. If only her cancer had not been stage four. I could have donated a lung to save her. As is often true, the

## Chapter Thirteen

cancer was diagnosed far too late. By the time we found out she was sick, the disease had spread to her bones and to her brain.

I still can't talk about my daughter's death—not with anyone. Every Sunday Rob and I sing in a choir at our church. The music makes me cry, makes me remember what I have lost with every fibre of my being. I have considered quitting, but I love this activity, so I've persevered. It's embarrassing though. I wonder, do the congregation think I'm insane? Look at the weird lady in the choir stall at the front of church. Why do tears stream down her cheeks every Sunday? Is she crazy?

The worst thing is that Rob cries too. He's a guy, for God's sake! If they think I'm nuts, how do they feel about him? This singing is cathartic though, for both of us. We've talked about how we always feel so much better after church. Week after week we go, even though I'm still angry with God (if there is one). I know we're both struggling to come to terms with our spirituality. I miss that part of my life.

In the last months of her life, Jen faced impending death with courage and love. As her husband, Michel, said at her memorial, "As her body failed, her spirit grew stronger."

If anyone believed in an afterlife it was my daughter. She lived and breathed the Bahai faith. I know she would be disappointed with me now and with my maudlin failure to deal with her death. "There are parallel universes, and I am still with you," she would tell me.

Still, I can't hug her, tell her how I feel, or celebrate Christmas with her. I can't describe how much her dad and I, her husband and young daughter, as well as her siblings and friends, miss her. I can't explain how losing her has changed our lives—not in good ways. I worry that I'm

## Chapter Thirteen

forgetting her voice. I wish I had recorded her talking before she died.

The other day at a session on spirituality (why do I attend these stupid things?) my friend Jane shared that she felt her dead husband's presence. She was walking in the bush and a cardinal appeared on the ground in front of her. Cardinals were always a symbol of the love she and her husband shared. Jane believes that her husband had been there in the forest, with her. Dear God, could someone please send me some kind of sign, cause I'm getting nothing. Even a vivid dream would be an improvement. What is wrong with me?

I understand that I have to get it together and God knows, I'm trying. I go through the motions. I put on a brave face and go forward. It is in the quiet times that I fail to adjust or make sense out of anything. There are few things that make me happy.

I find solace in my younger daughter Megan, our two sons, Dan and Andrew as well as our grandchildren, but I am terrified for them. I listened to a segment on CBC radio news the other day. A young woman in her twenties was on an elevator in a Toronto subway and her scarf got caught. She died of strangulation. I immediately thought of my Megan. Stupid, I know. The fact that she lives in Toronto and takes the subway wasn't really grounds for my assumption that it might have been her. Logic is not really my strong suit these days.

I hear about a fatal car accident on the 401 in Toronto, and I'm afraid for my son Dan. Please get a grip! There are two and a half million people in Toronto. My son is an excellent driver. What are the odds? Our youngest, Andrew, who is now 23, lives in Peterborough. There is not much in the news about that place—too small. Still, I worry about him. He's young—is he eating well? Is that

## Chapter Thirteen

job he has just taken safe? Is there too much toxicity in the plant? Cancer is always an option.

Funny that I no longer worry about Rob and me. We've had the most incredible, love filled lives. We've lived and worked all over the world, had eight postings in Tanzania, Ivory Coast, Egypt, Jamaica, the Philippines, France, Ethiopia, and Bangladesh. We've lived a life that most people can't even imagine. If we die, it would be okay. I just wish I could be sure that my kids and grandkids would outlive us and have healthy, long, fulfilling lives.

## Chapter Fourteen
### Milton Obote's Kids (1971)

Two weeks after our arrival in Africa, Rob and I were given our job assignments. Initially we had set out to change the world, to make a difference. What utter rot and nonsense. What had we been thinking? As flower children of the late sixties, perhaps we can be forgiven. We were, after all, part of the culture of those crazy times. We had no skills or experience, no real knowledge to impart, but we did have plenty in the way of *naïveté* and good intentions. Africa was going to give us more than we had ever bargained for—friendship, wisdom, patience, and adventure beyond our wildest hopes—whether or not we deserved it.

To say we were in over our heads was a bit of an understatement. I was assigned to teach 50 students, ranging in age from five to seven, at the Bunge Primary School in Dar. They spoke almost no English. Rob, with only an undergraduate degree in economics, was given a job as a special advisor in the prime minister's office dealing with regional development. Can you imagine? We were woefully under qualified. What wisdom can an oblivious 21-year-old Canadian impart to the Prime Minister of Tanzania: how to score a hat trick in hockey or cook with maple syrup?

Though I may not have been dealing with the prime minister, I had my own work troubles and cultural disparities to overcome in the classroom. Despite no training as a teacher, I was hoping to be as inspiring as Mr. Little was to me. I couldn't bring myself to beat the children despite being told that it was the preferred form of discipline. I was expected to teach through fear, but desperately needed to be loved. Miscommunication often

## Chapter Fourteen

occurred due to language barriers and differing customs. Each day provided a new challenge.

On this particular day, my problems were to come from two of my favourite students: Jack and John. The boys looked very much alike. Both had chunky, solid bodies and the same shy, winning smile. Their favourite activity was recess, when they would spend their time digging trenches and making sand castles or hanging upside down from the gym bars shouting, "Teacher, teacher, look!" I continually confused one with the other because they always seemed to do everything together.

But these boys weren't just any students, and their real names were not Jack or John; their African names might have allowed people to uncover their secret identities. I was taken into confidence by the family because it was my responsibility to make sure they came to no harm during the school day—on pain of death. They were the five-year-old son and six-year-old nephew of the deposed Ugandan president, Milton Obote. At the time, the early seventies, Obote was camping out at the palace with Julius Nyerere, the leader of Tanzania. Idi Amin, the man who had ousted Obote, was at the peak of his power in Uganda and was systematically killing or deporting vast groups of the population for both ethnic and political differences. For Obote and his family to stay in their own country would have been a death sentence.

Being young and *naïve* I don't think I ever considered that anything would go wrong. The children were in the classroom with me all day, and an armoured chauffeur driven car dropped them off and picked them up from school.

I wondered what their life in exile was like—living in hiding, away from friends and everything they had once known. It could not have been easy for the two little boys.

## Chapter Fourteen

They were never allowed to play without supervision, or go anywhere without body guards. Even at school two policemen were always lurking around our school compound.

It was difficult to oversee fifty active children while they played outside in the large, walled yard. And, I confess, on the day the event occurred, my mind was on the romantic dinner that Rob and I had planned for that night. I was going through the motions of patrolling the school compound with my student helpers Jamila and Joy holding my hands.

John raced across the yard, tackled me around the knees, and sent the two little girls flying. "What's wrong with you?" I shouted, shocked and unnerved by his unusual rudeness. For one awful moment he stood frozen, groping for the English words to explain.

All he could manage was, "Come quick, teacher, come quick!"

I flew across the yard in the direction of his pointing. In minutes the whole class was gathered with me under the baobab tree at the far corner of the compound. Jack was sitting in the sand, hunched over and whimpering, holding up a limp hand. I knelt beside him, my heartbeat pounding in my ears.

"Itchy, sore," Jack whined, indicating the palm of his hand. I carefully examined the area but could see nothing.

"He play with snake," John added.

I raced across the distance to the school and shot up the stairs. "Help, help," I screamed.

Mrs. Mbago, my officious head mistress, came out of her office looking annoyed to see the *mzungu*, the crazy white teacher, in such a state. "What on earth ..." she stuttered.

"Jack has been bitten by a snake."

## Chapter Fourteen

No more words were wasted. Her usually slow moving, obese body accelerated into immediate action. Time was not on our side: it could be a black mamba, a puff adder, a cobra, or even a Gabon viper. Regardless of the type of snake, bites in Tanzania were often fatal. The nurse and I were dispatched to the yard to check on Jack while the office staff concentrated on getting medical assistance and calling his family. The other teachers evacuated the children from the schoolyard.

When we reached Jack, the nurse applied a tourniquet to his wrist. The little boy seemed curious and amazingly cheerful for someone who had just been bitten by a snake. "How do you feel?" asked the nurse, checking his pulse and looking closely at her patient. "Where is the bite?"

"I good," Jack said with a lopsided grin, as he pointed to his unmarked hand.

"What did the snake look like?" I questioned, hoping to add to any knowledge that might help save the child. "Was it big?" I stretched out both arms to convey my meaning.

"Come, I show," John said, leading me by the hand and pulling me over to a big hole the boys had dug. Around the top they had used little twigs and sticks to produce a trap. Inside there were ten fuzzy brightly-coloured caterpillars.

"They itchy, sore," John pronounced, looking extremely proud of his language ability. "Jack touch too many snake," he added to clarify the situation.

When we returned to Jack, he was looking even more delighted with all the attention. "Caterpillars not snakes," I muttered to the nurse. She took one look at the expression on my face, put her arm around my shoulders and giggled.

## Chapter Fourteen

"Those particular caterpillars cause a burning and itching sensation in people with sensitive skin," she laughed. "I think we've found the culprit. Thank God."

I was so relieved that I started to chuckle just as the emergency team arrived with Mrs. Mbago. "This is the boy who was bitten," she shouted, her military voice booming above my giggles. Pointing to Jack, she regarded me with suspicion.

"Actually," I choked out, "It turns out it was not exactly a snake."

"Well, what was it then? Pull yourself together. This is serious and there's no time to waste." I looked at our British nurse hoping she might take over. No such luck.

"It was a fuzzy, green and yellow ... caterpillar," I said sheepishly.

"A what?" Mrs. Mbago said in disbelief.

"You know, one of those itchy types."

"Are you absolutely certain?" she questioned, looking serious.

"Yes. The kids have them trapped in a hole over there. That's definitely what it was," I answered, waiting for the tirade that would surely follow.

My headmistress threw back her head and laughed: a gutsy, natural, happy kind of laugh. She put her arm around my waste and said, "Thank God. You had better get back to your classroom and teach those children some English. Quickly!"

# Chapter Fifteen
## Spot the Dog in Tanzania (1971)

"Rob," I said, one day over dinner, "I have a problem. The only readers I have for my kids have been donated by the British Government. They're totally inappropriate because they feature two blond haired, blue-eyed kids—Dick and Jane. They do stuff like making pancakes and pulling red wagons. I'm sure my students have no idea what they're on about. I only have one white, Brit kid in my class, and even he has lived his whole life in Africa. Any ideas?"

"You could try to get money from the small projects fund at the Canadian High Commission. You should write a proposal. They're always looking for innovative initiatives to support. They're slow with that fund, so it won't happen quickly. In the meantime, you'll just have to work with what you've got."

Each day I listened to my students as they read, "See Jane swing." or "Look, Jack, look. See the yellow leaves falling from the trees." It amazed me that my kids never seemed surprised or bored by the antics of Dick and Jane. The reader also featured a cute little black and white dog called Spot. I imagined when the children read, "Go spot go," they could at least identify with the puppy. All kids loved dogs.

I began to feel that despite the challenges of teaching 49 non-English-speaking kids, I was making progress. The students started to read a few words and appeared to understand most of what I said to them. But I wanted more. The kids seemed to be just going through the motions. I wanted to hear laughter. I needed to be liked.

## Chapter Fifteen

I set up activity centres: a painting table with brushes, sponges, and palettes dappled with bright and pastel water colours; a craft bench where boxes and cardboard tubes could be turned into skyscrapers and freight trains; a math area for calculating angles and counting beads; a science corner for pouring, measuring, and weighing; a terrarium for observing small bugs and tropical plants; and a reading centre designed to invoke the spirit of Spot the dog.

I was gaining trust. There was sharing. "Teacher, teacher," Ahmed called proudly holding up a photo. "Look my family. See."

There was curiosity. "Teacher," asked Jamila, "You have husband, children?" And there were polite invitations to dinner which I eagerly accepted. People were kind. Attempts were made to make the new *mzungu* (crazy white) teacher feel more at home. The dark pools of my children's eyes had begun to focus. There were smiles, infrequent but present, in their soft, smooth faces. Better still, the kids would reach out and touch me, just a gentle, fleeting tap, a hand resting on my arm for a split second, but a measure of their trust.

"Teacher, I have a new puppy, and it looks like Spot, so that's what I called him," said Toby, the only white kid in my class. "Can I bring my dog in for show and tell?"

"Of course," I said. What a way to engage my students. I could just imagine the excitement, the thrill, and laughter a puppy would bring. I couldn't wait for Spot's visit. I thought, I really did, that a pup might just break the quiet reserve of my kids.

The dog, as it turned out, was not as young or as small as I had imagined. Toby's Spot was white with black splotches, but the resemblance to our storybook character ended there. In the reader Spot was a tiny ball of soft, fluffy, roundness—obedient and well-behaved. The

## Chapter Fifteen

animal in front of me was a gangly, bounding, barking parcel of pure, angular energy—the type of pup that jumps all over you and grabs your hand in its teeth to pull you into some game.

"Isn't he cute?" Toby asked, anxious to share his treasure with all of us. His little freckled face shone with excitement and pride. Spot strained at his leash, anxious to play with the kids.

At first, I was so busy helping to control the over exuberant pup that I didn't notice my class. It took a few seconds for me to sense that something was terribly wrong.

I handed the leash to Toby's mom and turned my attention to my kids. "Isn't Toby's Spot cute?" I asked. No response. The masks of my 49 students had dropped and what I witnessed was not at all what I had hoped for. The children, without exception, had looks of pure terror. Their eyes grew huge in their small faces. They rose in one unified gesture and scuttled backward towards the wall where they stayed pinned, as far away from Toby, teacher and the dog as they could get.

Ahmed started to wail and Spot responded by barking loudly. The sound in the room was ear-splitting as every child began to sob. For one awful moment I wondered what would happen if Spot broke from his leash.

"Toby, you and your mom please get the dog out of our classroom now," I shouted above the noise. Toby started crying, and I hated myself for sounding so harsh. Just as Spot was leaving, my overbearing head mistress came blustering through our door.

"What do you think you're doing?" she screamed at me, officious as usual. "Why is there a dog in this classroom? For goodness sakes children, stop that awful noise." As if

## Chapter Fifteen

on cue the sobbing disappeared, although several children still whimpered quietly.

"I'm so sorry," I said, more to my students than to Headmistress Mbago. "I thought it would be fun to have Toby bring his dog for show and tell."

"Dogs," said Mrs. Mbago in disgust, "are filthy creatures. They are not kept as pets in our Muslim homes. *Wazungus* (crazy whites) keep vicious guard dogs to ward off thieves, and they are terrifying animals. Dirty street dogs carry rabies. The children hate and fear dogs. I can't believe you haven't noticed."

\*\*\*

When I got home that evening Rob took one look at me and said, "You look like you had a terrible day. Wanna talk about it?" I explained what had happened, and my husband put his arms protectively around me. "That's awful," he said. "I thought all kids loved dogs. It was an easy mistake to make. Occasionally, I feel like we shouldn't be here. It seems we're doing more harm than good. Are you sorry we came to Africa?"

"Sometimes," I answered. "Everything's so hard to figure out. But mostly I'm glad we're here. I love my students, and it's gotta get easier. Just think of all the stories we'll have to tell our kids and grandkids."

## *Chapter Sixteen*

### Too Hot (1971)

"Toby put on your clothes!" I shouted, in shock. If you take off your underpants I will …"

The truth was that I had no idea what I would do. Forty-nine willing and curious, African and Asian, five-year-old faces looked adoringly up at me, waiting to see my reaction. Visions of headmistress Mbago roaring down from her office upstairs, clouded my brain. "Toby, I don't want anyone to see you like this. It is not allowed, and you will be in big trouble."

It wasn't fair. Toby, the only white kid in my class was more trouble than all my other students put together. He looked up at me in complete confusion. His Brit parents, psychology professors at the University of Dar Es Salaam, had taught him to do whatever came naturally and that meant taking off his clothes if he was too hot. Tanzania was, for him, only a temporary place, a phase in a life that would be comfortable and secure. The colour of his skin was all wrong for the unrelenting African glare. So was his attitude.

The ferocious Mrs. Mbago, our head mistress, took great pride in taking all the horrible tendencies of a colonialist minority and embodying them in a far more officious and convincing manor than any implant to her society could have imagined. Our school was run like a military camp only with less humour and camaraderie.

"Toby please," I begged. I could feel the tears welling up behind my eyes. God, please don't let me cry. How could one little kid defeat me? I even liked him. He was cute in a ragamuffin sort of way, small for his age, blond tousled hair and freckles covering his impish,

## Chapter Sixteen

grinning face. His were the only hugs I got in that classroom. Toby was the only child who wasn't afraid of me.

I knew what the parents of most of the kids in the class would tell me to do. "Beat him, miss, beat him." They had already instructed me to do exactly that if I had any problems with their children. Not that I would have had any trouble. Those kids barely spoke and then only deferentially, eyes focussed on the floor tiles. It had taken me weeks to figure out that they couldn't read but had just memorized every word in their readers.

"But miss, I'm so hot and Mommy always lets me take my clothes off in our garden. It feels so much better like this," he said gesturing towards his nearly nude little body. I looked down at him and then at the starched, navy shorts and pristine white, short-sleeved shirts of the other boys in my class. Their laced-up leather shoes and blue knee-high socks completed their school uniforms. I, too, questioned the logic of such a dress code. Toby was right. Nakedness was a far more sensible condition.

No argument there kid I thought as I stood red-faced, hair plastered to my forehead, sweat trickling from every pore of my body. But what I said was, "Toby, you are not in your garden, you are in school. You cannot just undress here. It's against the rules."

"But why?" he pleaded meeting my glare with an angelic, troubled look. Toby was not a brat, not at all. His parents' laissez-faire policy might have worked in England, but it was a hard philosophy to follow in a strict, elite, African public school.

"Look kiddo we can't just all undress. What would happen then?" Visions of fifty naked children running happily through the gates of Bunge Primary flitted through my head. The headlines in the Dar Es Salaam

*Chapter Sixteen*

English Daily News would read, "Freedom for repressed children. Fifty Tanzanian five-year old kids were seen parading, stark nude, in the streets yesterday led by one Canadian teacher and her wayward British student Toby."

"We can all take off our pants and shirts. Maybe Mommy can bring my plastic pool. That would be so much fun." This wasn't going the way I had hoped. How to explain why nakedness just wouldn't work here to one very intelligent five-year old? Already Toby had stripped down to his underpants. I wondered if the little guy could somehow sense my fear, my lack of ability to deal with the situation. By now the other students, obedient as they normally were, had begun to giggle. I was losing my grip. The day before my biggest concern had been that we were the noisiest class in the entire school. Ironic that such a small thing could have worried me. Boy, was I in trouble?

"Toby if you put your clothes on, I will play a game with the whole class. How about follow the leader?" My kids looked blank and then Ahmed started to unbutton his shirt. "No, I meant follow me, not Toby." Obviously, the game Toby was playing held more appeal than anything that I had to offer. I watched as Toby began to peel off his last article of clothing.

"How about hide-and-seek," I stammered. No one was paying any attention to me. They were all staring in awe at Toby. Finally, in desperation, I had to let him see my weakness, my lack of authority or knowledge. I had no choice. Honesty was my last hope. "Toby, do you like me?" My question had surprised him, so he stopped and looked up at me.

"Course I like you," he answered, looking confused. "You're way nicer than any of the other teachers. But miss, I'm too hot."

## Chapter Sixteen

"Toby, if you don't get dressed and anyone sees you like this I will get fired. Do you know what that means? It means I will lose my job. Everyone will laugh at me because I let you take off your clothes, and we will both be in big trouble. Do you understand?"

"Yes, I think so," He paused to consider the question. For a moment Toby surveyed his universe and the possibilities it presented. I held my breath realizing that I was completely in the grasp of a five-year-old boy's whims.

"Toby dutifully picked up his uniform and began to put it on. "But this is really too hot for me."

"For me too Toby," I agreed. It looked like Toby and I would get to stay in Africa, at least, for a while longer.

# Chapter Seventeen
## Recalling Jen's Celebration of Life (2015)

Today is the second anniversary of Jen's death. Can she really have been away from me that long? I have gone from avoiding the pain of thinking about her to being terrified that I will forget. Now I desperately cling to everything that allows me to bring her essence closer. With that in mind I am examining my memories—listening to Jen's favourite music, looking at old videos, recalling her Celebration of Life that occurred on November 30th, 2013.

I don't remember much about that day, but fortunately there are records: pictures, readings, written accounts of what people said. Call it morbid, but I'm spending hours with these artifacts of my daughter's life. I have come across what our daughter, Megan, and our son, Dan, said on that day. Instead of weeping, drinking too much and taking sleeping pills to hide from their words I find myself celebrating Jennifer. The realization that we have done a great job with our kids hits me full on. I am proud of every one of our four children. Maybe Rob and I have something to celebrate after all. In this moment, I push the guilt aside—I allow myself to bask in the beauty of my family.

Megan, Jen's younger sister by eleven years spoke first at her memorial.

*"I know if Jenny were here right now, she would want us to be doing this memorial with a gigantic mug of tea in each of our hands. Tea was her remedy for everything, as long as the mug contained more milk than tea, and at least six heaping scoops of sugar. I can picture her most vividly with her slender fingers wrapped around the biggest mug she could find, pulling all-nighters*

## Chapter Seventeen

*talking about life, beauty, spirituality, and love. She may have been the only person in the world who truly believed tea was an antidote for sleep. Whenever we were together, no time was bedtime. There was always too much to discuss, too many adventures for two sisters to have together.*

*It was precisely this attitude that gave Jenny such an exciting life. Well, that and the fact that she was born to two parents who treated world travel like it was takeout at an exotic restaurant. (Well, yes dear, we are due for another near-death experience. Maybe Thai this time? Or Jamaican?) But Jen was never one to be outdone; she had deep sea diving to do, dik-diks (tiny African deer) to adopt, and some Bangladeshi villages to save from arsenic poisoning with her water filtration system.*

*Travelling brings you to the doorstep of so many different souls and Jenny wanted to know all of them: their stories, their plights, their joy, and the sound of their laughter. She would always come away with new friends. It was impossible not to love my beautiful sister. And when she left, her absence was keenly felt. Jen always burned a little brighter than everyone else. Each moment was saturated with passion and every gesture was imbued with charisma. It was easy to get carried away by her laugh or be entranced by her grace. Her radiance warmed up even the coldest Ottawa winter.*

\*\*\*

*Our parents used to own a cottage on Buck Lake with a swampy pond in the back. While most little girls would have been concerned with making sand castles on the beach, my sister had a mission: she was determined to save the frogs from the leech infestation. Each day she would wade into the mud to catch as many frogs as daylight would allow. She would emerge covered in*

## Chapter Seventeen

*hundreds of big juicy leeches, just like the frogs in her bucket. Before taking the blood suckers off herself, she would attend to each of her green friends, sprinkling salt onto the leeches and poking them off with tweezers. Then, at last, when every frog had been helped, she would remove the bloated leeches from herself. The next day, she would repeat the process again. When asked why, she said, "Well, I'm a lot bigger than a frog and I have a lot more blood to give," as if it were obvious.*

*But that was just my sister. She was boundlessly giving and unflaggingly generous. And she wanted to save the world one frog at a time.*

*I remember coming home from elementary school one day and telling teenage Jenny that one of the girls in my class always looked like she'd gotten dressed in the dark. Jenny scolded me immediately. 'Those could be the only clothes she has,' she said. 'Or she could be colour-blind. Or maybe she just has a more unique fashion sense. Either way, you don't know her reasoning or her story. Don't be so quick to judge!' She was right, and it's a lesson I've carried with me ever since. My sister was never judgmental—she gave everyone the benefit of the doubt. She never said an unkind word about anyone. Although she did mention that people in Orillia like to go about the town in their pyjamas with just a hint of disdain. You have to draw the line somewhere!*

*Jenny made you strive to be a better person. But, despite my sister's altruistic nature and devotion to faith, my sister was ... endearingly flawed. There was a reason one of her nicknames was the late, great Jennifer. I don't believe early was a word in her vocabulary, in fact, the phrase "on time" may not have been in there either.*

*Getting a hold of her was impossible because she never ever answered her phone—a rare quality in an age where*

## Chapter Seventeen

*people seem to be attached to their mobile devices. In fact, when she finally got her own old-school flip phone, she somehow managed to accidentally melt it on the top of the stove. But, for all the planes missed and technology melted, she had many qualities that she passed on to her beautiful daughter Kaia. Jenny was an incredible mother. In Kaia I see Jenny's faith, strength, bravery, and kindness every day. The shining values Kaia carries are a testament to the way Jenny lived her life and to whom she was as a person. I'm also sure that Kaia inherited that mischievousness, Jenny's fly dance moves and her penchant for overly sweet tea.*

*My sister made me believe in magic. She protected me and took care of me. We laughed together and cried together. We were more than sisters. We were best friends.*

*I have always felt a bit guilty; felt as if Jenny drew the short straw. She battled with sickness, even before she was diagnosed with cancer. Life never exactly went according to plan. Luckily, she wasn't big on the whole planning thing anyway. She enjoyed every single moment she had. When she was faced with a dilemma or hardship, she did so with strength and bravery, and more than a few laughs.*

*When Jenny passed away—far too early—she left an indelible imprint on the world. Life seems bereft without her warmth. It seems like she had only just begun. She found the love of her life. She discovered what she wanted to do. She raised a beautiful daughter. Jenny had so much more to teach us. The loss of my sister is felt in all the moments that she will miss out on and all the memories we won't be able to create with her. She will never meet the children I hope to one day have, never watch her daughter fall in love, graduate, grow up.*

## Chapter Seventeen

*But I've learned something about love in the deepest moments of grief, something hopeful that I want to share with Kaia, Jen's husband Michel, my parents, my brothers, our family, and friends, during this difficult time. Even though my heart is broken, shattered into thousands of fragments, I know I can trust those I love to hold the pieces together until I can do so on my own. Jenny believed in the redeeming power of love above all else. She told me, on our last day spent together before her death, that it was all the love from everyone around her every step of her life that helped her get through every hard time, every moment of adversity, every difficulty she ever faced, with strength and grace. And so it is in this resounding love that I trust, because I can feel it, all encompassing, around me every day. I can feel her presence, as reassuringly as if she was holding my hand. I know she is with me, protecting me, loving me, watching over me every step of the way.*

*So, to Jenny I raise a teacup. I am proud of you for the life you lived, for the person you became. You are missed. You are remembered. You are greatly loved."*

***

Our eldest son, Dan (younger than Jen by three years and eight months) spoke second:

*"Hi everyone; and thanks for coming tonight. I'll try to make this quick but, obviously, it could be a bit tough to get through. My amazing wife, Kim, like most women compared to their men, is probably more emotionally intelligent than I am. She would tell you straight up she's just more intelligent than I am, but let's stick to the emotional bit for now —and she didn't want me to speak ... said she wasn't sure I'd make it through this thing so, based on that, we could be in for a rough ride, but please bear with me ... I wanted to say something for Jen.*

## Chapter Seventeen

*I could always make Jen laugh, and that's saying something because most everyone here knows me, and knows I'm probably not quite as funny as I'd like to be. I'll sure miss that quirky sense of humour Jen and I shared, but all of you are just going to have to crack more jokes and, more importantly, you're also going to have to laugh at all of mine. Okay, maybe laugh at some of them anyway.*

*I'm going to take a walk down memory lane. Everyone here knows I'm not exaggerating one bit when I speak to how kind, graceful, how much of a perfectionist (but how that perfection was seldom on time) and most importantly how loving and brave Jen was... To start, as you've heard from the story Meg told about Jen rescuing frogs from our old cottage frog pond, Jen was so kind that not only would she not harm a fly, she probably tried to nurse an injured fly or two back to health. And clearly, looking at what a spectacular little lady Kaia, Jen's daughter, has become, that kindness, caring, and patience made her an amazing parent too.*

*Jen loved to dance, I guess the difference between her and the rest of our immediate family being that Jen actually had real tangible talent to go along with the endless enthusiasm we all share for gesticulating madly to music. And Jen did not simply, as the saying goes, dance as if no one was watching. Jen danced with perfect abandon whether no one or everyone was watching, and if everyone was watching then they probably needed to get off their asses and out on the dance floor. So, as my cousin Tommy likes to say, hopefully we'll get to cut some rug here tonight and bust a move for Jen. She would like that. Not sure how to put this, but Jen was punctually-challenged, or perhaps time-deficient. Y'know what, let's be serious, I'm not sure Jen was on time for anything ever*

## Chapter Seventeen

*—especially, that is, before her time conscious better halves showed up in the form of Kaia and Michel. I mean I'm notoriously slow and often late, but compared to my lovely sister, I'm like a friggin Swiss watch. I guess Jen did not simply do things in her own time, the endeavours which Jen undertook were assigned no timetable and were completed only if and when they were perfect. With Xmas around the corner, it seems fitting to remember those perfect Xmas gift baskets Jen made my parents and her siblings one year. Those baskets were awesome, absolutely loaded with chocolate, candles, small gifts, tinsel, foil, ribbons ... Amazing. Of course, the only thing was that they arrived just before New-Years. Meh, we didn't care. Let's just say Jen knew that good things take time.*

*Of all the things I did know about Jen something I did not know, until she was diagnosed, was just how brave my sister could be. Jen's faith, and the great love she felt for and received from others, made her completely fearless in the face of what I now realize, and she well knew, was almost a daily game of Russian roulette. Jen weathered her treatments but also found the strength to live her life fully through this past spring, summer, and fall. In fact, Jen discussed her tough, tough chemo and radiation with jokes and the calm resolve others describe working through a difficult but everyday issue, like getting weeds out of their garden or a stain out of their shirt. And that's not because Jen did not know the medical details and impossible odds of what she was up against. Jen was too smart for that. It was because her bravery, faith and love made her totally unafraid of what was next. Jenny did not simply fight that disease, it could not hold a candle to her spirit, and she was so brave that she rose above it.*

## Chapter Seventeen

*To start to wrap this up, mostly I wanted to say that Jen was such a special person I think we can do more than just remember her. Raised by the same, if not devout then at least persistent Anglican parents, it's funny that Jen and I developed very different ideas of faith. Jen was, of course, devoutly Baha'i, while I was, and still am, searching for a different kind of high. I think we shared an idea of just how precious life is. So always live life to the fullest. If, instead of just remembering Jen, all of us here today can live with even a fraction of the grace, kindness, faith, and courage that Jen showed, be insanely and perfectly late for a few appointments, dance a little more, not care for meaningless material things, but instead occupy ourselves with treasuring and loving our friends and family at every opportunity, then Jen can live on through all of us in a very real way, and I guarantee the world will be a better place for it.*

*To Kaia, Michel, my mom and dad, as hard as this is for Meg, Andrew and I, I am sure it is tougher still for you. I know it's tougher still for you. I love you all dearly and I know I speak for everyone in this room when I say: if you ever need or want any help or support do not hesitate for one second to ask. I will do whatever I can.*

*Sphen (Dan's nickname for Jen), I love you and I know you would want us (in fairly rapid order) to go from mourning you to celebrating you. So, I'll say just that, let's celebrate tonight, for Jen. I love you all, and thank you again for being here."*

I am trying to move on, as Dan put it, "go from mourning to celebrating" my daughter. As Meg pointed out, I need to trust my loved ones, especially my husband, to hold me together until I am able to do so myself. Despite my kids' words I'm still fighting hard not to fall apart.

# Chapter Eighteen
## How to Save a Marriage (2015)

Just two years since we discovered that Jen had stage four lung cancer, I have discovered a new reality. When Jen died, I wanted to escape from everything familiar, my husband in particular. The pain of our shared grief was too much to bear. That feeling has gradually shifted. Now I must work to save our marriage. I want to. This story of our past, before children, is one way of connecting to my partner. When I write about our time in Tanzania, I remember how much we have been through and how much we need each other to survive. Not even the death of our first-born child should have the power to destroy us.

What I know is this: we are and always will be better together than separate. We are the parents of four wonderful kids and grandparents of amazing grandchildren. Despite our terrible loss we cannot afford to lose what time we have left in denial and grief.

That doesn't mean that we are not struggling. We are. You don't lose a child and get away with it. There is still so much shared guilt. There is blame. There is shame. There is doubt for both of us. Will our marriage survive?

As I write this account of our early days in Tanzania, I am spiralling down a rabbit hole of time, back to a kinder, happier place. I sit at our cottage on Christian Island, my soul's home. I can hear the waves lapping on the shore of Georgian Bay. The sky is blue streaked with puffy white clouds. The sun shines through the pine trees and paints spider web shadow patterns on the sand dunes that lead to the lake. The smell of sand, cedar and fresh water lulls me, assures me that the beauty of this earth goes on no matter what I'm feeling. The high-pitched drone of cicadas

## Chapter Eighteen

and the phoebe bird chanting "phoebe, phoebe, phoebe" distract me from my grief.

I am trying to breathe in and out, in and out—to let go—to live in the godgiven grace of this moment—to appreciate all the universe still has to offer—to write the early story of Rob and me—to document memories of Jen, so I will never forget her.

Stop with the panic, the resentment, the pain of all that I have lost. Smarten the hell up! I can't go on like this: crying all the time, unable to move forward with relationships, hiding behind a mask of fake smiles, hating parents who haven't lost a child, resenting my partner and myself for not having stopped Jen's death. It's easier to slip away, to stop caring, to let despair conquer.

I keep remembering the bad things, although there is so much to look forward to, so much good to appreciate. My mind will not cooperate. I'm drifting to the negative yet again—my anger the foremost emotion. I keep thinking about what my friend, Pat, said to me at Jen's memorial, "You are so brave. If I lost my daughter, I don't think I could go on." Silly woman! How could she imagine that I have a choice? Life doesn't just stop even though sometimes I would like it to. I am not brave, not at all. What I am is desperately sad.

I wish I could just stop—let the world disappear. Does Pat not understand that I still have to be present? This grief is not mine alone. Jen left a huge hole in the universe of the people that loved her: family, close friends. At least I am not alone in my grieving. These are my people, the people that I love, who are going through this madness with me. They understand.

Another friend, Susan, said that maybe Jen's death happened to teach me something. Is she nuts? Does she really imagine that for one moment I would entertain such

## Chapter Eighteen

a ridiculous thought? I'm way past the middle of my life. Jen had so much to live for and to give to the world. I could never benefit from the death of my beautiful daughter—never! That kind of comment makes me crazy, makes me wonder about the nature of human beings. It's hard to imagine that someone can really be that self-centred, that stupid. Do these women have so little empathy that they can't imagine what I'm going through?

My other least favourite expression that has been quoted to me since Jen died is: "What doesn't kill you makes you stronger." Does the fact that my daughter's death is almost killing me mean anything. Real death is physical. Spiritual death is different—a shutdown of the senses, a withdrawal from life, a despair that transcends reality. Is that not a kind of death, the kind that no one sees?

Another dreadful analogy is that cancer patients are warriors fighting the good fight, implying that if they lose that battle, they are weak and haven't tried hard enough to win. Cancer is an illness that can happen to anyone. Some survive, others don't. It has nothing to do with strength of character or the will to live. No one wanted to live more than Jen did. She died because she was sick with stage four lung cancer and that is an incurable disease. Think massive heart attack—no one says victims of that malady lost the battle.

I wish that all those people who make silly, unhelpful comments would just shut the hell up and leave me alone. I need to get back to writing the story of Rob and me in Tanzania—to focus on the two of us and how life was then.

# Chapter Nineteen
## *Mwalimu* (Teacher) (1971)

Rob and I originally chose Tanzania over other African nations because of president Nyerere or *Mwalimu* (teacher), as the local people called him. He was an enlightened leader who wanted desperately to fight ignorance, poverty, and disease in his country. To do this *Mwalimu* formed an African socialistic model that was applauded by leaders around the world. It was based on the idea of *Ujamaa* or family moving together. Nyerere argued that Tanzania was already socialistic because the country was an extension of village life where people shared resources and took care of one another. The idea of a nuclear family didn't exist in Tanzania. *Mwalimu's* theories made sense to us and seemed like a solution to the development problems of Africa, not just Tanzania.

After we'd been in Dar for two months, Rob came home one day looking discouraged. "You know," he said, "this socialism thing sounded great on paper, but it just doesn't seem to be working. The government is nationalizing things like butcheries, bakeries, small hotels and gas stations. They're kicking out the Asians and turning businesses over to people who have no idea how to run them. I lined up for ages to get bread just to be told that they're all out. That would never have happened when the Amlani family was running the bakery."

"What happened to them?" I asked.

"Not sure but they've gone. They also ran that guest house next to their bakery, and it's closed. I spoke to Sadru, the father, about a month ago. He was asking me tons of questions about Canada, Calgary in particular. Maybe they've already arrived there."

## Chapter Nineteen

"Ya and now no one knows how to run the bakery where we used to get our bread. Wonderful. Were they able to get money for their businesses?" I asked Rob.

"I doubt that they got much. It's difficult to get money out of the country. That's why the Asian owners of the *Twiga* hotel, where we stayed initially, asked us to pay them in Canadian dollars, offshore. That family are probably in Canada by now as well."

"That's so unfair to people who have worked their whole lives to make a living for their families. They should get more for their businesses. How else are they supposed to manage when they reach another country?" I asked.

"I agree," Rob answered, "but at least they're not getting killed on the streets like the Ugandan Asians under Idi Amin. Dar is going to be in big trouble if this continues. The East African Asians are the entrepreneurs and small businessmen here. God forbid that they all flee. There goes the butcher, the baker and the *dukas* (small convenience stores), not to mention the restaurants, the cooking oil distributors, the bars, and the petrol stations. The city will grind to a halt."

It wasn't only Asians who were complaining about the new socialist Tanzania. Our African friends were not very happy about it either. Larger *Ujamaa* collectives were being set up in the countryside to replace small traditional villages. Logically, if people were moved from their homes and taken to *Ujamaa* villages everyone would have access to schools, health care, agricultural equipment and seeds. It sounded like a wonderful philosophy, but not everyone agreed.

Rob and I, as well as his workmates and their partners, would gather at the Cozy Café in Dar to chill after work. The Cozy was an Indian restaurant and I wondered how

## Chapter Nineteen

long it would be before someone thought to nationalize it. The place was located in a charming outdoor courtyard with red, white, pink, and orange bougainvillea vines covering the walls. Bright yellow weaver birds darted in and out of their elongated, hanging nests, chirping and chattering noisily. Red and white checkered gingham table clothes covered the round tables and the atmosphere was relaxed, pleasant.

Our friends and their partners were a varied and interesting group of Asians, Africans, and expats. After a few drinks of either *konyagi* (local gin) and tonic, or Kilimanjaro, our preferred Tanzanian beer, the conversation at the Cozy would get interesting. "I love the short forms they use at the office," Rob joked one day after work.

"Ya," answered John Olomi, a Tanzanian from the Chagga tribe near Mount Kilimanjaro. "Like 'PA ' for put away, or 'BF' for bring forward."

"And then there is 'FYI' (for your information,)" added Gerry Lewisk another CUSO volunteer.

"My favourite is 'CCL'," Rob said, grinning."

"What's that one?" I asked.

"That would be, 'couldn't care less', answered Karim, an Ismaili Tanzanian of Asian descent.

"Don't forget, 'KYA,' said Gerry. 'Cover your ass'"

"On a more serious note, what do you think of *Ujamaa*?" Rob asked.

"My parents are terrified that they'll have to give up their home to go to an *Ujamaa* village," answered John Olomi. "Poor *Mwalimu* (Nyerere) is trying so hard to make things better, but most people in my area are very much against *Ujamaa*. Can't say as I blame them. Who wants to be forced to move? Most of us have lived our whole lives in our ancestral villages. Often families have

## Chapter Nineteen

their own small grove of coffee bushes or vegetable gardens."

"Hey, I've studied hard and hope to be able to travel, make great money, have a western style home and send my kids to university in the city," added Godfrey Ngoye. "I have absolutely no intention of living in an *Ujamaa* village and volunteering my time and energy to the betterment of the masses. That philosophy is way too close to the Chinese model. Have you seen those poor buggers in the Chinese camps who are here to work on the railway?"

"Ya," I answered. "They're all dressed in black pants, shirts and shoes, everyone exactly the same. There are no women and all they seem to do is work. Not a lot of fun. As far as I can tell they aren't even allowed out of those walled tent encampments. I've never seen any of them in the city, except in huge, escorted groups."

"If that's what we have to look forward to I, for one, am not buying. In fact, I haven't met many people who think socialism is a good idea," added John Olomi.

I looked at Rob and realized that we were both feeling a bit sheepish. All our wonderful ideas of what would work in Africa were based on idealism when the truth was that we had come here with no concept of the background, dreams or culture of the Tanzanian people. True, we were learning, but helping—no way. Even Nyerere, a true statesman who had lived and worked in the country his whole life and had a desire to save his people from hardship, didn't seem to be getting it right. Who did Rob and I think we were?

# Chapter Twenty
## Oblivia (1980)

Part of my guilt in dealing with Jen's loss is that I never understood her. In fact, sometimes she drove me nuts. I used to feel that any other mother would have been a better match. Was she switched at birth? I'm grounded, always early or, at least, on time. Time—oh God—she never got it.

Flashback. Kindergarten. Ottawa. Mrs. Giles her first teacher—"There's something wrong with your child. I call all the other children in from recess. They come. Half an hour later I realize that Jennifer is still outside playing, all by herself. It had occurred to me that perhaps she is hard of hearing, but I don't think that's the problem. She knows she's supposed to be in the classroom. She just doesn't care."

My face burns with the criticism. I'm angry. My child is perfect. Does that stupid teacher not have worse problems to deal with? She's obviously a bitch. Instead of admitting that Jen has a problem, we change her school. This time the new teacher tells me our kid is perfect: polite, kind, obedient, infinitely creative and absolutely adorable — just what we need to hear—same kid, different teacher. Weird.

I push my worries away and try to be the best mother I can be. My kiddo is artistic and loves to make a mess, so against my neat, programmed nature, we do crazy art projects. At Christmas, I put red and green paint in pie plates. Jen loves the tactile sensation of placing hands and feet in the gooey, slimy paint. Her face glows with pleasure, and she gets paint everywhere—in her hair, on her clothes, all over the basement. Her little hand and

## Chapter Twenty

footprints in the colours of Christmas, on the rolls of white paper, wrap all our presents—such messy but satisfying results.

Even though I'm trying to lose weight we bake together and give plates of Christmas goodies to the dentist, doctor, teacher, and friend's families—everyone. The smell of chocolate, cinnamon, cloves and ginger fills our home. Clouds of flour dust float in the air and land on every surface. I gain ten pounds. Jen almost never samples our wares, but takes such joy in giving our treats to others.

At school, I strove to be popular. Not my girl. She couldn't care less. Instead, she befriends kids who need her. There's one little boy in her kindergarten class that cries the whole day in a corner, if Jenny is absent and unable to mother him. "I hate it when Jenny's away," her teacher tells me. "She's my little teacher's helper."

In grade five, Jen becomes best friends with a child who has a hideous, huge lump—a birth defect—on her right cheek. Jenny feels sorry for the little girl. "Kids are mean to Louise," my daughter explains. "It's not fair. Not her fault. I wanna make it better."

"I get that Jen, but Louise is mean spirited, unkind and a bully with you. You don't have to put up with that kind of behaviour from her. You're, kind and charismatic. Anyone would be lucky to be your friend." Jen, of course won't listen. The final straw comes when her, so called, friend starts to follow Jen home and, one day, beats her up.

Our solution is to move our daughter immediately to an alternative school across town. Jenny is perfectly suited to her new environment, but continually misses the school bus in the morning. We, of course, have to drive her to school. The tension in our home mounts because both Rob and I have jobs, schedules. "Damn it, Jenny, hurry up!

## Chapter Twenty

You're making everyone late," is a familiar morning refrain.

Even our six-year-old son Dan, who's never late for anything, is frustrated. "Mommy," he asks, "Why can't Jen just be on time? It's not fair. It makes you guys mad all the time." Rob refers to our daughter as The Late Great Jenny B, or sometimes in total frustration, Oblivia.

The alternative school has less emphasis on time-oriented activities, less competition. Jen is allowed to work and study on her own terms, and excels. When she's left to choose her own book, she reads for hours. Instead of rote math she's given real problems to solve using measurements and numbers. She's challenged, motivated and successful.

Still some things have to be completed on time, so my mom sits with Jen all one night to finish her science project on moulds. For months, we've had moulds growing on oranges, garbage, plants, and plates of food. All of us are sneezing. Her finished project proves amazing: intricate drawings, scientific explanations well beyond a ten-year old's scope, and an oral presentation that is clear, precise and emphasizes all that Jenny has learned. It's worth all the work, all the hours, because Jen wins first prize at the science fair.

"She's such a perfectionist. I'm not surprised that she won," my mom comments looking proud but worried. "She's going to have to change a bit when she gets older. She can't always leave everything to the last minute. I wonder: if I hadn't been here to push her, would she have completed the project at all?"

I begin to understand that Jen is amazing, but completely different from all my friend's children. A second science fair project at the alternative school leads to a disagreement between us that is typical of our

## Chapter Twenty

different personalities. "Mom," she confides in me after school one day, "I have a great idea for the science fair this year. I need something original to win again. I want to grow bean plants in the same sun, soil and light conditions, but treat them differently to see if that has any effect on their growth."

"Sweetie," I plead with Jen. "They'll all grow the same way. You won't win the contest, you'll probably fail."

My daughter ignores me and before long she has nine bean plants, each with the same growing conditions. She carefully puts a black sticker on the three plants she will treat badly, a red sticker on the three plants she will completely ignore and a white sticker on the ones she'll lavish with attention and praise.

To the ill-fated beans she is critical. "You're stupid. You're ugly. I hate you," I hear her shouting. Later, she's with the lucky plants. "You're strong and beautiful. I love you," she tells them. She also sings and plays classical music for her favoured beans. With the neutral plants there is complete silence, but she sits with them for an equal amount of time.

Jen meticulously documents the emotional treatment of the plants, the only variable that is different. I give up worrying and realize that she will be given enough marks to pass just because of her scientific process. Rob is more doubtful. "This is stupid. There's no way the plants will grow differently. She might not get a passing grade."

Both Rob and I are wrong. To this day I can barely believe the result of her experiment. The plants that were praised prospered and grew to be about eight inches high. The ones that were left alone achieved about five inches of growth. The ones she was mean to only grew a bit and one died.

## Chapter Twenty

"I told you it would work Mom." Jen doesn't win at the fair, but her experiment is very impressive. She receives tons of accolades for creativity and innovation. Her mark is an A. Both Rob and I are left feeling proud and amazed. But she has worked far too hard and has left everything to last minute. Jen is exhausted. Once the fair is over, she succumbs to a terrible flu and is ill for two weeks.

"Oh God," laments Rob. "Will she ever learn to work smart?"

## Chapter Twenty-One
### Masai Warrior (1971)

There were times in that faraway African place when I could almost imagine that I was home in Ottawa. I would close the shutters to block out the bright-white glare, burn incense to smother the smell of dust and turn up the volume of Joni Mitchell singing, "I wish I had a river to skate away on." I remember my escape into Tolkien's book, 'The Hobbit'. Somehow the lengthy description of hairy hobbit feet and the diminutive Bilbo Baggins fighting the mighty forces of evil made it easier for me to create a mental landscape far removed from my African reality.

There were other times when I felt unreal, a sort of white ghost like figure wandering in a foggy, yet sun-filled dream place that only existed in my head. Our first up county trip to the Serengeti Game Park was like that. The female lions sprawled on their backs, feet up in the air with their furry white stomachs exposed. They looked more like kitties than predatory beasts. I wanted to get close to them.

The half-eaten carcass of a torn wildebeest, smelling of rotten flesh, lay, fly ridden, beside the great cats as they licked their soft brown fur and stretched, yawning in the sun. Camera in hand, I inched forward until I was only feet away. The lions didn't even acknowledge my presence—just went on basking comfortably in the hot afternoon sun.

Rob's voice, shocked, urgent, reached me, as if from a great distance. "Stop! You're far too close. Back up slowly." I felt annoyed, jerked from my innocent, mindless reverie but, I did what I was told.

## Chapter Twenty-One

On that same trip we went to Moshi, a cool mountain town at the foot of the mighty, snow-capped Mount Kilimanjaro. We stayed in the bungalow of another Canadian volunteer couple. To our delight, the view of the mountain, blue, green, and white tipped, greeted us the very first morning. It rose up alone out of the flat, grass blown landscape and loomed above us. An hour after sunrise the mountain was shrouded in clouds.

That evening we sat on the porch, sun-downers (*konyagi* and tonic) in our hands, and waited to see Kili again. As the sun sank lower and the birds sang louder, the mountain appeared like magic. I got out my camera and took shots from every angle, anxious to share the majesty of the moment with friends and family back home.

Moshi, although tropical, was nothing like Dar es Salaam. The air was crisp and had a clean, fresh pine scent. It was a treat to burrow down under the covers at night to keep warm. "If only we had been posted to Moshi instead of Dar, I'm sure I would be much happier," I told Rob. "Maybe we could get a transfer."

On one of the days of our visit we went swimming in a mountain pool, and I was really cold for the first time since I'd left Canada. "Gotcha," Rob teased as he jumped up from under the water and grabbed me round the waist. There was no one around and the fire-red flame trees cast their reflections on the smooth, dark surface. Brightly coloured birds—turquoise, scarlet, yellow—darted and dove. Their voices echoed and danced with the sound of the rippling water.

I wanted to stay there. That world seemed more vivid, alive and colourful than anything I had ever imagined. For a moment I could almost forget the beggars, the rats, the putrid smells and my own inability to cope. I felt cocooned in the peace and beauty that can be Africa. The

## Chapter Twenty-One

sun was still strong despite the chill, so we pulled ourselves up onto the rocks and lay wrapped in each other's arms, until the warmth returned to our bodies.

Too soon, it was time for me to leave Moshi. Rob was staying behind to help plan development projects. But my school holiday was over, so I had to return to my students in Dar, on a rickety *Tata* bus, by myself. "Are you sure you're up to this?" Rob asked. "You do realize that you'll be sharing the trip with crates of chickens and maybe a goat or two?"

"Don't worry. I'll be just fine," I answered dreading the trip and worrying about making it all the way from Moshi to Dar alone. I got on the bus clutching my suitcase so hard that my fingers were numb and carefully selected a seat by the window, close to the front, as far away from the noisy, smelly animals as possible. They were relegated to the roof and the back of the bus.

I sat quietly and slowly got my bearings. This was going to be an adventure. I leaned happily out the window and grinned at my husband, who was standing below me looking very uncomfortable about our agreed upon arrangement. "Hey, I'll be okay. Promise. It'll be fun."

"Sounded fine yesterday, but I dunno. Maybe we could find another way to get you home, but I just can't think of a solution," Rob said, looking very young and out of place beside the bus. I was so focussed on him that I smelled rather than saw a person sit down beside me.

I turned and looked in astonishment at a nearly naked, young Masai warrior. His hair was dyed ochre red from mud and cow dung, as was the custom, and in one long, thin, elegant hand he held a sharp spear. In the other hand he had the severed, still bloody tail of a lion. "I kill lion yesterday," he said by way of introduction.

## Chapter Twenty-One

The Masai proudly offered to let me hold the lion's tail. "We don't have weapons in Canada," I stammered, sounding stupid even to myself. By now the overpowering odour of bodies and animals had begun to upset my stomach. I fought the impulse to gag and put my head out the window. The fresh air and comforting sight of my husband greeted me.

Then I did the unthinkable. I started to cry; not just a civilized, quiet, teary cry but a loud sobbing that split the air of the bus. People stared at me with open curiosity. I could feel as well as see the looks of concern and caring on their faces. My Masai took off his red cape and draped it around my shoulders.

The thought of what I did next still embarrasses me to this day. I flung the offending garment at the surprised Masai teenager, stood up, squeezed past his lanky, stork legs and crashed my way out of the bus. I launched myself into Rob's arms and continued to wail.

"What the hell," my husband managed, holding me. "Don't cry. Everyone's looking at us. We will find another way to get you home."

From the safety of my new vantage point, I ventured a glance at the crowd. I had become a spectacle, an object of curiosity. "Look at the strange young woman from far away," everyone's gaze seemed to be shouting.

"Oh no, what have I done?" I said, looking at the Masai who had moved to the window seat and was staring down at me. Tears pooled at the corners of his dark, sensuous eyes. His lower lip quivered. The air of pride and dignity from his successful lion hunt had slipped. The warrior seemed ashamed as if this incident was his fault instead of mine.

"Are you okay love?" Rob asked. "Let's get you out of here. What happened anyway?"

## Chapter Twenty-One

"No wonder they call us *wazungu* (crazy white people)," I said. Rob looked confused.

# Chapter Twenty-Two

## Wind and Water (1988)

"Oh God, I don't know what to do with my teenager," my friend in Ottawa tells me. "She's transformed from a cute little kid to a monster; spends days in her room, swears non-stop, is sullen, refuses to go to school and says she hates me. I worry that she's smoking or taking drugs. I don't know how much longer I can take her behaviour. What's your secret? Jen's such a wonderful kid, but then so was my Jessy before she got hormones."

I'm silent—no answer. I shrug my shoulders. What am I supposed to say? Jen is excelling at school. Her teachers love her. When she's not glued to a good book, our daughter spends her spare time pursuing dance and drama and is begging to take up scuba diving. She has nice friends. Serious boyfriends haven't appeared on the radar. Polite and caring, Jen helps with chores, babysits for her two younger siblings and tells us lots of stories about her experiences at school. She's constantly late and a perfectionist—some things never change—but we have nothing to complain about.

Puberty has hit. Jen has mild acne, braces on her teeth and her hair is wild and floats, Afro-style, around her head. She's all legs and arms—gangly. That my daughter will someday become a stunning, graceful and beautiful woman is not evident in her teens. Regardless, Rob and I could not be prouder of our eldest daughter. We must be doing something right.

When Jen graduates from her alternative school after grade six, our family is posted to Jamaica. "Aren't you worried that Jen will have trouble coping?—such a bad age to move a child," her teacher says.

## Chapter Twenty-Two

"No, Jen's used to our lifestyle, and we always have each other. We're an extremely close family. She and her brother Dan are best friends, and now we have our baby, Megan, who Jen adores. We come home every summer and sometimes for Christmas to be with extended family. Because we're moving to an island paradise, practically everyone we know has promised to visit."

Despite my assurances to her teacher, Jen clings to her best friend, Margaret, at the airport and cries all the way to our new home in Kingston, Jamaica. I begin to worry that this move might be harder than previous ones. Will my teenager adapt to her new environment? She's become shyer lately and less confidant.

We're at a High Commission welcoming party in Kingston when we hear the frightening news. Hurricane Gilbert is bearing down on us. We've only been in our new house for two days and in the country for two weeks. We're coping with a High Commission pack up kit—dishes, bedding, household items. Our shipment from Canada, as well as our new car, are sitting on the tarmac at the port in Kingston. If there is a storm surge, we'll lose everything we own.

Will our family be safe? On the way home we brave the crowds to stock up on food and water, then race home to see our neighbours boarding up their windows. We live on a compound with three Jamaican families. There's a shared pool and all of the homes are palatial. We've not met the people we will spend our lives with for the next three years.

"I know what we can do," Dan, our eight-year-old, says. "We can go to the basement. We'll be safe there."

My mouth hangs open. Rob looks stunned. Jen hugs her little brother close and gives him the bad news. "Sweetie, there are no basements here." Dan's lip trembles

## Chapter Twenty-Two

as he tries not to cry. "We can go into the cupboard under the central staircase—safe and lots of room. We'll take food and water and pretend we're camping. It'll be fun. We'll read 'The Lion, the Witch and the Wardrobe' by candlelight, and you won't have to go to school for days."

Dan grins and looks excited. Our new neighbours arrive with tools, plywood and duck-tape to help us prepare for the storm. With help, we board up some windows and tape the others to prevent broken glass from flying around. Mr. Paisley, our neighbour, tells us, "We haven't had a hurricane for fifty years but this one's going to be major. They're predicting winds of 320 kilometres and the eye of the storm will come directly over us." As we stand in our yard chatting the sky is blue and there isn't a hint of wind. "I've been watching the forecast," he adds, "hoping that the storm will change direction—unlikely at this stage."

Now we just have to live through this nightmare. At least it's daytime when the hurricane hits. It sounds like a freight train charging through our living room—an enormous, ear-splitting roar that goes on and on, unrelenting. Our windows whistle and our house shakes. My kids are terrified—eyes wide open, trembling, huddled together under the stairs. We hug each other and hope for the best.

By the time I'm brave enough to go to the window and glance outside there are huge satellite dishes flying through the air. The roof on a house across the street from our compound is gone. The storm has uprooted a royal palm in our yard; its carcass lies, fronds down, in the swimming pool. Electric wires hang useless but dangerous; they drape over houses and lawns. The rain and wind pummel our windows and water streams under doors—our house, which is modern and well-built, groans

## Chapter Twenty-Two

under the strain, and I wonder will it hold up. Will we lose our roof? What then?

Hours after the storm hits with such fury, the world seems to stop and rest; there's an eerie silence—no bird song, no wind, no rustle of nature—nothing moves and the blue sky radiates warmth. Sun scorches the ground and reveals the damage that the hurricane has dealt. We venture outside. The air is thick with humidity; steam is rising from the grass. The eye of Hurricane Gilbert will continue to lie directly above us, granting a temporary and artificial peace, for about one hour. Our neighbours, wave to us from across the compound. Everyone seems to be fine.

When the hurricane hits again it's coming from the opposite direction, so the winds lash the back of our home. Because the front of our house has held out, we begin to relax. Jen and Rob, the ultimate optimists, seem more excited than scared. "Wow, this is cool—our first hurricane. I can't wait to call Margaret. She's not going to believe it," Jen says.

"Doubt we'll have phone lines or electricity for a long time," I answer. "Remember, we still have to survive the next half of the hurricane before we can tell anyone anything. The second part will be just as bad as the first. We should go back under the stairs. What was that noise?"

A crash from upstairs brings looks of terror from all of us. Newspapers in the living room blow off the end table. "Oh no," says Rob. "I think a window broke in one of the bedrooms. I'm going up. You guys get back under the stairs now!"

Minutes later Rob shouts, "Julie I need your help."

When I arrive in our upstairs bedroom the place is in chaos. A large front, bay window has blown out. "I want to try to board up the hole," Rob tells me.

## Chapter Twenty-Two

"You can't—too much wind. Forget it!" Rob listens to me for once in his life. Instead, we pull down a shower curtain, ram it into the door jamb between the bedroom and the hall and slam the door shut. We're sacrificing the bedroom but saving the situation. The bedroom door into the hall does not get the full force of the wind, so our solution seems to work. We go back downstairs and tell the kids that the problem is fixed. I'm not sure I believe that we will survive, but I know Rob does—'nothing can go wrong' is his motto. The kids seem calmer. It's me who is most likely to lose it.

When the storm is finally over, I no longer recognize the landscape. There are few trees left standing; the pool is filled with green leaves, tree limbs and garden furniture. The gazebo has blown away. Everything in our compound, except the four houses, is destroyed. It's impossible to go out to the street, although we can get to our three neighbours. People are out sharing stories, ice cream for the kids and alcohol for the adults.

In the aftermath of Hurricane Gilbert, Jamaica has to deal with curfews, looting, lack of supplies, no electricity or water—the list goes on. Miraculously, we have water. Our area is called 'Waterworks'. The water tower looms on a hill above our house and so no electricity is needed. Gravity gives us water. Our friends from the Canadian High Commission are coming to us to have showers.

It's September and school should be starting, but the hurricane has prevented that. The High Commission decides that non-essential spouses and children need to be sent home as soon as possible, and a week and a half after the storm the kids and I, against our wishes, are on a plane for Toronto. We stay with my brother and his family in Pickering. Jen and Dan go to school with their cousins.

## Chapter Twenty-Two

There's not enough room in grade seven, so Jen is tested and allowed to attend grade eight.

Three weeks before Christmas and three months after Gilbert, we're allowed to return to Jamaica. Rob, as head of the Canadian aid program, is still working long hours to deal with the aftermath of the hurricane. When we arrive, he's there to greet us. My husband carries our luggage across the tarmac and loads it into the High Commission vehicle. Home at last.

That evening Rob has prepared a wonderful meal. We sit at dinner, grateful to be together. The kids go to bed and Rob and I cuddle in the living room. "God, I missed you guys," he says.

"Me too," I answer. I look at Rob. "Are you okay?" I ask. His face is red, and he winces in pain when he moves. "What's wrong?"

"Don't know, but I think you better phone the High Commission doctor? It just started, but I have incredible pain in my abdomen—worse than anything I've ever experienced."

I call, and luckily for us the Canadian doctor comes immediately. He examines Rob and declares that he needs an operation—now. Rob has a strangulated hernia. Flying him out is impossible; the hernia could burst. Because of the hurricane the hospital is not operating at its full capacity, but Rob is taken immediately and has surgery. His drip bag is hung on a coat hanger. The electricity comes from a generator. I'm not filled with confidence.

At home, later in the evening, I sit crying on the couch. "What's wrong, Mom," Jen asks, putting her arm around my shoulders. "Dad's going to be fine. It's a good thing we are home though and could reach the doctor."

Jen's right. Despite the circumstances the operation has gone well. Rob's recuperation time is minimal. I'm

## Chapter Twenty-Two

grateful to have a healthy, happy family. We've just survived a hurricane and an operation. How lucky are we!

Several months later, with the clean-up from the hurricane behind us, I'm relaxing on the porch of our Jamaican home when the phone rings. "Do you have a minute?" Alan our friend and neighbour asks. "There's something I think you should know. When we were diving with Jen the other day, she really scared me. She's a natural underwater—relaxed, strong, confident and in her element. I was taking underwater photos of the kids and when I focussed on Jen to get a close up, I noticed that she was stroking a sting ray—the dangerous kind. I got a picture so I can show you. There was nothing I could have done to help her. I would have only made the ray nervous. Had it decided to sting Jen she could have died. The girl has no fear—none—which is not unusual in kids her age."

"What should we do?" I ask. "She loves diving."

"I think she needs more diving lessons asap, so she'll learn to identify the dangers under the water. She hasn't a clue."

The direction of our life in Kingston changes. We get scuba training for both Jen and Dan. We spend hours with our friends Alan and Alison, watching our kids and their son John learn to scuba dive in pools and then at the beach. At home, while my two older children are at school, I swim with baby Meg every day. Our shared pool has no fence around it, so she needs to learn to swim — fast.

By the time she's two Megan is as comfortable in water as she is on land. We have a diplomatic cocktail party around our pool. Our little one toddles out of the house, and jumps straight into the water, clothes and all. The ambassador from Sweden, in his three-piece suit and shiny black shoes, launches himself into the pool to save her.

## Chapter Twenty-Two

Meg is not impressed and fights the poor guy with all her tiny strength, while she shouts, "No touch me." We're mortified.

Jen, who was supposed be watching Megan, comes running out just in time to see the action. "I'm so sorry." She says to everyone. "She got away from me and ran straight out here before I could catch her. Good thing she can swim like a fish."

Our Swedish diplomat has the grace to roar with laughter. "You're kidding," he sputters. "Meg's so little. I've never seen anything like that. Do you guys spend all of your time in the pool?"

"Pretty much," Rob says. "Sorry about your suit."

## Chapter Twenty-Three
### Mzee (Old One) (1971)

I loved Rob's parents. Who wouldn't? It didn't take me long to realize that my husband and I were at the centre of their universe. They adored their son and because I was his wife, they had to love me too. However, the thought of their imminent visit to our home in Dar es Salaam was daunting. They lived in Kapuskasing which is north of the arctic water shed. They had never been outside of North America.

Cec and Phyll arrived at the airport in full winter gear. In mid-November, they'd come from minus 25 degree centigrade temperatures to plus 35 in Africa. Poor souls. They were lugging more suitcases than I had ever seen and were wearing winter coats, heavy boots and scarves. They looked ridiculous. Aliens from Mars could not have been more out of place.

I knew we were in big trouble when the first words out of Cec's mouth were, "Everyone is black." Big surprise there. We were, after all, in an African country. Who would have thought that people might be black?

"Dad," Rob said trying to make his father more comfortable. "Our mayor, in Kap, is black. He was my teacher and choir master. You know he's a great guy."

"That's true," said Rob's dad. "I don't have anything against black people, but there are no white people here. Only us. It just feels strange, that's all."

"Take off those coats and boots, or you're going to fry. The car is close, just outside in the parking lot. Let's get you home," Rob instructed heading to the exit door.

We drove out of the airport in our ancient *Roho (Renault-4)*. The car was in such bad repair that we could see through the floor boards to the road below. Phyll and I

## Chapter Twenty-Three

sat in the back with the guys up front. I noticed that, exhausted as she may have been, Rob's mom managed to keep her feet up and never placed them on the floor of our vehicle. I didn't blame her one bit.

We arrived at our home, the Oceanic Motel. Our volunteer organization, CUSO, had not been able to find us permanent lodgings, so we had a temporary suite of rooms. Sounds exotic but it was far from that. The first thing my mother-in-law did was to inspect the kitchen. Oh, dear. It was clean, at least as clean as was possible. She immediately opened the cupboard and, of course, hordes of beady-eyed, antennae-flailing cockroaches poured out.

Was she shocked? You bet she was. However, Phyll didn't overreact. She simply asked me if we had any insect repellent, took the can of DDT and began to bomb our home with it. Not just the kitchen, the whole apartment. It's a wonder that Rob and I have not died from a toxic overdose of chemicals long ago. "I'll fix this," she pronounced, always a woman of action. We didn't see another cockroach for at least three days.

Their first morning was pleasant and relaxing. Rob's parents slept well despite the heat. Dressed in summer clothing, they looked refreshed and ready for their big adventure. We went to breakfast in the downstairs dining room and were served, as usual, fresh papaya with lime (something they had never tasted), a fluffy omelette with onion and tomato, and delicious Tanzanian highland coffee. "This is perfect," Cec exclaimed, beaming. "I'm so glad we've come for a visit."

Fortunately, Rob's mom and dad had arrived during my winter school break, so I could devote all my time to them. "Shall we go to the market and buy some fresh veggies for dinner?" I asked.

## Chapter Twenty-Three

"Sounds like a great idea," Cec answered. "Can't wait to get out there and see how the other half live." I wasn't sure what he meant by that, but it was clear that the market was an acceptable idea.

"Do you mind if I stay home?" Phyll asked.

"Sure. The bleach and bug spray are under the sink," I answered.

"Great and can I make some soup for lunch?"

"That would be lovely," I replied. I wondered if Phyll was going to stay at home for the whole visit, doing my chores.

When Dad and I arrived at the market it didn't take me long to realize that my usual shopping spree had taken on a new flavour. All the vendors asked me who the elderly gentleman was. They shook his hand and wished him well. Cec was in his element; so much attention and respect. "What are they calling me?" he asked.

"*Mzee*," I replied.

"What does that mean?"

"It means old one." I answered.

"Hey, I'm not that old. I'm only 64."

"I know Dad, but you have white hair and people have immense respect for age here. It's a badge of honour."

"That's odd," said Cec.

Maybe so, I thought, but it was kind of sweet. I soon figured out that if I let my father-in-law bargain the prices would come down. He could get great deals. He also loved to talk and conversed with everyone. I learned that the pineapple vendor had three kids and two wives. Who knew?

Laden with more fresh fruit and vegetables than I'd ever purchased at one time, we hopped into the *Roho* and sped towards home. "Dad," I said "be a bit careful driving.

## Chapter Twenty-Three

The road rules here are very loose and people drive differently."

"Yeah, of course," my father-in-law said sounding insulted. "I have never had an accident." Just at that moment we stopped at a major intersection. Even though I couldn't drive, I noticed immediately that Cec was looking the wrong way before pulling out into traffic. I realized, too late, that because we were driving on the opposite side of the road his natural inclination was to look left, but the traffic was approaching from the right. I felt the car surge forward and thought, "We're in big trouble."

My first shock was to hear Dad say, "Oh shit." I had never heard him swear before. It was completely against my concept of the dignified man that I knew. I felt a jolt and saw that we had been sideswiped by an oncoming vehicle. Dad and I were shaken up but in one piece, so we slowly got out of the car. Across the side of the other vehicle was scrawled the logo, 'Bank of Tanzania'.

It was my turn to think, oh shit. Could we not have picked a regular citizen to bump into? The bumper and front of the big black Bank of Tanzania Mercedes was smashed completely in. Our car was totalled.

It was a miracle that no one was hurt. The driver of the other car spoke no English, but it was clear to us and to him who was at fault. The police arrived, took measurements, made notes and then told us we were free to go. However, Cec would be charged with reckless driving and called to court. We exchanged papers and found a local taxi to take us home.

And then we waited and waited. A week went by. Rob and I had visions of his father being put in jail or, at the very least, prevented from returning to Canada. After ten days, we finally received a summons to court. My father-in-law was obviously trying to make an effort to appear

## Chapter Twenty-Three

calm, but he looked grey. To be in a foreign country and charged with an offence was more worrying than any of us cared to admit.

The courtroom was full of people. Some were crying. We registered and sat down to wait our turn. Case after case was heard, and sentences handed down. One man was given a life sentence for murdering his wife's lover. Another was told that he could either serve a thirty-year prison term or go to Mozambique to fight for Frelimo (The People's Liberation Army of Mozambique) against the Portuguese. The man chose jail.

"Why are they making us wait so long?" asked Dad. "Holy, moley, it was just a little accident and no one was hurt. This is terrible. I just want to go back to the motel."

"Me too dad," Rob answered "but we have no choice." Rob went up to try to talk to someone in authority and was told, none too kindly, to sit down and wait our turn. Rob was looking furious. I began to worry that he might lose his temper.

Two hours went by and there still seemed to be a steady stream of cases. "Are they ever going to get to us? What do you think they'll decide to do?" Dad asked.

It was well into the afternoon and the courtroom was almost empty when Cec's name was called. I gripped the edge of my seat and prepared for the worst. Would he be fined heavily? Could they give a foreigner a jail term? Would my father-in-law be allowed to return home as planned, or would his flight have to be delayed?

The proceedings came to a temporary halt as a very old and dignified individual made his way to the front of the courtroom, and climbed into the judge's chair. Rob and I looked on in wonder as the judge motioned specifically for Cec to come close. Then he hugged Dad. "Welcome to our country," he said. "I am so sorry about this

## Chapter Twenty-Three

unfortunate incident. Do not worry. Your fine is very small, less than ten dollars in your money, and we hope you will visit Tanzania again. It is beautiful, is it not?"

"Very beautiful," said Dad, "And thank you for your concern."

"I am ashamed to have taken so long to appear. It is the first time I have been asked to come out of retirement to try a case and I have been out of town for several weeks visiting my brother in Arusha," explained the judge.

"But why did you need to come? I'm sure there are lots of other judges." Dad asked.

"You are old, an *mzee*," said the judge, "but I am older. We needed to find a judge older than you to try your case. It is a matter of respect. You are also a guest in our country. We hope this will not take away from the enjoyment of your visit with us."

After the trial we were invited to the judge's quarters to have afternoon tea. We sold the *Roho* for scrap metal and bought ourselves a *piki piki* (little motorcycle).

# Chapter Twenty-Four
## Don't Disturb the Elephants (1971)

"Wo!" said Rob, staring in fascination at the Polaroid photo of a Volkswagen Beetle with its hood completely squashed in. "An elephant did that? It sat on a car?"

"Do not disturb the elephants by honking your horn," the sign under the photo at the entrance to Mikumi Game Park read.

"That's a little scary," I added.

"The problem is," said Juma, one of the park wardens, "the elephants like to walk in the middle of the road and tourists get impatient. To tell you the truth the elephants in this park are sometimes a little drunk on over ripe bananas, and they can get a bit crazy. They hate loud noises and people tend to honk their horns. The elephants get annoyed and that can be dangerous."

Reality was beginning to set in. The nagging voice of many people back home echoed in my brain. "Africa is dangerous. Why would you want to go there? Stay at home and be safe," they'd pleaded. Here we were taking Rob's parents into danger. I figured we could wipe out all four of us on one drive through this wild park.

"Rob," I stammered, "maybe this isn't the best of ideas. This car we rented is a wreck. Why don't we hire a guide and take a game drive in one of the Land Rovers? We'll probably see more animals that way, and it will be safer."

"Oh, come on," said Rob. "Where is your sense of adventure? Anyway, it's way too expensive, and it won't be as much fun."

I suppose I had asked for this. I'd wanted a husband who would do anything and go anywhere, a husband who was fearless and carefree. For me Mikumi Game Park was the realization of a lifetime, one of the main reasons I had

## Chapter Twenty-Four

come to Africa in the first place. Our little, ancient, hunk of junk Peugeot rental sputtered as we pulled away from the entrance gate. I tried not to worry.

The game lodge appeared off to the right on the top of a hill. I was immediately charmed by the place. Low, graceful buildings built of traditional materials, thatch and timber, blended with and rose above the open savanna. I could imagine sitting at an outdoor table on the patio having mango juice with lots of ice as I gazed down over the plains and watched herds of wildebeest.

Several exotic Masai warriors with their red capes stood, stork like, at the side of the road. Tall, very slim and completely masculine, they had stopped to stare at us. Their necks were weighed down by copper necklaces, and they all held sharp looking spears. The scene was reminiscent of the pages of National Geographic.

Mikumi loomed ahead of us as we put putted away from the entrance onto the bumpy, dirt road. A dry parched landscape greeted us; miles of sweeping yellow grass interspersed with twisted acacia trees. Heat waves rose, mirage like, from the road's surface, resembling suspended pools of shimmering water. The Peugeot lurched forward and dust entered the body of the car through the open windows. Twisted, tortured looking thorn trees dotted the horizon and tsetse flies began to buzz around our faces.

"Did you bring the bug spray?" Phyll asked, hopefully.

"Sorry, no." I answered. "That spray is too strong to be used in a confined space like this."

"Rob are you sure this is a good idea?" I said, coughing and rubbing my eyes. "Don't tsetse flies cause sleeping sickness? That can be fatal you know. In our orientation seminar they said to avoid tsetse flies. They're really dangerous."

Rob's parents looked horrified but said nothing.

## Chapter Twenty-Four

"Stop worrying," answered Rob. "What are the chances? The flies aren't really biting, just swarming around."

We rounded the bend and saw two giraffes looming above an acacia. They had to bend down to eat from the top of the tree. The gentle giants simply gazed at us with their limpid eyes and kept on munching. Termite mounds created small sandcastle bumps on the otherwise flat surface of the land. Grey monkeys screamed wildly as they leapt and swung around the tall baobab trees. They seemed to find our presence annoying but still stopped to stare while they picked lice from each other's hides. Their long tails hung down from the branches as they popped the little bugs into their mouths.

"Oh my God, look at the that!" Rob shouted, as we turned the corner. A lone lion raced across the plains and took down a young zebra at the edge of the herd. Rob pulled the car up. We were so close, only a few yards away. This is what dreams are made of, I thought. My heart raced and all the risk, the planning, the leaving family and friends was worth it. It was like being a child again. The excitement, the thrill was beyond description.

Phyll and Cec didn't look quite so enchanted. Sweat was dripping from their faces, and they were frowning. I suspected they would have been much happier sitting on the patio of the hotel observing the game over a glass of lemonade.

Rob stopped the Peugeot beside a heard of zebra. Out came my camera. I hoped that I could capture on film the psychedelic vista of black and white striped zebra running across the grass lands, looking like one large canvas of shifting movement and colour.

"I probably shouldn't have turned the engine off. I hope the car will start," Rob muttered.

## Chapter Twenty-Four

I was beyond caring by then and completely enthralled. Notions of danger had deserted me. The air smelled of hot earth with a hint of jasmine. A lilac-breasted roller bird darted around the car flying on its side to show off the iridescent blues, purples, and greens of its plumage. The car started, and the engine was turning over nicely as a graceful herd of Thompson's gazelle entertained us with their bounding ballet, their white, black, and light brown coats blurring with the swiftness of their movement.

On the left side of the road a herd of African buffalo were feasting on the long grass. They raised their heads and stared in our direction. "Those buffalo look deceptively docile, a bit like overgrown cows," said Rob. "Did you know that they are called Black Death? They kill about 200 people every year, more than any other animal in Africa, including lions and crocodiles."

"Good to know. Could you drive a bit faster?" I begged. Had my husband not seen the looks of terror on his parents faces? I wished that he would be a bit more attentive to their moods. But Rob was completely oblivious and had no idea that his parents did not feel the same way.

"Look at those axe pecker birds on the backs of the buffalo. They remove ticks from the animal's nose and ears," Rob explained.

"That's gross. That bird has its beak right inside the buffalo's nostril," Cec said. Maybe Rob's father wasn't as worried as I had thought.

"They're the only animals stupid enough to get that close to those beasts," Rob joked.

We came to a large dome shaped hill and drove up the incline as the car sputtered and burped ominously. On our right was a circle of four huge elephants, giant ears flopping, bums touching and eyes looking outwards.

## Chapter Twenty-Four

"Look guys," said Rob. "There's a baby under their legs, in the centre. They're protecting their young. Wow! What a sight."

"There's another baby on the other side of road," I commented innocently.

"Oh no," yelled Rob. "We're separating a baby from its mother?"

"Drive," I screamed as the bull elephant trumpeted, almost splitting out eardrums. The mother threw her trunk up and charged straight for us. We were slightly ahead, but she was rapidly narrowing the gap. Dust made it almost impossible to see as we inched up the next hill, but it was clear that the elephant was gaining on us.

"Julie, turn around and get a picture out the back of the car," Rob shouted over the noise of the trumpeting giant.

"Just shut up and drive," I yelled as I turned and snapped the picture. The car groaned up the hill gradually losing speed. The elephant continued to gain on us, her massive trunk moving up and down as she screamed in anger. Thoughts of my family back home filled my brain. If we died, I would never see my parents and five siblings again. At twenty-one, I had so much to live for, so many things I still wanted to do. I would never get to teach in Canada, never get to create the family we had planned. We couldn't die, not like this. Everyone would be furious at us for taking such awful risks and for paying, not just with our lives, but also with the lives of Rob's parents. I wondered what sentiment would be stronger with my loved ones in Canada: grief or anger.

The elephant was mere feet away. Rob seemed uncharacteristically terrified as he bent tense and low over the steering wheel. I think it had finally occurred to him that we might be in danger. The car, instead of gaining speed, continued to slow down. There was a very good chance that the old Peugeot would not make it to the top

## Chapter Twenty-Four

of the hill before the elephant. Why had we not taken the reasonable option of a guided game drive? The mother shrieked again in anger and frustration as we crested the hill and began to gain speed on the downward slope.

"Thank God," Rob sighed and put his foot to the floor. We sped up and left her behind us in the dust. It was at that moment when I realized just how much danger we were putting ourselves in. It wasn't just the elephants. We took risks every day, stupid risks. Most of those risks were avoidable, and I decided from that point on I would try to be more careful. The challenge would be to convince my husband that he wasn't invincible. I would have insisted that we drive straight back to the lodge and get in a park vehicle, but we were already halfway through Mikumi.

"Are you okay?" Rob asked the three of us.

"What do you think?" I shot back. "We could all have been killed."

"Unlikely," Rob answered. "I admit that was scary. Next time we'll go in the Land Rover and hire a guide. Maybe we would see more and learn things about the animals."

None of us spoke much on the trip back to lodge. We saw a giant herd of wildebeest across the plain and some Thompson's gazelle leaping gracefully through the tall grass. When we finally arrived back and Rob and I were alone, he said, "Don't be mad. You have to admit that it will be fun to tell our children and grandchildren the crazy story about how we were almost killed by an elephant."

"Ya and I have the photo to prove it. If we live that long."

# Chapter Twenty-Five
## Metamorphosis (1991-1992)

We have returned to Ottawa after our posting to Jamaica. I'm pregnant and completely exhausted. The world is a fog of days spent folding laundry, making meals and caring for my young family while trying to fit in substitute teaching days. I'm a mess emotionally and overwhelmed with our move back from Jamaica, a posting I loved.

Jen is in grade ten and helps as much as she can. She races home from high school at lunchtime. I worry that she should be spending more time with kids her age, but the truth is our daughter is far more comfortable with adults than other teenagers. She's not adjusting well to Canada and is in full awkward teenager mode.

Long, lanky limbs and hair twice the size of her face—huge, curly, unruly hair which refuses to be tamed - Afro hair in shades of red and blonde. Jen hates her hair and everything about the way she looks. She won't let anyone take her picture. Her mouth is full of silver braces, so she refuses to smile and dons a smirk—a protective stance against a world she doesn't understand. Her fashion sense is a weird mixture of all the places she has called home: Egypt, Ivory Coast, Jamaica. She wears long, hippy skirts and bright-coloured blouses with puff sleeves in a world of tight, blue jeans and body revealing t shirts.

With no idea of the cultural practices required of a Canadian teenager, she stands too close to talk to friends, and they are intimidated. If she had been born somewhere else, had a different accent, they'd understand, but our daughter looks and sounds completely Canadian. "Jen," I

## Chapter Twenty-Five

try to explain, "Personal space is different here. Back up a foot or two when you're talking to people."

One day my daughter comes home in tears. "Mom," she says, "I tried to hold my girlfriend's hand and all the kids laughed and called me gay. I'm not gay and even if I were, so what? I don't understand." My young teenager can work a diplomatic crowd better than I can. Adults love her—polite, articulate, knowledgeable, sensitive, smart. Kids in west end Ottawa think she's super weird—a mixture of childlike innocence and adult worldliness is not normal here, although it worked just fine in a Jamaican private school. It breaks my heart to see my child suffer such extreme culture shock. This transient life of ours has cruel consequences for Jennifer.

After our youngest child, Andrew, is born on April 6th, I can't imagine coping without Jen's help. At 16, she's like his second mom. Most weekdays after school, she rushes into our home and calls, "Give me the baby. Go have a nap. I'll start dinner."

I know Jen should be out with her friends instead of babysitting for me, but nothing I say convinces her to try to reach out. At least she still has her close friend, Margaret, from her few elementary school years spent in Ottawa. Margaret lives across town and goes to another high school, but the girls are inseparable and spend weekends and evenings at our house, usually playing with Megan, our five-year-old, and Andrew, the baby.

After one year at our local high school, Nepean, Jen transfers to Lisgar in downtown Ottawa, to be with Margaret. "I can't stand the Ottawa valley girl mentality at Nepean, the narrow-mindedness. I'll never fit in no matter how hard I try. The students are so hopelessly monochrome. Lisgar has more foreign students, diplomatic kids like me, as well as my best friend. I know

## Chapter Twenty-Five

I have to commute and take Japanese to get in, but it'll be worth it," she assures us.

Jen is happy downtown. She makes several new friends from foreign countries like India and Ghana. Margaret is always with her. In grade 11 Jen's transition into a beautiful young woman begins. Off come the braces to reveal perfect teeth. Her hair and skin calm down and her stick figure develops revealing curves and grace. I'm not sure when it occurs to me that my daughter is stunning—ugly duckling to majestic swan—far too pretty for her own good. Boys show up like moths drawn to the flame, but Jen has no idea that she's attractive. Her attitude of nonchalance just makes her more desirable.

Margaret, Jen's best friend, has also transformed from a chubby teenager. Now with her straight, blonde hair that hangs past her waist, her huge blue eyes, peaches and cream complexion and her new slim body, she's getting lots of male attention. It terrifies Rob and I to let the two girls out of the house—innocent, gorgeous, oblivious—will they be safe?

The worst thing they ever do is to stay out late, drinking coffee at Starbucks in the Byward Market. Rob and I wait at home worried that Jen and Margaret are in trouble. They don't arrive home until after three in the morning. "Damn it, Jen. Where were you? Mom and I were frantic with worry. I've been driving around for hours looking for you. What were you thinking?" Rob yells as the two young ladies waltz through the front door.

"Could you not have called?" I ask.

"Sorry," they both mumble, looking surprised.

"Is it really so late? We were talking. Guess we just lost track of time," Jen says.

At Christmas Jen is acting secretive and elusive. We're supposed to go to Rob's Canadian International

## Chapter Twenty-Five

Development Agency Christmas party. He's so excited about showing off his lovely family of four amazing kids. On the day of the party Jen shocks us. "I can't come," she says."

"But I promised that you would be there. Everyone is expecting you," Rob says.

"Sorry, not possible. I have something I have to do," Jen answers. Rob is hurt by Jen's reaction, and I'm confused. This is not like our daughter. What's going on?

"Dan," I quiz my oldest son, who, at 14 knows Jen in a way that we never will. "Do you know anything about this? Why won't she come?"

"I wish I could help, but Jen hasn't confided in me either. She must have a good reason, but I have no idea what it is," Dan tells me.

We give up and go to the office party without her. Over the Christmas vacation Jen seems exhausted and mentally absent, although she hasn't been away from our house much at all. We're worried, puzzled.

The day before New Year's Eve our daughter presents us with gift baskets of homemade preserves, cookies, Christmas cake, wine, special vinegar, jams, fudge —the list goes on. She has made most of the goodies from scratch in my kitchen. How had I not noticed? She's stayed up night after night preparing our gifts and, of course, did not finish in time for Christmas.

We are humbled by Jen's efforts. How could we not have guessed that Jen's intentions were good? We've been miserable to her the entire Christmas period, disappointed by her strange behaviour. She really is such an unusual but wonderful person—always unfailingly kind and good but never, ever on time. Rob and I should have had the faith not to have second guessed her intentions.

# Chapter Twenty-Six
## Remembering Graves (2016)

Jen never did have good luck with health. I get angry all over again when I remember the disease that destroyed her life in her late teens and early twenties. She lost ten years to Grave's disease. Then she recovered and got on with what should have been a very long and successful life. After a second start—a wonderful new marriage, a baby, the completion of her teaching degree, a job in Dhaka—cancer ended her health a second time. It just seems so unfair.

My mind flips to her struggle with Graves' disease which began in Ottawa, in 1996, when she was only 19. I remember Jenny's words and think that I should have been there for her, should have done something:

"Mom, there's something terribly wrong with me," Jen whimpers and flops down on the motel couch, head in hands. "I can't sleep. My heart's racing night and day, and I'm losing weight even though I'm eating well. I feel anxious all the time. I can't concentrate. I don't know what to do."

"Oh God, I'm phoning our family doctor right now," I tell my daughter.

I set up an appointment with Ben. He's been our doctor since Jen was a baby and he and his wife are personal friends. They were in the same babysitting co-op and were the first people we left baby Jenny with. He's also worked with "Doctors Without Borders" and stayed with us, on his way to South Africa, when we were living in the Ivory Coast, West Africa. Jen will be in good hands. Ben cares about us and our family, or at least I believe he does.

## Chapter Twenty-Six

He has kids too and understands our lifestyle. I trust him to diagnose what's wrong with our daughter.

Rob and I, as well as our three other kids, are leaving in the morning to complete the last year of our posting to the Philippines. Jen has to remain in Ottawa to attend Carleton University, where she's studying anthropology. I hate to leave her like this. She seems lost, vulnerable, pale and thin—completely alone and overwhelmed.

Our family have always had each other as we moved around the world. Now we're leaving our eldest to cope alone, and she's clearly not well. Should I stay home? I have a teaching job in Manila. Danny is in high school. Meg is going into grade three and Andrew is only three years old. I can't abandon them, can I?

Jen is responsible, smart and in second year university. It's time for her to fly, to leave the nest. I tell myself this, but I have a lurking premonition that I shouldn't go—not now. Rob is supportive and worried, but also doesn't see that we have any choice but to return to the Philippines.

In the next year abroad, I try desperately to talk to Jen every day, but often she won't answer my calls and when we do connect, she's strangely distant. "I'm fine Mom," she tells me, but little else.

The next summer when we arrive in Ottawa, we go straight to see her. God, I've missed my eldest child. I almost don't recognize Jen because she's covered her face in white, clown makeup—a mask. She's so thin and her hair clings in strands to her head. I hug her to me but can feel her pushing me away.

"Good Lord Jen, what's going on?" Rob pleads.

"I wish I knew Dad?" she answers defensively.

My previously fastidious, attractive daughter looks like she's been living on the street. Her apartment is a hovel. She hasn't been going to school. It's like our child walked

## Chapter Twenty-Six

out of the house one day, happy, glowing, smart, capable, and returned the next, another person.

We're confused, devastated. It's clear that she's in trouble. Fortunately, our posting in Manila has come to an end. Jen's happy to move back into our family home. Together we will work this out.

"It's been a terrible year, but now I think I know what's going on," she confides. "Our doctor thinks I'm mentally ill and, I confess, I do feel like I'm going crazy. He sent me to a psychologist, but that hasn't helped, so I'm not going back.

"I've done some research on the net, and I'm pretty sure I have Grave's disease. I have an appointment to see an endocrinologist this week, and we should have some answers.

"I know how shocked you must be, and I am sorry."

A month later our daughter receives a diagnosis of severe Graves' disease (hyperthyroidism). With further reading we realize that before Graves' disease was discovered a huge number of the people in mental institutions were there because of this insidious condition. Their mental issues were based on a physical condition.

Jenny's medication helps but only marginally. She's struggling on, pursuing her degree, but has not returned to her former self and still persists in wearing hideous, pancake makeup.

Where once Jen didn't overly dwell on what others think, now she's lost her self-assurance and lacks confidence. "I feel ugly, unlikable, and always on edge," she tells me.

"Jen, you're smart, beautiful, talented. I don't understand," I tell my daughter. "People have always been drawn to you. You're a wonderful young woman."

## Chapter Twenty-Six

"You're my mom. You have to say that," she answers as tears fill her electric blue eyes.

It's at that point in her life, when she is most vulnerable, that Mo appears.

# Chapter Twenty-Seven
## Moster (1997)

It's January in Ottawa and 25 degrees centigrade below zero. The sun is shining, and the sky is robin's-egg blue. Huge, carrot shaped icicles hang outside our front window sending sparkling prisms of coloured, rainbow light in all directions. I can smell the wood-smoke from our fireplace as orange flames dance behind the grate. Outside, pristine white snow lines our driveway and footpath.

"It's sort of beautiful," I venture to my husband and daughter.

"God, I hate winter," Rob says glaring at me. "Fine for you at home, inside looking out. Not sure the car will start but if it does, Jen, do you need a ride to Carleton? I can drop you on my way to work."

"Thanks Dad. I hate this weather too !—so much—but it's only 8 o'clock, and I don't have a class till 1:00. I don't want to hang around waiting for the bus on a day like this though."

"I can drive you later in the old Saab—hope it makes it though," I say, not realizing my offer will change all of our lives.

When we arrive at Carleton in time for Jen's class, she jumps out of the car and runs, books piled high in her arms, toward the entrance, wanting to avoid the frigid blasts of winter. Please be careful, I think. Watch where you're going. It's too late. Books fly in every direction as Jen crashes into a guy wearing a long, black, wool coat and dress shoes. He looks out of place at the university where the costume of choice is blue jeans, sweat shirts, ski jackets, scarves, toque, and heavy winter boots.

## Chapter Twenty-Seven

The young man picks up Jen's books and smiles at her. He's her height, dark skinned and slight. He resembles an Indian movie star with his longish, shiny black curls, huge coal brown eyes and finely chiselled features. The guy is gorgeous, I observe as the two young people look at each other with extreme interest and then proceed through the doors of Carleton.

Not being intuitive, I have no inkling of how this encounter will end up. Two weeks later, there's no doubt that Jen has fallen hard. "Can I invite my friend Mo for dinner? I really like him," she asks, and we agree. The truth is that Jen is not at her best, still suffering from Graves and wearing a mask of white make up. Maybe this new interest will help her.

A week later Rob has made a scrumptious feast for Jen and Mo. The aroma of curry, ginger, chicken and coconut fills our home as we wait for them. The appointed dinner hour arrives but still no guests. "Has Jen forgotten after all this work?" Rob says looking hurt and angry.

Hours later our youngest kids are in bed, we've eaten dinner and are listening to music in front of a roaring fire when the phone rings. "Hi Mom, sorry we didn't make it. We were talking and lost track of time. Can we come now? I really want you to meet Mo."

"But Jen, it's ten o'clock at night. Dad and I have to work tomorrow. Dad's pretty pissed-off. He made such a lovely dinner. Maybe another time."

"Please," Jen pleads.

"Rob they wanna come now. Is that okay with you?" I ask, covering the mouthpiece of the phone with one hand.

"Now? You're kidding."

"They'll be here really soon," I answer.

"Okay, but they better hurry. I'm exhausted."

## Chapter Twenty-Seven

I hang up and we wait and wait. Finally, two hours later we give up and go to bed worrying about our daughter. She's 20 years old, trustworthy and sensible. She'll be fine, we tell ourselves. Although Jen is often late, it's totally out of character for her to be unkind and disrespectful. Not showing up for dinner at all is just weird, but the truth is she's not been acting normal lately.

It's after one o'clock when Rob and I are woken up by our front door slamming. Jen's voice comes wafting up the staircase accompanied by a deep male response. Then Jen does something that shocks both of us. She turns on the stereo full blast. Rob sits bolt upright, leaps out of bed and walks to the bedroom door.

"Turn the music down. It's the middle of the night. What are you thinking?" he screams down the stairs.

The music gets marginally softer but is still preventing us from sleeping. We twitch and turn. Finally, Rob loses it. "That's it," he says, throwing his housecoat on and heading downstairs. I follow.

Jen and Mo are on the pullout couch necking. "I think you'd better leave," Rob says to Mo.

"Sure," Mo answers, glaring spitefully at both of us. Not—"I'm sorry." Not—"Nice to meet you." Rob and I are appalled at his behaviour, shocked by his disrespect.

The cocky young man in our living room exudes fumes of marijuana, cigarettes, and alcohol. He gets up off the couch, winks at Jen, grabs his long black coat and prepares to leave. Our daughter says nothing. She just stares at us in shock. She looks dishevelled but is clearly sober, unlike her friend. There's an ominous silence as we all freeze in a frame, a fateful moment etched in time and memory. The only sound comes from the clock ticking in the hall.

## Chapter Twenty-Seven

Jen grabs her coat, scarf, and mittens, and bends down to zip up her knee-length winter boots.

"Where do you think you're going?" Rob shouts.

Jen says nothing as she follows Mo out the door.

# Chapter Twenty-Eight
## To Leave, or Not to Leave (1998)

Jen stays away for days but eventually comes home. "Mom and dad, Mo loves me and I love him," she tells us.

"But sweetie, you know nothing about this man. When we met him, he was drunk, stoned, and obnoxious. What about his family?" I ask her.

"He's devout Muslim, but he loves me enough to overlook my religion. He hasn't told anyone about me, but he will soon."

"You still don't know if his parents will accept you. You need to find out these things before you proceed with a serious relationship that could end in disaster," Rob tells our daughter.

"Don't be so dramatic, Dad. This is about Mo and me, not about our parents on either side."

"Are you kidding? That is the most naive thing you've ever said," Rob shouts.

"You guys are being racist."

Rob's face is scarlet, and he's breathing hard. "You know we're not racist. Many of our best friends are Muslim. That's not the issue and you know it!"

"Jen," I plead. "We just want what's best for you. It's Mo. He doesn't seem very nice, to be honest. Anyone who is that rude to the parents of the person they profess to love isn't very smart or very kind."

"He makes me feel beautiful and loved. I care deeply for him."

"What a lot of rot. You just met the guy. You're not acting like yourself. We really need to get to the bottom of this Grave's disease situation before you make any decisions that will affect the rest of your life," Rob pleads with our daughter.

## Chapter Twenty-Eight

"Sorry guys," Jen answers. "This is my life, not yours. Mo is here to stay! You can either accept that or not, but that's what's going to happen. Please, I love you. Back me up. Don't make me choose between my family and the man I love."

The room is so quiet that I can hear the hum of the refrigerator in the kitchen. Our little white poodle, Muffy, appears and jumps on Jenny's lap. No one speaks. Muff licks Jen's hand and looks adoringly up at her.

"Okay," says Rob. It seems we have no choice. We'll do our best to support you despite our doubts. I just hope that Mo realizes that I will kill him if he does anything to hurt you. Just for the record, I still believe that you are not well enough to make life altering decisions. You're not thinking straight."

After that, Mo comes to our home regularly. I try to like him but fail. He makes my skin crawl and is often drunk or high. He does, at times, make an effort to be civil. Jen continues to wear white mask makeup and seems to be losing weight. She's frail. At meals, she picks at her food.

Despite everything, the relationship continues and my dread increases. Rob finds an assignment with the Organization for Economic Development (OECD) in Paris and takes a leave of absence from the Canadian Government so that he can fulfill his dream of working in the City of Light. The truth is that if Rob doesn't leave, he's going to have a nervous breakdown. He's not sleeping or communicating except to rant about Jen. He's obsessed with the plight of his eldest daughter and there's not a damn thing that he can do to make things better.

## Chapter Twenty-Eight

I'm reluctant to follow my husband abroad because Jen is still sick and Dan, our 18-year-old son, is in grade 12 and can't come with us. He wants to finish his final year of high school in Ottawa, so we have no choice but to leave him on his own for grade 13.

Ironically, although Dan is four years younger than Jen, I know he'll be fine. Jen would be too if only her health was better, and she wasn't with Mo. I stay back in Ottawa for four months, but each day without Rob is difficult. My two little kids miss their dad and cry for him constantly. Meg, who is ten, is angry with me. "I want my daddy to read to me," she pleads every night at bedtime. "Why can't you just take me to Paris? This is your fault."

I'm living in Ottawa, but I rarely see Jen. She's with Mo all the time, and they avoid me. By the end of July, Rob and I have to make a decision. If I'm going to Paris, I must get our two youngest children in school by the beginning of September. Finally, we decide that Meg, Andrew and I will join Rob in Paris.

Before I leave, I cling to both of my older children. "Mom," Dan tells me. "Stop worrying. We'll be fine. I can't wait to visit you at Christmas. Paris ! Wow! A dream come true. It'll be great."

Jen doesn't seem so sure. She clings to me and cries for ages running her white makeup mask and black eye shadow. I'm clearly not getting through to her. Maybe Paris will help. Maybe she'll figure out that she deserves far more than the jerk she's with. Maybe she'll sort out her medical condition. Since she isn't allowing me to get close while we're together in Ottawa, maybe things will be better with our absence.

"See you at Christmas," Jen says as Meg, Andrew and I head for the departure lounge. Mo is not with her, but Dan is. I wave, walk away, and dissolve into tears. My two

## Chapter Twenty-Eight

youngest children look shocked by my behaviour. Having to say goodbye to their brother and sister can't be easy for them, so I put my shoulders back and try to get control.

"I'm being silly. Sorry. It won't be long before we'll all be together again," I tell Meg and Andrew, stifling my tears. "We'll have such a wonderful Christmas."

## Chapter Twenty-Nine
### Housing Problems (1971)

"Julie and Rob, if your housing doesn't come through you have got to leave Africa and come home," Rob's father blustered."

"Dad, relax" Rob countered. "It will all work out. Most of the other CUSO volunteers have been allocated housing. It's just a matter of time. Don't worry."

"This is not funny. They are going to kick you kids out of your unit at the Oceanic Motel at the end of the month, and you still have nowhere to go. Your mother and I are not leaving here until we know you have a safe place to live!"

Housing for CUSO's in Dar was on ongoing problem. Some volunteers, after more than a year in the country, were still living in hotels and motels, some paying with their own money. No way we could afford to stay without CUSO covering our housing costs. It was particularly frustrating because CIDA (Canadian International Development Agency) people, under the auspices of the Canadian Government, regularly jumped the queue and got housing on arrival in Tanzania while we NGO (Non-Governmental Organization) types were left waiting.

Rob arrived home from work ecstatic. "We have a home at last!"

"Thank God. It's about damn time," Rob's Dad exclaimed. "Now we can go home knowing that you have housing. Mom and I are so relieved."

The next day the four of us got into a taxi and went to see our flat. Gerry, our CUSO volunteer friend, lived on the bottom floor and met us at the door. "You can't live

## Chapter Twenty-Nine

here. You've been allocated an apartment on the fourth floor," he said immediately. "These East German apartment blocks are a concrete slum. I have water, but anything above the ground floor doesn't have a drop, and it's not like there's a community well or anything. It's also way too dangerous for a foreign woman. Julie, you'd be targeted and wouldn't have a moment's peace. I'm fine because I'm alone and six foot four—a strong guy. This just won't do for you two."

Although I was trying to keep an open mind, I was shocked by the housing development. I'd come to Africa to see flowers, birds, trees, and wildlife, and this place was a desert with no vegetation for miles around— just sand, dust and flat terrain. Groups of malnourished kids with fly-ridden eyes stood around staring at us. It was beyond horrible. But hadn't we come to Africa to help? If this was home to Tanzanians, why were we any different?

"Look," said Gerry. "Living here has been a challenge even for me and I have water. You're dreaming if you think you'll survive. Turn the place down. It'll mean waiting for heaven knows how long, but you have no choice."

"Thanks, Ger," said Rob. "Good to know, but we will get turfed from our apartment in the motel at the end of December. It's either accept this or return to Toronto. We have no job prospects back home, and it's too late to apply for post grad studies."

Rob's Dad had been uncharacteristically silent. I think he was in shock, but he finally found his voice. "I'm not leaving you kids here. No way. You're coming home. CUSO is going to hear from me when I get back to Canada. How can they even think of putting our Canadian young people in such a dangerous, dirty, disgusting situation?"

## Chapter Twenty-Nine

Ilala flats could have been a slum anywhere in the world. Without any trees, the sun beat down relentlessly and all of us were soaked to the skin with sweat. I couldn't imagine what the inside of the apartment would feel like. There were tiny windows on the front side of the building only, which would mean that there would be no airflow. I guessed that the temperature, especially on the upper floors, would be unbearable.

We trudged upstairs. The apartment was hot, dark, airless. Cockroaches, antennas flailing, scurried across the floor and big, black, bottle flies swarmed and buzzed around us. The smell of urine and feces made me gag. Garbage and leftover food were scattered everywhere. I did not want to give up and go home to Canada, but it would be impossible to live here.

"Okay, okay, I get it Dad. We can't accept this. I won't let Julie live here. I know it's dangerous and dirty. Don't worry, I'm not that irresponsible."

"Good," said Cec. "So come home."

"No," answered Rob. "We will decline the housing allocation, but we are not coming home."

"Where will you live? Mom and I aren't leaving without some answers."

"I'm not sure yet, but there's absolutely no way we're giving up."

The answer to our dilemma came the next morning. Our CUSO friends, Paul and Cathy, had recently been allocated a one bedroom home close to downtown Dar. "Come and live with us again," they said. Ironically, they'd lived with Rob and me for two months in our two-bedroom motel suite before they were assigned housing. The arrangement had worked out remarkably well.

Now that we had nowhere to go, Paul and Cathy were glad to reciprocate. They had a large screened-in porch at

## Chapter Twenty-Nine

the front of their house that would be perfect for us to sleep in, so we gladly accepted their invitation.

"We can share costs, save money, and we already know we're compatible," Rob explained to his parents. "It'll give us time to work this out and find our own place."

"Be reasonable kids," said Rob's mom. "You can't live on a porch."

"Yes, we can," I piped up. "It's just temporary. The Tanzanian Government will come through and give us decent housing before long. We can't give up now. We've only been here six months and things are just starting to make sense. We'll be fine. You'll see."

"There may be nothing we can do to convince you to come home," said Cec, "but we are not happy. We'll be discussing this with your family Julie. I will also write a letter to the editor at the Toronto Star and my MP explaining how irresponsible CUSO is with our Canadian young people."

Our struggle to get housing was not over, but at least we weren't headed home quite yet. We'd won the argument, but Rob and I both understood that our solution was only temporary.

# Chapter Thirty
## Shoe-less (1999-2000)

"They should be landing now mom," Andrew shouts as he runs into the living room of our Paris apartment, his blond hair tousled and his eyes shining. Our seven-year-old has been anticipating this visit from his big sister and brother for months. Transition to a new country and school has not been easy for Megan or Andrew, our two youngest, and they have both missed their older siblings.

Our apartment is classic Paris with its wrap-around balcony, white crown mouldings, fireplaces in every room, wooden floors and floor to ceiling windows. We like to watch old movies set in our new city, so that we can see love and murder in apartments just like ours. The scent of coffee brewing streams into the window from our downstairs *pâtisserie*.

"I can't wait for Jen, Dan, and Mo to see where we live. They're going to love it!" As I utter the name Mo, my heart beats a bit faster. It's the first time Jen's boyfriend has spent any time with us and I wonder how the two-week visit will go. For the last six months in France, I had been hoping that Mo would disappear, but Jen seems even more committed to him now. It's time to stop fighting and accept her young man.

Transatlantic travel and taking public transport to reach us in Paris is easy for our world travelling children, but not so for poor Mo. Although his family is from Pakistan, he was born in Toronto and this is his first airplane trip—first time to leave Canada.

When the kids finally arrive, Dan knocks on the door to our flat. He has tons of luggage at his feet, and looks frantic. He greets us with, "Help! Mo's stuck in the elevator. Jen's trying to pull him out, but it's not working."

## Chapter Thirty

All of us cross to our ancient elevator, which consists of a small cage with sliding, accordion, metal doors that you open and close manually when you enter or exit. Somehow Mo has managed to get his shoe caught in the doors.

"Not working. Ouch!" Mo says to Jen, so she stops trying to pull him out.

Were all in shock, frozen in a state of inactivity. The smell of bodyodour fills the hallway. A minute later Dan says, "Mo, take off your shoe. I'll go get the *concierge*." He turns and runs down the stairs.

Jen gets down on her knees, unlaces the offending shoe and pulls Mo's foot out. He's set free. "Stupid elevator," he mutters and, one shoe less, follows us into the apartment. It's everything I can do, now that the drama is over, not to roar with laughter. My reaction reminds me that I have to work hard at liking this young man that my daughter has chosen as her partner.

When Dan returns with the *concierge* of the building, we explain the situation. She grins from ear to ear. *"C'est dommage. Desole."* (That's too bad. So sorry). She heads off to retrieve the offending shoe, looking pleased with herself. I can imagine her telling anyone who will listen about the stupid foreigners on the fifth floor who can't even manage a Parisian elevator.

We have made spaghetti for dinner. Mo excuses himself and comes back with a bottle of hot sauce from his suitcase, which he pours all over his food. He drinks more than his share of the red wine, and when it's done asks for more. By the end of the meal our daughter's boyfriend is tipsy and slurring his words. Jen, who has not had much to eat or drink, looks embarrassed by her friend's behaviour.

## Chapter Thirty

"Shall we sit in the living room?" Rob asks. "I'll make a fire."

"Man, this place is great," Dan says beaming. "I'm going to try to get an internship here, so I can come for the whole summer. What do you think?"

"I'll talk to my friend, Mark. I bet he can get you a volunteer job with United Nations Environment Program (UNEP)," Rob says.

"Must be nice to be so entitled," Mo says, smirking.

"That's not fair," Jen answers. "Dan's taking environmental and civil engineering and would be a perfect fit. Besides, he's not asking to be paid."

Mo looks smug but says nothing. Andrew saves the day by inviting Mo to play cards. I look at Jen, but her expression gives nothing away. Is she beginning to realize that her partner's not a good match for her?

The next day I can see that Mo is trying to ingratiate himself into our family. He smiles constantly and makes comments about how lovely our apartment is. More importantly, he does not drink. "Where do your folks live?" I ask him.

"In Toronto," he answers, and then squirms in his seat on the couch. Clearly, he's not comfortable discussing his family. Further questions disclose that he has a sister, but despite our curiosity we learn little else.

At dinner that night, Jen says, "Mo and I have an announcement to make."

I look over at my husband. He clenches his jaw and scowls. God, is my daughter pregnant? I wonder. What next?

"We would like to get married this summer, hopefully in Huntsville," Jen says.

Mo is silent and avoids eye contact with any of us. Tension fills the air.

## Chapter Thirty

Meg saves the day. "Great. My first wedding. Can I be a bridesmaid?"

Jen hugs her little sister. "Of course you can, sweetie."

Rob looks ill. I'm trying my best not to cry. This is not what we had hoped for our first-born child. I'm searching for something supportive and cheerful to say, but the words just won't come.

Finally, I manage a feeble "congratulations", but Rob has still not said a thing. Jen looks hopefully at her dad, but he remains silent.

Dan asks Jen, "Where exactly in Huntsville?"

"I was hoping to get married at Camp Tawingo. There's a lovely outdoor chapel. Wouldn't that be perfect?"

"Sounds like a plan," Rob manages, still looking dismayed despite his words. "How do you feel about that?" he asks Mo, who has yet to look up.

"Anything to make her happy," he mumbles.

I want to shout at Mo—"her!—are you kidding? My daughter has a name." I say nothing.

We decide to get a live Christmas tree. It costs a fortune. The minute we bring in into our living room it begins to drop needles. By Christmas day the tree is bare. Our celebration is a bit like the naked tree in our living room—so many dropped questions, so many lost dreams for our daughter.

I am still grateful to have all of our children with us. We exchange gifts and celebrate the big day as we always do. Mo has his own stocking and seems to appreciate the efforts we have made to include him.

The year 1999 is coming to an end. On New Year's Eve we want to go to the *Tour Eiffel,* but Jen has had a vision. She maintains that there will be a bombing. Had anyone else said that to us, we would have laughed, but this is Jen. She has a sixth sense that none of us can

## Chapter Thirty

understand. We listen to her because things happen that she predicts.

Instead, we all go to our local restaurant, *Vavin*, early in the evening. We have oysters and champagne like real Parisians. Later, Jen, Mo, and Dan are invited to a New Year's Eve party at *Le Lucernaire*, a quirky café/theatre across the street from our apartment where they party till dawn. Rob and I sit in front of the fire and drink ginger-ale out of special pink wine glasses, to toast the New Year with our two little ones. Not a bad way to bring in the new century.

A terrorist carrying explosives is arrested at the *Tour Eiffel* that night. No bombing happens.

# Chapter Thirty-One
## Tanzanian Wedding (1971)

Rob came home looking agitated. "Bad day?" I asked as he ran into the house.

"We have a problem. John Olomi has just asked us to his wedding in two weeks. He's marrying Angela, the girl who always comes with him to the Cozy Café. You've met her. She's lovely."

"That's great," I replied.

"Great? Do you have any idea what a wedding here entails? Just for starters what are we supposed to wear? What will we be doing at the ceremony and the reception? What the heck are we going to buy them for a present? I'm not exactly in my comfort zone here, and I don't want to blow my friendship with John."

"It can't be that different," I said, trying to appear calmer than I felt. "Why don't you just ask him what's expected?"

Rob did his best to prepare us for the big event, and so on the Saturday in question we were both looking forward to the wedding. John had assured him that it was to be a very North American-style event, nothing out of the ordinary, but we still entered the church feeling a bit nervous. We sat down to the left of the centre aisle and looked around. There were bouquets of white lilies at the end of the front pews and white satin bows tied to the ends of all the other rows. The old colonial church glowed with dark wood and sunshine. The slight scent of incense added to the atmosphere. All normal, so far. However, at 2:45 PM, 15 minutes before the ceremony was supposed to begin, there was no one in the church except for Rob and me. "Oh no," said Rob, "I must have the wrong church."

## Chapter Thirty-One

He took out the invitation and looked at it closely. "This is the St Johns Anglican Church, isn't it?"

"Absolutely, but maybe there are two churches with the same name," I answered.

"I doubt that," Rob assured me. This has to be it. So, what are we supposed to do now? I knew this whole thing was a mistake."

"Come on Rob, don't panic. Let's just relax and see what happens. Everyone is always late here."

Ten minutes later two other white couples entered the church and sat down across the aisle from us. "Hi guys," I greeted the strangers. "Excuse me for asking but are you here for John and Angela's wedding?"

"No," one of the women answered. "We've come for the wedding of Ruth and Gilbert."

"What time is that wedding supposed to start?" Rob asked.

"Two fifteen," replied the women.

"Are you sure?" Rob inquired. "Here's my invitation, and it says clearly that our wedding is going to take place at two o'clock. That seems a bit close"

We compared invitations and both looked correct. After that we sat quietly for another ten minutes, wondering what to do, when our friend Gerry came sauntering into the church and plunked down beside us. "Man am I glad to see you. Those other couples think that their friend's wedding is taking place here at two fifteen," Rob explained.

"Weird," said Gerry. "I thought I was late. Guess not."

"Have you ever been to a Tanzanian wedding Gerry?" I asked.

"Never," he answered. "Maybe it's fashionable to be late, but what about the other wedding?" Gerry looked confused. At two forty-five the church was full of people,

## Chapter Thirty-One

and we recognized some of the Tanzanians from Rob's office.

At three o'clock, a full hour late, Angela and John finally arrived. It took another fifteen minutes for them to get organized, and just at the point where the ceremony looked like it was starting another bride and groom arrived. "Oh, oh," I stammered. "What now?"

Another fifteen minutes passed. John and the other groom, plus an assortment of best-men and groomsmen, gathered at the front of the church, with the priest in the middle. The bridal march started and Angela, on her father's arm, with her bridesmaids behind her, started down the aisle. She was dressed in a high necked, long sleeved, North American-style, traditional, white bridal gown with exquisite lace. The fabric fitted closely at her waist and fell gracefully down to her feet accenting her slim, tall figure. The lace vale surrounded her face like a halo. She looked, as all brides seem to, radiant and happy as she walked slowly down the aisle.

Angela joined John, and they held hands at the front of the church. The rest of the wedding party stood to one side. "Guess it's finally about to start?" Gerry whispered. He was wrong. There was silence for ten minutes and then the bridal march started up again. The second bride, resplendent in her own white gown, with her attendants, walked down the aisle and joined her own groom at the front. When both couples, and their wedding parties, were in place by the alter, it was rather crowded. "Is the priest gonna marry both of them at the same time?" asked Gerry.

There was another ominous silence. Thinking back, I believe that the priest was trying to figure out what to do. Finally, he started. He asked, "Do you John and you Gilbert take you Angela and you Ruth to be your lawfully wedded wives ?"—Totally confusing, but I think everyone

## Chapter Thirty-One

got the point. I couldn't help but wonder if, legally, Gilbert had just married both Angela and Ruth.

After the wedding we proceeded to the church hall. "Good grief," said Rob, "I hope we aren't about to have a double reception. The hall is small. This should be interesting."

Fortunately, we had the place to ourselves. Not a word was said about the ceremony and, as much as I wanted to, I was afraid to ask what had happened. Had doubling up been intentional? The hall looked like any wedding reception venue except the windows were open, and I could smell the scent of jasmine in the garden outside. Round tables with sparkling white table clothes, fancy napkins and cutlery, were set up around the room. There was a dance floor in the middle. The wedding party sat at a long rectangular table at the front, looking out at all the guests.

After the speeches Angela came around carrying a huge tinfoil covered box and handing out what I initially thought was wedding cake, until I focussed and saw blood on the napkins being passed around.

"What is that?" Rob asked. "Holy cow!"

"Exactly," commented Gerry. "It appears that Angela is handing out raw meat in napkins."

All of us were handed blood-soaked lumps of God only knew what. "I hope nobody puts this under their pillow," Rob said with a grin. He grabbed the meat and put it in his mouth.

"Yuck," I whispered. "Is that safe? You better not get dysentery or amoeba."

"Actually," said Rob, "it's rare goat meat, not beef. Try it. Best damn wedding cake I've ever eaten."

I held my breath, closed my eyes and popped in the goat. Surprisingly, it was delicious. "And I thought John

## Chapter Thirty-One

told you this was going to be a very North American style wedding," I said. "Yum."

"Angela and John are from the Chagga tribe. I guess this is a local custom in their area," Gerry explained.

"Ya," said Rob "and I, for one, love it. I hate stupid wedding cake, gross stuff. If I ever get married again, I'll make sure my next wife hands out raw goat."

"Shut up Rob," I said. "Come on, let's dance Gerry. I love that West African beat."

# Chapter Thirty-Two
## A Canadian Wedding (2000)

During the rest of Mo's Christmas visit to our Paris apartment I begin to understand why my daughter loves him. He relaxes, plays with Andrew, goes out on the town with Jen and Dan. He's more polite and doesn't drink too much. He's sexy and gorgeous. He even makes us delicious curry for dinner one night. I realize that being Muslim and loving a white Christian girl can't be easy. Is he being forced to choose between his wife and his family? When it's time to leave he says, "Thanks so much for your hospitality. I've had a great time."

"He's not so bad," I tell Rob. "He obviously loves our daughter."

"Sorry, but I totally disagree. He only cares about himself. I don't trust him. Not much we can do though other than prepare for this wedding next summer."

We hear from Jen fairly consistently throughout the rest of the winter and early spring. She admits that she is still struggling with her health. "They don't seem to be able to get my medication for Graves's right. I have high blood pressure, feel anxious and can't gain any of the weight I've lost. I hope I'll feel better by the summer."

Soon it's time to get home and put the final touches on the wedding plans. The ceremony is going to take place, as Jen requested, at Camp Tawingo, in the outdoor chapel, in early August. The reception will be held at Hidden Valley in a ski lodge overlooking Penn Lake in Muskoka. Everything is set.

On the day of the wedding Jen is dressed in a full length, heavy, gold silk gown with intricate embroidery and bead work; tightly fitted at the waist to accentuate her

## Chapter Thirty-Two

slim figure. The sleeves are long and the neckline a v shape. Our daughter looks stunning.

"Mom," she tells me," I had my hands hennaed. That's Mo's tradition and I think he and his family will appreciate the gesture." Jen's long, slender, piano hands look exotic, exquisite—covered with intricate, lace-like, golden flower pattern tattoos.

Mo has chosen a full length, open, black silk embroidered coat with black pants and a white silk shirt. He looks a bit like a Spanish conquistador, or Zorro without an eye patch. He's almost as pretty as my daughter. The two of them would fit well in a Bollywood movie. They're enormously attractive, and their attire is beyond amazing, if a little different.

Two of Jen's bridesmaids are draped in gold and maroon silk saris and the third, our 12-year-old daughter Meg, has a long skirt and a short blouse with a bare midriff, in similar fabric and colours. She looks like a genie who just escaped from her bottle to grant her master's every wish. Andrew, who at seven is the ring bearer, is reluctantly wearing a gold brocade suit and gold sandals. He looks cute but is clearly mortified.

Mo's best man and attendants are wearing smart, black suits and white shirts. Our son Dan is in the wedding party. I smile when I imagine that he has something to do with the simplicity of the men's attire. I bet a brocade suit was suggested and vetoed by Dan early in the wedding negotiations. Poor Andrew didn't have any choice.

We've tied bouquets of wild flowers around the trees that surround the outdoor chapel. The tall pines tower over the forest enclosure creating a glade of shimmering green splendour. The blue, smooth lake is visible down the hill. Guests are gathered on benches that face a flat platform where the groom, plus the priest (a close family friend

## Chapter Thirty-Two

who looks like a cheerful Santa Claus) stand. There's an aisle between the seats where Rob leads his lovely daughter to her chosen mate.

It's a beautiful wedding, a gorgeous day. Everything goes off without a hitch. Well, almost everything. We have invited and paid for Mo's family, who allegedly consist of about 30 people, to attend, and not one of them shows up. I'm left wondering if Mo invited them. Are they protesting the marriage of their son to a white, Christian, Canadian girl or do they even know he has chosen a wife? Has he told them about our daughter? Somehow, I doubt it.

# Chapter Thirty-Three
## East African Christmas (1971)

"And so, this is Christmas," the words of the song assured me, but it sure didn't feel that way. Christmas had always been a big deal in my family. As the oldest I was responsible for helping my parents with wrapping, tree decorating and putting together toys before the little ones woke up on Christmas morning. With five siblings, our routine of stockings and gift opening took all day and was the highlight of my year. I couldn't help thinking about what I was missing here in Dar es Salaam and was spending a lot of energy trying not to cry. My throat ached with the effort of remaining cheerful.

Rob's parents were still with us. It wasn't fair. Rob had them, but I was half a world away from my family. Cec and Phyll were not happy because of our decision to remain in Dar. They were scheduled to return to Canada right after the New Year when Rob and I would have to leave the Oceanic Motel and move to Paul and Cathy's porch. Christmas was going to be a nightmare.

"That looks nice," Rob said to his mom as he observed the Christmas tree shape she had fashioned from Christmas cards stuck to the wall. I was thinking that a real Christmas tree would look better than the hopeful attempt Phyll had made. What a joke. It would've been better to have nothing. Resentment built in my gut. Intellectually, I knew I wasn't being fair, but I really didn't care.

Memories of Canada invaded my mind. Most of the time I was able to block my homesickness, but Christmas was the catalyst that brought my thoughts crashing down. I missed everything: the smell of wood-smoke from our cozy fireplace in the living room, the six stockings hung

## Chapter Thirty-Three

on the hearth, the perfectly shaped spruce Christmas tree with coloured lights, all the ornaments representing special memories from my childhood, the pottery crèche on the coffee table, and my loved ones as they eagerly anticipated the arrival of Santa Claus. It was just sad that I couldn't be with my family in the afternoon as they raced down the toboggan hill and, in the evening, played monopoly.

Nothing about Dar at Christmas felt authentic. The oppressive heat, the stupid bugs, the dingy motel, the constant chirping and rooster crows, even the smell of jasmine just ticked me off. Had I been able to teleport myself back to my home in Toronto I would have, in a nanosecond. I had forgotten that I hated the cold, mistrusted the commercialism of Christmas in Canada and found the racing around and sleep deprivation of the season hard to take. From where I stood that day, my memory painted a perfect picture of all the Christmas celebrations past.

"So," said Rob, jerking me back to the present, "Since it's Christmas, what do you want to do today?"

"First we should open our presents." said Cec.

"We could go out for dinner later," Rob added. "I also booked a call to Canada for 3:00 this afternoon. It would be nice for you to talk to your family Julie. We should also phone my sister. I wonder what she's doing without us. And, if you'd like, we could try and find a church that has a Christmas day service."

"Sounds good," said Cec. "We'll have a great day, but I sure miss the snow and our home. I wish you guys would just give up and come back."

"Dad," Rob snapped. "We have already discussed this ad nauseam. You know our plans, so please let's not talk about it anymore. Let's try and enjoy the day."

## Chapter Thirty-Three

Rob's father looked annoyed but resigned. I thought Rob's mom might be going to cry, so I suggested the two of us go outside to the garden to pick some red bougainvillea which would make our apartment feel more festive.

Outside I began to feel better. "It's beautiful here, isn't it?" I asked Rob's mom. Just look at the blue, blue sky and the sun that just keeps on shining. I hate the snow, the darkness, and the freezing cold temperatures in Canada. We really will be fine, you know. Try not to worry. If things get too bad, I promise we'll be sensible and come home."

"I know," answered Phyll. It's just that we worry, and we miss you so much."

I was reaching up with my scissors to cut off some red flowers on the wall above my head when I felt a terrible burning sensation on my right shoulder. I turned my head and saw a foot long, segmented, black centipede with crazy, red legs clinging to me and thrashing around while it bit deep into my flesh.

"Oh God, oh God!" I shrieked, flinging my basket. I took my left hand and swiped it across my shoulder dislodging the offending insect. "Help," I screamed. The guys rushed downstairs and ran gasping up to us.

"What's wrong?" Rob asked wide-eyed.

"I've just been bitten by a Tanzanian train," I screamed at him. "We have to get to the hospital. That's as bad as a scorpion bite, isn't it? I don't want to die!"

Rob took my hand, and we ran to our *piki piki* (little motorcycle), leaving Rob's parents gaping. We arrived minutes later at emergency and, to our relief, the doctor didn't seem too concerned. He gave me some painkillers and said to bathe the wound in warm water and baking soda. "You'll be fine, not to worry. It's not a fatal bite,

## Chapter Thirty-Three

although it might cause discomfort and a burning sensation for the next couple of hours. Take the pills. That'll help."

Merry Christmas, I thought angrily, although I had the grace not to say anything. When we got home Rob's parents looked pasty white, and they'd obviously been fighting. You could cut the atmosphere with a knife. "Guys it's not as serious as we thought," I said, embarrassed to have caused such stress. "Let's go to the CUSO office and make those calls home."

Rob had carefully booked overseas call time in advance with Tanzania Post and Telecommunications Authority, and we didn't anticipate a problem. We were wrong. Our operator in Tanzania immediately got through to the overseas operator in Montreal who explained that all the lines within Canada to Northern Ontario were occupied. She couldn't put us through. We tried to connect for two frustrating hours and finally gave up.

By then we were all so demoralized that no one was talking at all. We drove toward home in tense silence until Rob, always the optimist, suggested that we go to church. Praying seemed like a good thing to do so we agreed. The only service late in the day on Christmas was at the Mission to Seamen in the port area of Dar.

"Can't you find an Anglican church?" Dad asked.

"This will be like an Anglican service," answered Rob. "When you think about it, Jesus's disciples were fishermen, weren't they? Seems kind of appropriate somehow." That shut Cec up, and he managed a feeble grin.

The chapel was a small room that looked out onto the harbour. "How lovely," Phyll remarked.

Elegant Arab dhows from Zanzibar, heading for the Gulf, competed with modern cargo ships for dock space.

## Chapter Thirty-Three

The quality of the light in the late afternoon was translucent. The rays of the sun reflected through the stain glass windows and spilled onto the alter. The hymn, "I Saw Three Ships a Sailing" sung by the small congregation was strangely haunting.

For the first time that day I felt at peace. Everything fell into perspective. We were going to be just fine. This was our dream and Rob and I were not going to give it up. Most of the people in the congregation were seamen a long way from home, and they were homesick too. What we were feeling was perfectly normal. Our time in Tanzania was a gift not to be wasted.

"Look," remarked Rob's dad. "Under the alter cloth. What is that?"

Two tiny kittens, one pure black and the other white with black spots, popped out from under the alter. "How adorable," Phyll said. "This really is a very special Christmas. I know I shall remember my experience here forever."

"Let's celebrate," said Rob. "We do have so much to be grateful for."

We went to the Agip gas station on Ocean Road, which had an adjacent snack bar with a distant view of the water. It was far from fancy but had surprisingly good Italian food, and the stuffed *filetto* was the best I'd ever eaten. Our Christmas dinner was different but delicious.

When we got back to the Oceanic hotel we popped the cork on a bottle of Israeli, bubbly wine and made a toast to family, friends, and Christmas celebrations past and present. We remembered all our loved ones in Canada, held hands and said an evening, prayer: "Come Lord Jesus be our guest, our morning joy, our evening rest, and with this daily prayer impart a love and joy and peace in every heart."

## Chapter Thirty-Four
### Goodbye, Paris, Hello Addis (2000-2001)

Our Paris interlude is over. The Canadian government decides that all its executive officers on leave of absence abroad, including Rob, have to either return to work for the Canadian Government or stay with the organizations that are employing them currently. Rob has no choice. He will have a great pension if he puts in the rest of his time with CIDA (Canadian International Development Agency) but not if he leaves the government now.

He bargains with CIDA to avoid a return to Ottawa. The solution is to approve a posting to Addis Ababa, Ethiopia, starting in September. I manage to get a job as the head librarian at the International Community School in Addis. We're excited to go back to the Third World where we have spent most of our lives.

Jen is married, but her health is still not good. Dan is in university. Meg is furious. She has loved Paris and doesn't want to leave, but at 13, I know she will adjust. Andrew, at eight, doesn't really understand. He'll be fine if we are.

Our first year in Addis Rob and I, with our two youngest kids, return to Canada for Christmas. It's wonderful to be together—my whole family reunited. The seven of us, (Mo is part of the family now), drive from Ottawa to Huntsville to be with my parents, who arrange for a horse-drawn buggy ride into the woods. There's a full moon that night, and it is minus thirty degrees C. I imagine that fairies are dancing and throwing sparkling diamonds of light on the white, snow-covered forest. The scent of pine trees, newly fallen snow and the bonfire that we are headed to, make me want to stay at home forever.

## Chapter Thirty-Four

Why do I insist on going abroad? Our only problem is Mo. He's dressed in formal black dress shoes and a long, unlined, black, wool trench coat. The man is going to freeze! By the time we reach the fire he's shivering, and his lips are blue. We're miles into the forest. There's nothing we can do except huddle around the bonfire for a long, long time, drinking hot chocolate and eating melted maple syrup candy. When we climb back on the horse-drawn wagon, Mo looks a little less tragic.

Back in my parents' lovely home on the frozen lake, around their floor to ceiling stone fireplace, it's easy to see the humour in the situation, but I am struck again by the reality that my son-in-law does not fit into our family's lifestyle. How will Jen and Mo make their marriage work? He still has not introduced his wife to his family. Things are not looking good—at least not to Rob and me!

During all of this time my daughter is loving and loyal to her new husband. "Mom, he's working so hard to make a life for us." How, I wonder, do you make a life for your wife while hiding her from your mom, dad and sister, not to mention your aunts, uncles, and cousins? Jen is still moving out of their Ottawa apartment whenever his family arrives for a visit.

"Take everything of yours with you," the bastard tells our lovely daughter. Clearly, he wants to deny her presence in his life. Jen is so vulnerable, so naive. She's still suffering from Graves and has lost her, 'I can do anything,' attitude. She seeks her husband's approval for everything. Jen is a shadow of her former self, and I'm terrified for her.

After Christmas vacation I cling to my eldest daughter before we leave for Addis. "Take care of yourself," I plead. "You know we are here for you. Dan lives close,

## Chapter Thirty-Four

and he will help if you need anything. Call if you have a problem. We love you."

As we board the plane, my heart is aching. I wish I could kidnap Jen—bring her to Addis with me. I don't trust this man she's married, and I know she's not well, not herself. Why can't the doctors just make her better.? God, how complicated can it be?

Back in Ethiopia we communicate regularly. It is in the words she doesn't say that I know things are not what they should be. I know, too, that Jen doesn't want to worry us. She keeps our conversations light and cheerful, but my gut tells me that all is not going as she planned.

# Chapter Thirty-Five
## Life on the Porch (1972)

Rob's parents were gone. As difficult as our time with them had been, I felt bereft. A sense of abandonment, loneliness invaded my thinking. Cec and Phyll had tried so hard to get us to come back to Canada. Had we made an error? Rob was hurting too, I could tell. He seemed to be always busy, distant, and would stay late at work. He'd remain in the living room, alone, brooding long after I had gone to bed. Rob had stopped looking at me with longing, soft, sensual eyes. He'd stopped reaching out for me at night when we were sleeping. I missed him.

I began to wonder if the sacrifice required to fulfill our African dream had been too much for our relationship. What would be left of us when we got back home? His parents had created a rift, a weak link between us. I am his wife, I thought. He is supposed to be strong, self-possessed, my leader. The concept of Rob, helpless and dependent on his parents, was a vision I would have given anything to avoid, but it was too late.

We were exposed and vulnerable. Rob was no help. He was as lost and scared as I was. He was young, naive, and thousands of miles from home just like me. I hated that he could do nothing to change our housing situation. All his ranting, the angry words, the idle threats couldn't make the situation any better. I felt myself hardening at the edges, more brittle and unsure than I had ever been. Could this bond that I believed would last forever be broken? So many CUSO marriages had already ended. One out of three couples that were posted with us hadn't survived. Would we end up just another casualty of a difficult posting?

## Chapter Thirty-Five

The Tanzanian government, annoyed that we had turned down their housing option of Ilala flats, were ignoring us. We wondered if we would ever be allocated a suitable place to live. "If this isn't resolved soon," said Rob, "we will have no choice but to leave." He spoke in staccato, measured, abrupt language. Instead of discussing our next move, my husband was telling me what we would do. How dare he?

I knew he was right. We couldn't go on without a place to live, but I was just beginning to feel at home. I'd fallen in love with my students and had made friends among my Tanzanian counterparts. Rob was enjoying his job and was beginning to understand how things worked. Our almost new, shiny, black 125 cc Honda motorcycle (*piki piki*) was proving to be a great means of transportation. Life, after eight months in Tanzania, was getting easier.

Our temporary accommodation, Paul and Cathy's porch, was another story. We had no privacy. We were intruding on another couple. All four of us had believed that our living arrangement was temporary, yet we had been in their home for almost two months.

One night we awoke to the sound of Cathy sobbing. "Great," said Rob. "What are we supposed to do now?"

"Should I go and knock on their door? Maybe I can help." I whispered.

"Are you nuts? Back off. Maybe they just had a fight. It's none of our business!"

The crying escalated into wails of agony. "Oh my God, what do you think is wrong with her? I have to do something," I insisted.

At that moment Paul and Cathy rushed onto the porch fully dressed. "Sorry, to disturb you guys," said Paul. "Cath forgot to take out her contact lenses. They've been

## Chapter Thirty-Five

in far too long and something is terribly wrong with her right eye. We're off to the hospital. See you in a bit."

Two hours later Cathy returned with a large white patch over her eye. "The contact scratched the cornea," she explained. "It was terribly painful. At the hospital they put in drops, and I'm feeling much better, just a bit of discomfort. No lasting harm though. Apparently, the cornea repairs itself easily and naturally. I'll be fine in a few days."

The real trouble in living with another couple was the tension it created between Rob and I. Paul and Cathy were nice people, and we got along well. It wasn't their fault that we never relaxed. There was no door to close on the porch and sound travelled easily between the walls. We couldn't even fight or make love without feeling nervous and exposed.

"I have to get out of here," Rob shouted one Saturday afternoon.

"Where do you suggest we go?" I snapped back.

"'Planet of the Apes' is playing at the National Theatre downtown. Let's go."

"'Planet of the Apes'. You're kidding. Gross. I hate stupid movies like that."

"Hey," returned Rob, "Don't be such a snob. That's our only choice, and I'm going with or without you."

At least the theatre was air-conditioned. We got a break from the oppressive heat, but we saw almost none of the movie. We spent the entire time bickering about whether to go home to Canada or stay in Tanzania. By the time we were halfway through the movie neither one of us had any idea of the plot. People were glaring at us for raising our voices. We tried again to focus, but failed. We left the theatre. I suspect we didn't miss much.

## Chapter Thirty-Five

My school, Bunge Primary, was very close to where we were living and so was the Kilimanjaro hotel. After teaching each day I didn't want to go home, so I would make my way to the hotel pool, swim lengths, read and then sleep under an umbrella for an hour or so. It was a solitary routine that allowed me to relax. Rob couldn't join me because he had to work later. He arrived home stressed.

Our friend, Paul, was a computer programmer at the Tanzanian treasury, implementing the first public service pension plan. The computer he worked on was the size of a small house. In this day and age, we can do more functions on a cell phone. Cathy worked as a math teacher at Dar es Salaam Technical college. They were quiet, intellectual, analytical types, and they loved to play games, so in the evening, after dinner, the four of us would sit around a monopoly board or a deck of cards. That did nothing for Rob.

"I hate stupid games," Rob whispered to me after we had gone to bed. I'm not sure how much longer I can stand this."

"Come on," I answered. "It's not that bad."

Not everything was terrible during those days on the porch. One Sunday the four of us packed up Paul and Cathy's VW van with snorkels, fins, a cooler, and our bathing suits. We headed out Ocean Road towards *Mzizima* fish market. There we caught the *Kigamboni* ferry across the harbour to a beautiful, white, sandy beach with a reef just offshore.

The reefs around Dar, in the early seventies, were untouched and magnificent. That day we saw schools of brightly coloured tropical fish darting in and out of the vibrant coral as well as huge, ugly faced barracuda. At up to two meters in length, with their fang-like teeth, they

## Chapter Thirty-Five

resembled sharks. Because they weren't dangerous, we were able to swim so close to them that we could look into their eyes. It was a magical day.

Slim, tall Cathy, with her long, straight, light-brown hair pulled up in a ponytail, Paul, lanky and well over six feet tall, and Rob and I, were just Canadian kids a long way from home. We probably looked very out of place at that time, on that amazing beach, but we were living a dream and having an experience of a lifetime. It was also a moment in time that can't be recaptured today. The coral is all but destroyed. Most of the fish have disappeared with pollution, over fishing and irresponsible divers.

That night I drifted off to sleep only to be awakened at four in the morning by a mechanical clicking sound. I tried to shake Rob awake. "Go back to sleep," he murmured. "I'm exhausted." It had been a long day of sun and sand, and I was tired, so I laid back down. Again, the sound came, louder and more persistent, accompanied by a hissing whisper in Swahili. I cautiously peeked over the window sill into the driveway.

"Rob," I said shaking him harder. "There are two guys out there, and I think they're trying to steal Paul and Cathy's van."

"You have to be kidding," Rob whispered, sitting up and peering out. "Oh my God, you're right. They're trying to hot wire the car."

Two burly, tough looking men were busily messing around under the hood, only 25-feet away from our heads. The only thing between the bad guys and us was a porch screen. "Crap," I hissed. "What if they have a gun! If we try to stop them, we might be sorry."

"What are we supposed to do? Nothing?" asked Rob, incredulous that I would even contemplate such a solution.

## Chapter Thirty-Five

"It's just a car," I answered. "I'm not prepared to die for a van. Be quiet, and maybe they won't notice we're here."

At that moment Rob stood up and screamed at the top of his lungs, *"mweze, mweze, mweze"* (thief, thief, thief). Given no choice I joined my voice to his. Paul and Cathy came tearing out of their room in their pyjamas looking stunned. The thieves looked up at the porch and hesitated. We all held our breath. Our fate hung in the balance that night.

Fortunately, the bad guys grabbed their tools and ran off into the darkness. "They were going to steal our car," said Cathy, incredulous. "Thank goodness you live on our porch."

"Thanks for doing that," added Paul. "Lucky for us that they ran away though. I just hope they never come back. We'll have to report this in the morning."

Ya, and if they do return I hope to be away from here and in our own place, I thought. "Frankly," I said, "I confess that I would have done nothing. Rob was the one who screamed."

That night didn't help our marital relationship one bit. I felt resentment curdle in my stomach. Why was Rob always the hero? Why did he persist in taking such terrible risks? It would've been far more sensible to do nothing. What he had done was brave perhaps, but sometimes there is a fine line between bravery and stupidity. We were all lucky to have survived the encounter, and that evening could have just as easily ended in tragedy.

## Chapter Thirty-Six
### Ladder Cove (1972)

"Why don't just the two of us take our snorkelling gear and head off to the ocean? A Brit volunteer mentioned a small shore line cave that is underwater at high tide, but exposed when the water is low. You have to crawl down a cliff face to get to the cave, but there's an attached ladder to help you out. What do you think?" Rob asked.

What I thought was, 'you've got to be kidding. Caves terrify me. I'm also not so keen on heights and scrambling down sheer cliff sides.' I should have mentioned that to Rob but our relationship had been so strained lately that I wanted to cooperate, so what I said was, "Sure, sounds like fun."

Besides, we really needed to get out of the house and away from Paul and Cathy. They were great people and had saved us from having to return to Canada, but we were just so different. Paul would be sweeping up the floor under the dining room table before we finished eating. Their place was immaculate, austere; no books or magazines, no nick-knacks, no clutter of any kind.

Because I was nervous about messing things up, I became clumsy. I seemed to spill more beverages than I consumed. I dropped plates, forgot to pick up books and generally began to feel and act like a sloppy person. Rob, not the neatest guy in the world, was even worse. He didn't worry about leaving papers, books, and clothes around. For him that was just normal. The tension in the house was mounting.

We roared off on the bike early in the morning, noticing that the tide was out but not at its lowest point. After parking at the edge of a hidden cove not far from

## Chapter Thirty-Six

town, we looked out from the top of the cliff and saw calm, clear water and a reef not far from the shore. Everything was going well until I focussed down to the beach below, straight down, 30-feet. My knees began to shake just imaging what the descent would be like. Rob looked at me. "Don't worry. I'll go first," he said. "Just don't look down."

The ladder started at the top of the cliff but ended about 5-feet above the ground. Rob scrambled down like an agile monkey and then jumped onto the sandy beach which bordered the cave. He looked up at me. I was suspended on the ladder and couldn't make myself take another step. "You're okay. Don't panic. Just step slowly, one rung at a time. I'll catch you if you fall."

"Thanks a lot," I snapped. I held my breath and made it, trembling and cursing, to the bottom of the ladder. "What do I do now?"

"Turn around and jump. It's easy."

"What if I break my ankle?" I whined.

"Julie, for heaven's sake, it's not that far down, and I can grab you before you hit ground."

I was contemplating returning up the ladder, but I didn't want to disappoint Rob, so I turned, closed my eyes and flew forward. The sand was soft and I landed easily. The cave behind us, jutting into the limestone cliff, was just deep enough to provide protection from the blazing sun. The shallow water lapped at the entrance and the soft white sand sparkled. The blue sky and turquoise ocean stretched out in front of us. There was nothing claustrophobic about this cave. "It's so beautiful and private." I whispered.

We sat on the sand and gazed out. "Wow. This is great." Rob said, sounding excited. We donned our snorkelling gear, which Rob had carried down the ladder

## Chapter Thirty-Six

in his backpack. The depth of the water was perfect, so we were able to walk a few steps, avoiding the sea urchins' sharp, black spines, and then swim almost from the shore. The reef was all we had hoped for. There were so many small to medium fish of all colours of the rainbow, as well as coral of all kinds. I felt like I was floating in an aquarium that had been over stocked. Fish kept bumping up against my mask and darting all around my body.

Rob swam over and touched my arm motioning for me to look at an amazing coral. It had at least fifty fluorescent green tubes with tips of bright orange. I pointed out a large, silver angelfish with black stripes. Both Rob and I had completely lost track of time. We weren't worried about sunburn because we had worn t-shirts over our bathing suits. The water was warm, sultry, clear, and calm, so we relaxed and just gazed at all the wonders of the ocean.

We continued like that for ages. Being fit and young, I don't think we had any idea how much time had passed. To this day I can't really say how long we'd been swimming when I began to think about being a bit tired and thirsty. "Rob," I called, taking off my mask, and treading water. "Maybe it's time to call it a day. I'm kinda done. This has been amazing."

The tide had continued to go out. We were quite far from the beach. In minutes, we realized that water had become too shallow for us to swim over the reef. "Now what?" I asked.

"No problem." said Rob, "just take off your fins and carry them in."

"We can't walk over this. There are too many sea spines. There's sharp coral everywhere. We'd cut our feet to ribbons in minutes. It's too shallow to swim. What are we going to do now?"

## Chapter Thirty-Six

"I don't know." Rob had no answer, probably for the first time since we'd been together. I felt bile rise in my throat as my stomach flipped over. I gagged. Rob just continued to stare at me.

"We have to swim out to the deeper water and wait until the tide comes in a bit. After that we can swim to shore," I said.

"Do you have any idea how long that could take?" asked Rob.

"None, actually. I haven't a clue. But it's our only choice." I was a much stronger swimmer than Rob. This ordeal was going to be far more difficult for him than it was for me. I'd spent my summers at our family cottage in Muskoka and had become a lifeguard in my teens. Rob, on the other hand, hadn't had much swimming practice. He was also slimmer than I was and would feel the cold before me.

"The best thing that we can do for ourselves is to stay calm. We're buoyant because of the salt. We can just float out here for ages, as long as we don't panic." It wasn't often that I took the lead. Rob looked a bit surprised.

"OK. boss," Rob said with a lopsided grin. "I guess you're right. How do you feel?"

"I'm fine. We can do this. We'll make it." We wasted no more time talking, put our masks back on and swam out to look at the ocean. We floated, treaded water, snorkelled and periodically held on to each other for what seemed like hours. I had completely lost the ability to estimate the length of time it took for the tide to start coming in, but come in it did.

Finally, the ocean near the shore was deep enough for us to swim back to the beach. We were both so exhausted and thirsty that we lay on the sand, at the mouth of the cave, saying nothing and sharing water from the thermos

## Chapter Thirty-Six

we'd left at the bottom of the ladder. When the beach began to disappear under the incoming tide, we were forced to get up and move. Rob hoisted me up to the bottom rung of the ladder and I began to climb with no thought of heights or danger. Rob leapt up on his own, behind me. We reached the top and our motorcycle with no trouble.

When we got back to Paul and Cathy's, we went straight to bed and lay in each other's arms for the rest of the day and all through the night. Sometimes danger can put a new slant on life. The important things became clearer. I stopped doubting Rob and he calmed down. Our decision to return home would be based on whether we were assigned suitable housing. Fate would decide what our next move would be. We were young, in love, healthy and having the adventure of a lifetime. That was enough for the moment.

# Chapter Thirty-Seven
## Dance Therapy (2015)

I am at a Zumba class in Orillia, more than two years after Jen's death. I'm dancing my heart out. I'm addicted to this activity which I do several times a week. It's the one time in my day when it's impossible to think about my daughter—far too busy trying to follow the instructor's next move. Gotta keep up with the pulsing salsa beat. My complete focus does not allow for intruding thoughts of any kind.

The second the music stops, and I exit through the gym door, thoughts of my daughter are waiting to pounce on me. As I walk, talk, write, or try to sleep, wherever I am, whatever I'm doing, they creep up on me, stalk me, torment me. My eyes are sore from tears that spring unbidden.

When I was a child, I had a recurring nightmare—I am walking in a jungle. I sense something behind me. I glance over my shoulder and see a huge, orange and black-striped tiger. At first the animal moves slowly and keeps a distance between us, but as I begin to run the tiger closes the gap, crouches, and leaps. At the end, just before I wake up sweating, shaking, I can feel the cats hot, putrid breath on the back of neck, but he never gets to eat me alive.

Thoughts of Jen's death are like that tiger. Although they threaten to rip me apart, they do not have the power to destroy me unless I let them. Like in the dream, life will go on for me, for my family. Babies will be born. Joy will happen. Love for each other will hold us together.

I remember the last day I was with my daughter before we knew she was sick. The two of us were at Zumba. I, the proud mama, stood behind Jen so I could watch her

## Chapter Thirty-Seven

with awe while she danced. She moved with such grace and rhythm—a butterfly flitting across the room, barely touching the floor—no jagged movements, just colourful symmetry—a choreographed wind dance.

It's not just me who was watching her magic. After class a woman approached us. "You should be teaching this class. I loved watching you," she said to Jen. "Where did you learn to move like that?"

Jen giggled a bit self-consciously. "I've studied dance for a long time," she answered.

"My daughter danced in the Jamaican Dance Theatre Company for a couple of years. They performed Cats all over the island. She was one of the stars."

As soon as the woman disappeared, Jen looked at me. "God Mom! Did you have to give her my life story? That was embarrassing!"

I still have a video of Jenny dancing in Cats. Her tall, slim frame, wild, curly, halo hair, her natural grace makes her shine in that performance. Although there were many young people on the stage, Kingston Daily Gleaner singled out her performance. Even though she was very white, the leading arts critic assumed she had to be Jamaican. I watch that video again and again—too often.

The next day, after my Zumba class with Jennifer, Rob and I left for a holiday in Ethiopia, a former posting of ours. Two weeks later we got an email from Jen. Something was seriously wrong with her.

She'd been suffering from a persistent dry cough for months—maybe even a year. Although Jen sought medical attention months before, she hadn't gotten around to completing all the tests. Her teaching rounds, in her final year of teacher's college, demanded so many hours. Rob nagged her constantly to do something, but sadly

## Chapter Thirty-Seven

she'd ignored him. Being ill just wasn't an option if she was going to graduate.

When Jen began to cough up blood she went immediately to the hospital. The x-ray showed a large tumour in her left lung. As soon as we got the news, we flew home. We got the final verdict days later. Stage four lung cancer. She was given 11 to 13 months with treatment and six to nine months without.

Jen was diagnosed in early March and died eight months later in early November. She tried all the treatments available. She wanted so much to live. There is one thing for which I will be eternally grateful. Her death was quick and painless—she died of an aneurysm resulting from secondary brain cancer.

Days before her death she rode her bike to Mariposa Folk Festival, attended art shows and visited our beloved Christian Island cottage on Georgian Bay. Although she had lost her hair from chemotherapy, Jen wore a cute wig and was still lovely. No one would have guessed that she was ill.

She knew she was dying, though. At the end she'd lost so much weight and found it almost impossible to eat anything. She had extreme pain in her lungs. The cancer had spread to her bones. Pain kept her awake at night even though she took heavy-duty painkillers. Jen never complained. She remained braver than all of us to the end.

Although we lost her far too soon, I am grateful that our daughter was never bedridden and was able to live each day fully to the end of her life.

## Chapter Thirty-Eight
### Whistle Blower (1972)

"I'm an idiot." I pronounced one night at dinner. "I've just volunteered to be the coach of the men's Dar es Salaam Technical College basketball team."

"Wow, you're brave. I have trouble teaching them math, and it's a compulsory subject. Good luck," commented Cathy.

"Brave?" shot Rob. "Stupid might be a better word."

"Hey," I said. "What do you mean?"

"I'm supposed to be your husband. Remember? Since when don't you ask me about stuff like that? You'll be busy every weekend. How's that not a bad idea?"

"But they weren't going to be able to have a team unless they could find a coach. They're really good. They deserve a chance," I argued.

"So, what's wrong with the 30 male teachers I teach with?" asked Cathy sarcastically. "They're just using you. They're being lazy because they know one of us stupid foreigners will step up to the plate. I bet they didn't think it would be a woman, though. Way to go. This should be interesting. Apparently our team, Dar Tech, has a very good chance at defeating the Crows this year."

"Who are the Crows?" Rob asked.

"They're a combination of the Americans at the embassy and the marines," explained Cathy. There's a huge rivalry between the Crows and Dar Tech."

"You have to be joking," Rob remarked. "Those guys are well over 6-feet tall and Julie, you're five feet three inches with heels."

## Chapter Thirty-Eight

"Maybe I could help you," said Paul. "I'm well over six feet. I played some basketball in high school, but my back just couldn't take it. I'd love to coach though and I know all the rules."

"Ya Paul," but I teach a bunch of those guys. Not cool," argued Cathy.

Paul looked disappointed but let it go. Rob just looked annoyed. I knew I hadn't heard the end of his complaints.

Our first practice went smoothly. It became clear to me after about five minutes that the guys on the team were not newcomers to the sport. They could out jump, out shoot, and out play me with their eyes closed. They sped around the court and completely ignored my presence. But, for the purpose of the regulations, they needed a coach, any coach. I was more like their mascot.

During the break, Hamid came over to me. "Thanks for doing this," he said. "It means a lot to us. I do think we have a shot at the championship this year." Hamid was a year or two older than I was and a great guy—warm, friendly, supportive and terrific looking. He was also the team captain and everyone looked up to him.

"That's okay," I answered, "but there isn't anything I can teach you guys. I had no idea the team was this good. You need a professional for a coach, not me."

"Actually," Hamid remarked, "all we need is a warm body, preferably a teacher, to come with us to practices and games. It's the only way they'll let us play. Pretty stupid but it's the rule. Are you married?" Hamid asked, giving me a side glance out of his warm caramel eyes.

"Ya, for more than two years now," I answered, feeling awkward. What had my marital state to do with anything?

"Why haven't you got any kids?" he asked.

## Chapter Thirty-Eight

Hey, I thought, this is getting a bit personal. "We don't want any at the moment. Lots of time for that," I answered.

Hamid looked shocked, although I had no idea why. "Want to come out with me for a drink after the practice?"

"Sure," I said. "We can discuss basketball plays. If you want, I could show you another way to set up a defence."

Later at Hasani's House of Cold Drinks in downtown Dar, I ordered a banana shake and sat down with Hamid. "You're beautiful," he remarked. I choked on my drink and turned bright red. I had not seen that coming. It seemed that guys worked faster here than in Canada. They didn't seem to care much about husbands. They were also clearly prone to vast exaggeration.

"Your husband is very stupid. You should have at least one baby by now and be at home taking care of your family, not out here coaching men's basketball," he said, reaching under the table to squeeze my knee. My effort to pull the chair back didn't do much good. His arm just reached out farther to grope some more.

"Are you trying to say that I should be barefoot, pregnant and in the kitchen?" I joked pushing his hand away.

Hamid chuckled. "Ya, of course. What else? That's what real women are for."

"Look, why do you think your male sex makes you better than me?" I demanded, beginning to feel annoyed. I want a career, kids, and a husband. There's no reason I shouldn't have it all."

"Good luck," answered Hamid. "You'd better go home to Canada then. You outsiders think you can change us, but you can't. Women, our women, get it."

"Hey it was your team that begged me to be a coach," I said.

## Chapter Thirty-Eight

"You volunteers are all the same. Of course, we let you be coach. None of our Tanzanian teachers want to spend their weekends at our games. They want to be home with their families. Too bad you don't have one."

"Oh my God. You're a male, chauvinistic pig! I thought you were my friend. Listen buddy, I'm married and one husband is more than enough for me. I don't want kids yet, and I have to go."

"Don't be mad. I had to try because you're so beautiful. I dream about you every night. Your husband is not too bright. You need a real man."

"That's just creepy." I stood up and ran out of the restaurant leaving my drink untouched.

My next encounter with the team was at a game between the Crows and Dar Tech. Hamid acted as if nothing had happened between us and so did I. The two teams waited at the gym for the ref to show up. Half an hour later—no ref. "What do we do now?" I asked.

"Has anyone got referee papers?" inquired the captain of the Crows.

"I do," I answered.

"No problem then. You'll be our ref."

"But girls' rules are totally different. I don't think I can do this."

"Sure, you can," all the guys agreed. "You'll be fine."

I took the ball to centre court for the toss. I was two heads shorter than the players, so it was difficult to throw the ball up and keep it in the middle. The Crows triumphed and Hamid screamed, "Not fair, bad toss." No one listened and the play continued. About two minutes into the game one of the Crows rammed right into a Dar Tech player sending him flying. I blew my whistle. Nothing happened. Both teams completely ignored me. I

## Chapter Thirty-Eight

blew my whistle again, as loud as I could, with the same result.

I shouted, "Foul, foul. Stop the play." No response. I ran out into the middle of the floor, jumping up and down shouting, waving my arms and blowing my whistle. Still nothing. The game went on. The Crows scored a basket and the play finally stopped so that the ball could be thrown in at the end of the court by Dar Tech. No one paid any attention to me at all. I felt invisible. I gave up trying to control the game and walked off the court.

I sat on the sidelines and watched. The Crows won by a score of 20 to 16. After the game the captain of the Crows approached me. "Thanks for doing that," he said with his strong American accent. "The game couldn't have been played without a ref."

"Ref, you're kidding." I shot back. "I was just a spectator."

By the time I got home I'd decided I couldn't go on pretending to coach the Dar Tech team. I told my story to Paul, Cathy, and Rob. They laughed their heads off. No sympathy there. "What am I going to do now?" I asked.

"Well," said Rob. "One thing's for sure. You're not going back there. No way."

"Cath," said Paul. "Would you mind if I took this on? I've always loved basketball and there's no way they would mess with me. It might be fun. I'd like to try. Clearly Julie needs out of this."

"I guess," answered Cathy "but you already coach swimming at the university. That's a bit much, don't you think?"

"How bout we switch. Julie, you have phys ed swimming qualifications, right?" Paul asked.

"That's true," I answered, but wouldn't it just be more of the same. Will the guys listen to me?"

## Chapter Thirty-Eight

"These men really want to learn how to swim," said Paul. "They're so grateful, and I think they'd respect anyone, even a woman, who isn't afraid of water. It's not much of a challenge though. I confess that I find it a little slow, but you might really enjoy it. The students are real gentlemen. They'd love you."

"That's what I'm afraid of," said Rob, but the deal was struck.

## Chapter Thirty-Nine
### *Dik Dik*—Richard the Second (2001)

Jen arrives at Bole airport in Addis Ababa for a short visit. As soon as I see her in the arrivals lounge, I know something has changed. I look at her walking, head held high, slim, graceful with her dancer's stance and body. Nothing different there. Everyone in the vicinity is staring at her. She has this way of drawing all the attention to herself, like sucking air out of the room. She doesn't mean to. Is it charisma, glamour, grace?—I'm never sure what quality makes everyone aware of Jen.

I love my daughter. I'm so proud. I take her in my arms and hug her tight. I can smell her blue water perfume, feel the warmth of her body. Her heart beats against mine. God, it's good to be with Jen again. She looks healthy, wears almost no makeup and has gained a bit of weight. She's a bit pale and tired, of course, after 17 hours in the air. Still, there's something new that I sense but can't quite figure out.

Rob, who has been at the luggage carousel looking for Jen's suitcase, races up and hugs his daughter. "Too bad Mo couldn't come. Thanks for joining us. I hope he won't miss you too much."

"He doesn't care," Jen answers. "He wants a chance to visit his family without me. It's so good to see you guys. Where are my sibs?"

"Meg and Andrew are home. They've been preparing for your visit for days. Dan got here yesterday and worked out at the gym right after he arrived. We tried to tell him to take it easy—the altitude here zaps your energy and takes some getting used to. He's okay, but completely out of it today. He'll be fine soon," Rob explains.

## Chapter Thirty-Nine

"Dan and I have seen quite a bit of each other, but it feels like forever since I saw Meg and Andrew. I hate being so far away from them," Jen says. "They're so young. I'm missing their growing up."

"Well, you're here now. Let's get you home. Tomorrow we're off to the Bale Mountains to stay at the Swedish Lodge. If we're lucky, we might spot the endangered Abyssinian wolf. Then we'll go to a cottage on Lake Langano. We can swim there—the only bilharzia-free lake in the country. It's going to be such a great holiday," Rob says leading both of us to our parked car.

Our family reunion is wonderful. Everyone is glowing with mutual love and happiness. My world, at that moment, is perfect. I'm still struck with the feeling that something about my eldest daughter has changed. I just have no idea what it is.

As we set off to the Ethiopian Highlands the weather is cool, clear, sunny. The trip in our embassy rented four-wheel drive is spectacular: vast stretches of open African savanna, thick tropical forests, round *tukuls* (mud huts with thatched roofs), women dressed in long white gowns with brightly coloured warm shawls, black and white monkeys with long tails leaping in the trees.

The Swedish Lodge, when we arrive, is more than we expected. There's no electricity, but a huge dining lounge with a butcher block table, comfy couches, and a floor to ceiling stone fireplace greet us. There's also a wood-fired sauna out back, and basic but clean bunk rooms where we'll sleep. There's a kitchen where our generous hosts will cook what we provide. There's no restaurant, no grocery store, so we have brought our food with us.

I could be anywhere. It wouldn't matter as long as I have all of my children together, healthy and happy. We're in the wilderness, on the equator, literally on top of the

## Chapter Thirty-Nine

world—so high up that it snows here occasionally. The air is crystal clear, clean, and there are no noises other than the sounds of nature. The birds wake us early in the morning. There are other noises too, that we don't recognize: a growl, a clashing of horns, weird grunts.

We check out our room and realize that it's short on sleeping space—four beds aren't enough for our whole family, but Dan has brought his individual tent and Rob and I have our camping gear. Jen, Meg, and Andrew will stay in the room and the rest of us will set up outside.

The first night, Rob and I are alone in our tent, high up on a hill above the lodge on the Senetti Plateau, or as the locals call it, 'the Island in the Sky'. "This is incredible," Rob says. "God, we're so lucky. How many people have ever experienced this paradise? I feel like I can reach out and touch the stars—so high and clear. Did you hear that? There's wildlife everywhere."

"Ya, I guess, but the animal noises are scary, and we're completely exposed to heaven only knows what. I wouldn't give this experience up for anything though." Too exhausted and content to worry anymore, I fall into a deep sleep.

Next morning the sun, beaming into my eyes, interrupts my happy dreams. I sit upright and there, just outside the screened in front door of the tent, is a huge warthog with giant tusks. He's staring at me, a foot and a half away from my face. I shake Rob. "Wake up. We have a visitor. Don't make a sound."

"Oh crap. He's huge," Rob whispers. "Now what?" The warthog looks curious but calm. We remain frozen, locked in the moment, not daring to move until the beast turns and trots off with his tail in the air. We go outside and see that the warthog and his friends have dug a trench around

## Chapter Thirty-Nine

our tent. It looks like a moat without water. "Wo, that was cool," Rob says.

Back at the lodge we check on our family. Dan has had a peaceful night in his tent. Jen, Meg, and Andrew seem to be fine, except Meg says, "Jen threw up early this morning."

"Are you okay love?" I ask.

"I'm fine," she answers. "Must have eaten something that upset my stomach. I feel great now."

We stay at the lodge for several days. Rob decides that it would be fun to pay for a goat to be roasted and shared with the community. Everyone in the area arrives with contributions of bread, rice dishes, greens that we can't identify, and fruit to share. It's a feast. People sing, tell stories, enjoy the sauna, dance and get drunk on local booze.

Jen loves this sort of celebration, this mixing of cultures: dancing, talking, sharing, eating exotic foods. Despite that, she excuses herself early in the evening and goes back to the bunk room. Although she seems tired and doesn't eat much, Jen appears to glow. She hasn't mentioned her Grave's disease once. Her medication must be working better. She's clearly happy.

After the lodge we travel north to Lake Langano to stay at a cottage for a few days. On the way there we see a man with tiny deer and a for sale sign. "Stop Dad," Jen shouts. "We have to take that poor little *dik dik* (deer) with us, or it's going to die," Rob reluctantly agrees. We pay and put the baby animal in the car.

The poor thing is crying in high-pitched squeals and trembling in Jen's arms. At less than a foot tall, the *dik dik* is light brown with huge black eyes rimmed with white that look at us in terror. Tiny bumps, that will someday be

## Chapter Thirty-Nine

horns, lie between his ears. "Oh, Mommy, he's the cutest thing I've ever seen," Meg says, patting the deer's head.

"Do you think he'll get along with Munch Bunny? Can we keep him?" Andrew asks.

"Sure," I answer, but I'm thinking that this baby was probably still nursing when it was taken and may not be able to manage solid food. I wonder what we're we supposed to feed it. God, it's so fragile. So tiny. I just hope it will survive.

I say nothing about my doubts. We name our new pet Richard the Second (*Dik Dik*) and put him in the screened porch when we arrive at the lake. His cries are breaking our hearts. We will do whatever we can to keep Richard the Second alive.

Late that night I get up to check on him. I find Jenny and Meg asleep on the porch, lying wrapped in blankets, encircling the deer. He's quiet for the first time, cuddled up against their warm bodies. I worry that my girls won't get much sleep on the hard floor but, not wanting to wake them, I go back to bed.

After our vacation we return to Addis. Richard the Second seems to be doing fine. Jen sets her bed up in backyard and refuses to leave the deer. We feed the baby berries and leaves. We learn that *dik diks* get most of their water from food and don't drink like other animals. They are the smallest deer on the planet. We're told that it was a mistake to buy Richard. Our choice will just encourage other poachers to steal and sell more animals.

"What were we supposed to do though, just let him die?" asks Dan. There's no answer.

Jen tries to hide it, but she's nauseous in the morning and often throws up. I've had four kids. I recognize the symptoms. Should I confront my daughter with my newfound knowledge? Does she know she's pregnant?

## Chapter Thirty-Nine

The day before Jen and Dan are flying home Richard's tongue turns black and that evening our little *dik dik* is dead. "I want to hate the person who took this beautiful creature from its mother too soon," Jen tells me with tears streaming down her face. "But maybe that poor man had a hungry baby to feed. I guess I can't blame him."

The day of our kid's departure comes. After a wonderful visit there is a feeling of sadness in our home. The imminent separation and the loss of Richard hangs in the air, but if I'm going to discuss my daughter's pregnancy, I have to do it before she leaves. "Sit down hon. Can we chat for a minute?"

"What's up Mom? Why so serious?"

"Sweety, are you pregnant?"

"No, I don't think so, although I have been throwing up a bit. It's probably just the change of air, water, the altitude. Dan was nauseous the first few days here."

"True, but that was because he overexercised too soon in this high altitude, and he was better by day three."

"Well Mom, I guess we'll find out soon enough."

# Chapter Forty
## Enter Kaia (2002)

I call Jen shortly after she arrives home in Ottawa. "You're pregnant, aren't you?" I ask.

"Yep, due in August."

"How are you feeling? I wish I was there with you."

"I'm so tired all the time and nauseous in the mornings, but I guess, according to what I'm reading, that's normal. Nothing to worry about. I've stopped taking the medicine for Graves' disease. My doctors say I have to take it, or I'll be at risk. I do not accept that. If it's hurting the baby—forget it."

"Are you sure that's wise? Please don't do anything to endanger your own health. Oh Jen, I'm so happy for you. Wow, our first grandchild. How did Mo take the news?"

"Mo was shocked at first, but he seems okay now. He's convinced that we're having a boy—seems super important to him."

Jen calls regularly in the next few months to tell us that all is progressing normally. In June, we arrive home in Ottawa excited to see Jen and Dan. My first stop is Jen's apartment. I walk in, hug my daughter, feeling her huge belly pressed up against me, and look around. The place is a mess. There's a double mattress on the floor in the bedroom, the sink is blocked up, and dirty dishes are stacked on the floor by the bath tub.

"I've been washing the dishes here—the kitchen sink hasn't worked in months." Jen explains, embarrassed. "Mo has been working a lot—haven't seen much of him lately. I was really ill for a while because I refused to take my medication for Graves. I would have destroyed the

## Chapter Forty

baby's thyroid function. I just couldn't do it. I've just started taking my pills again—had to—and am feeling fine now."

"Jen, I wish I'd known you were so sick. I would have come home. You know that." Guilt makes me dizzy, weak in the knees, so I sink onto the couch. "Has Mo helped you while you've been so ill? Why are you sleeping on the floor? What did you do with the bed we bought you? Why hasn't Mo gotten someone to fix the sink? You can't bring a newborn back to this hovel. How could Mo neglect you like this?"

Jen puts up her hand. "Wo, Mom, get a grip. The baby and I are fine. You should be grateful." I pinch my hand hard to suppress my rage and force myself to be quiet. Rob is about to arrive. He's out buying food and I dread his reaction.

"Mom, I know what you're thinking. I've given notice to the landlord. Mo's not happy but I can't bring a baby back here. Will you guys help us find a new apartment? I need to get something for August first, before the baby arrives, on the tenth or so."

"Your due date is August tenth, your birthday? Same day I had you? Bet the baby is a girl."

"Mo's convinced it's a boy. Won't even accept any other possibility. All I want is a healthy baby, but just between you and me, I would love to have a girl first."

At that moment the doorbell rings and Rob comes in carrying groceries. He looks around; his eyes are huge, and his face turns red. He puts his arms around his daughter and pulls her close. "You can't stay here Jen."

Jen, Meg and I spend the next weeks, during the day, cleaning up the apartment, finding a new place and buying baby clothes and furniture. We almost never see Mo, but my eldest daughter assures us that he's around. Rob's

## Chapter Forty

working at his agency's headquarters in Hull, Dan has a summer job and Andrew is in day camp, but our whole family, minus Mo, spend happy evenings going out to dinner, cooking and walking in Gatineau Park. Jen's feeling well, looking healthy and is excited about the baby.

August tenth arrives. Still no little one. We celebrate Jen's 26th birthday at a quaint Italian restaurant without Mo and Rob. Rob has had to return to Addis, but Andrew, Meg and I have remained to be present for the birth. Dan's summer job is in Ottawa, so he's with us too. I try not to worry about Mo. Surely, he will show up for the birth of his baby.

On the evening of August 11th Jen goes into labour and Mo arrives. We all trek to the Ottawa Civic Hospital and Jen checks in. Everything is ready for the baby's arrival. Jen has decided to invite a small village to attend the birth. Against my better instincts she's insisted that Meg, at only 15, as well as her best friend, Margaret, Mo, and I be present. I can't imagine having all those people around me. The only person I wanted when I gave birth was my husband.

Jen has her heart set on a natural birth and, if all goes well, I agree with her choice. However, I know my daughter, and she is stubborn. "You know, love, if you're tired or overcome with pain there is no shame in having an epidural. The main thing is to deliver a healthy baby."

Her labour goes on all night and into the next day. Jen is exhausted. How is she going to push the baby out? The doctor on duty is a young resident who seems to know nothing. "This is my first delivery," he tells us.

In the early hours of August 12th, the intern comes to the birthing room and says, "the fetal monitor is showing that the baby may be in distress. I'm trying to get the

## Chapter Forty

obstetrician of record to come to the hospital, but if he doesn't show up soon, I need to do a Caesarion delivery."

Jen looks horrified. Just when the resident is about to take Jen off for the C-section her own doctor arrives. He does a quick examination, takes an internal blood sample from the baby's scalp, tests it and declares that everything is fine. "Young lady," he tells my daughter, "I know how much a natural birth means to you, but I am going to insist that you have an epidural. You've got to rest so that when you wake up you will have enough energy to push. Your blood pressure is too high because of Graves' disease, and we also need to deal with that. There's really no choice. It's either an epidural or a C-section."

I look around at the four spectators in the birthing room. Everyone except Mo looks shocked, especially my teenage daughter. God, what was I thinking? I should never have allowed her to be present for this birth. Meg's face is as white as a ghost, and she has tears in her eyes.

Mo has been dozing in the chair for the entire time. Does he not care? Is he stoned? Drunk? Could he not be more supportive of his wife? I suppress the desire to slap him. That would wake him up. Jen falls asleep immediately after the epidural and everyone relaxes a bit.

When Jen wakes up, she says she has to push. The baby is born shortly after. "You have a beautiful, healthy baby girl," the doctor declares. The little one is placed on her mother's chest and Jen shines with pure joy.

Mo is another story. "I was so sure we were going to have a boy," he says looking sad. He doesn't offer to hold the baby.

"I'm going to call her Kaia. It means ocean." Jen tells us. She shoots Mo a look of utter disdain, a kind of screw-you-asshole look. Then she lifts her chin, smiles serenely and puts Kaia to her breast. I know this baby will be a

## Chapter Forty

source of comfort to my daughter. I know that Jen is going to make the best mother ever, with or without her husband.

My focus turns to my youngest daughter Meg. "You okay, hon? That was a far more difficult birth than I had with any of my four children. I really wish you hadn't been there."

"Don't worry Mom. I'm fine, but I'm going to have an epidural as soon as I get pregnant," Meg teases, laughing. "Mom I'm an aunt. Can you believe it?"

As soon as Jen and Kaia are out of the hospital we go to my brother's home. Tera, Jen's cousin and close friend, is having a shower for her and has invited the whole family. Mo is sulking because the baby is a girl and refuses to come with us. Jen is so enchanted by her newborn that she barely seems to notice or care what her husband does.

After the shower Jen checks her messages. "Mom, we have to go back to Ottawa immediately. The hospital got some later results back for the baby and her thyroid is not functioning properly. God Mom, I knew it. I shouldn't have taken my Graves medication at all, not even at the end of the pregnancy."

We drive directly to the hospital and Kaia is admitted immediately. After extensive tests the doctor declares that the baby's thyroid, a week after her birth, is now normal. Jen and I hold on to each other and cry with relief. "Thank God you only took the medicine after you were seven months pregnant. Good call love. I'm so proud of you. I admit, I thought you might be making a mistake. Talk about intuitive," I say through my tears.

Mo is not with us. Jen has been unable to get in touch with him.

# Chapter Forty-One
## Swahili Love Poems (1972)

Dar es Salaam was becoming my home. It was happening, a bit here, a bit there, but I was finally relaxing and getting over my yearning for Canada. The constant, slight nausea had disappeared and the ache of missing loved ones faded and drifted away with the realization that my time in this magical place was going far too quickly. It would end before I knew it. I was falling in love, not with a person, but with a place.

My mind was calmed by the salt, soft waves of the Indian Ocean. There were no glass windows where we slept, only screens, so gentle breezes blew through our porch home day and night freshening and cooling the hot tropical air. The scent of the night flowering jasmine bush lulled me to sleep. The frangipani trees that bordered the driveway greeted me in the morning with their soft, white petals and their sweeter than any perfume fragrance. The Tanzanians call frangipani "Swahili Love Poems". How appropriate.

Cock of the Rock, our yard rooster, strutted his red, blue, and green iridescent plumage and crowed us awake at dawn each day, without fail. "Damn thing," Rob commented. "I wish he would just shut up so that we could occasionally sleep in. My birthday is coming. Maybe we can ask Cathy to cook him."

" Beats our alarm clock back home waking us up in a cold, dark room," I said.

"At least I could stop that from ringing. That bird never quits," commented Rob.

While I was experiencing a heightened sense of smell, touch, taste and sound Rob was getting more and more frustrated. For him optimism was a usual state of mind,

## Chapter Forty-One

but I found we had switched roles. I was feeling a euphoria that was beyond me. The residential section of Dar where we were living was a paradise in those days; a tropical, fresh, fragrant garden of Eden. I knew I wanted to stay in Dar, but as Rob continued to remind me, if we failed to find somewhere to live, we had to leave.

My teaching was giving me more joy than I had anticipated. I was improving daily thanks to the other standard one teacher, Priscilla Strutt from London, England. She had finally accepted me after an initial period when she'd been very cold and distant. Apparently, the teacher who proceeded me had taken advantage of her assistance, and then left after about three months, without a word of goodbye or a thank-you. It took some time to build a relationship, but after that Pris did everything she could to help me. As an experienced teacher her advice and assistance were all I needed to move forward in my job.

I knew it was wrong and tried not to show it, but I had two favourite students, Jamila and Godfrey. Jamila's grandfather had been the sheik of *Kilwa Kivenge*, a little island south of Dar. We saw his hand-crafted bed in the national museum. Her ancestors were Arab traders who sailed dhows between the Arabian Gulf and East Africa. Wide, high cheekbones, ebony skin, raven black curls and deep, dark brown eyes that reflected her every mood combined with a shy kindness that made Jamila everyone's friend.

If she was away there was one child in the class, Habib, who would sit in the corner and refuse to come out. Jamila had a motherly influence on him, even though they were both seven years old. He adored her and followed her like a puppy. Jamila loved to act out plays with our homemade classroom sock puppets and to read and tell stories, not

## Chapter Forty-One

just to me, but to the other students. I called her my little assistant. She was a natural leader. I often wonder if she became a teacher later in life.

Godfrey was a Christian from the Chagga tribe near mighty Mount Kilimanjaro. Creative, fun-loving, always laughing and a delight to be around, he was full of great ideas. "Teacher can we make ABC cards for the wall? We have many kids. We do it quick and it look good. We all make one." Godfrey suggested. "Good idea maybe?" he asked.

"Wonderful idea" I answered. Soon the entire classroom was decorated with student art pieces on six by eight-inch cardboard, each one representing a letter of the alphabet or a number between one and ten. The kids were able to use their own art to learn the alphabet and numbers.

Pris and I divided our one hundred children into groups of ten and set up learning centres in our adjacent classrooms. The students rotated through the stations allowing the two of us to wander around and give assistance to individuals. Pris was a master teacher from England, a cockney ('born within the sound of the bells'), a girl from a working-class background who wanted to learn more about socialist Tanzania. She and her London-Irish husband Tom used to argue about who was more working class. Since Tom had a doctorate in geography and taught at the University of Dar es Salaam and Pris was a teacher, I wasn't sure whether either one of them qualified. Being Canadian, the idea of class structure wasn't something I knew much about.

Bunge, my school, continued to be a challenge regardless of all the help I was getting. We worked six days a week from 7:15 AM until 2:00 PM. By 12:00 the heat and humidity made it difficult to teach or to learn.

## Chapter Forty-One

The walls of our classroom only extended up to six feet; above that was open to the elements. The tin roof protected us to a certain extent, but during the monsoon season the water would blow sideways and wash over the tops of the walls and into our classrooms. It was impossible to keep mosquitoes out, and I constantly worried that my kids would get malaria. The play yard was dusty in the dry season and muddy during the rains. The students would come in from recess, happy as clams, but always smeared top to toe in dust or mud.

On Saturday the children left at 11:30, and then it was the teachers' job to clean our classrooms as well as the bathrooms and common areas in the school. The word janitor didn't appear to be in the Swahili dictionary. On one occasion I found a small, black snake in the cupboard that held papers and notebooks. It looked at me with reproach and then slithered away. Cockroaches crawled out of every drawer, every cupboard, every available space in that school. I gradually came to accept the flora and fauna, as well as my duties as school cleaner.

When I initially arrived at Bunge Primary, the only writing the kids did was on slates with chalk. I got the Mission Administered Fund at the Canadian High Commission to donate paper, crayons, and pencils, as well as water colour paints, brushes, and supplies for the Gestetner to copy worksheets for the children. Pris managed to conscript an old piano, which we placed in her room. She would take half of the kids for singalongs, while the other half would join me for puppet shows or story time.

Luckily, it didn't take much to amuse those kids. The crazy thing was that despite the large class sizes and less than optimum conditions, the students seemed to be learning at a normal rate. Oddly, my kids were

## Chapter Forty-One

recognizable from Pris's because they spoke English with a Canadian accent, while her children emulated her Cockney drawl. Amazing!

"It's not fair," I said to Rob one evening, "I'm finally beginning to relax and enjoy Dar. Why can't the government just get their act together and assign us housing?"

Rob sighed. "Sadly, they're saying it's our fault. According to my boss we should have accepted Ilala flats. You know I couldn't have done that, don't you?"

"Of course, but with CUSO (Canadian University Services Overseas) supporting our decision I thought they'd cave and find us another place to live."

"They may still come through but unless it's soon we're gone. This whole *ujamaa* thing is getting worse. Soon we'll be eating cabbage for dinner every night. Everything else seems to be unavailable. Then there's my Asian friends. I see them at work one day and the next they disappear—no idea where they've gone. So much for socialism."

I had almost given up hope that we would get housing when Rob came home one evening with a bottle of pink Israeli bubbly. "We need to celebrate," he shouted from the front door. "We have housing, at last."

"Really," I answered not daring to hope. "Is it housing we can live in?"

"Sure is," Rob returned. "We got a Kinondoni flat. Dick Jones, another CUSO volunteer, has the flat two floors above ours, and I've just been over to see it. Julie, you're going to love it. It's perfect and surrounded by trees and flowers. Poinsettia bushes grow all along the walk way at the entrance, and we have the main floor flat, so we can sit outside in the evenings. It couldn't be better."

"Does that mean we can stay?" I asked.

## Chapter Forty-One

"Ya, I guess so, although I had another surprise for you before this came up. I managed to book a flight home next month, in June. I got tickets on Egypt Air for five hundred Canadian dollars each. Not bad, eh?" Rob held the precious tickets up in the air and did a little victory dance.

"How did you get the tickets for such an incredibly low price? Egypt Air is safe, isn't it?" I asked.

"Ya, of course it's safe. I was lucky. Someone told me about this Brit accountant, Hunter Greatbatch. He has an office at the *Mnazi Moja* (One Palm Tree) Branch of the National Bank of Commerce, close to where I work. I popped down the other day and made a deal. We pay in Canadian dollars (hard currency) and get a huge rebate in Tanzanian shillings. I finalized the deal today, at lunch. I hope you don't mind that I went ahead and bought the tickets. Greatbatch was leaving tonight for a vacation in London and I wanted to get it done."

"Now what are we supposed to do?" I asked alarmed.

"Easy," said Rob. "I could only get return tickets, and they're non-refundable, so I guess we'll just go home to Canada for a month this summer and come back for a second year. We can reassure our parents while we're there."

"So, what are you waiting for? Crack open the champagne Rob." No bottle of bubbly had ever tasted better.

## Chapter Forty-Two
### Lod Airport Massacre (1972)

We were going home—just for a visit but still ... Dar, Nairobi, Cairo, London, Toronto. For most of the stops we would stay in the airport, but we'd have two days in Cairo to see the sights. We had been in Dar for almost a year, and it was time to see family and friends again. We boarded the Egypt Air flight home on the night of May 30th, 1972.

If only I had taken pictures of Rob and me at that time. Rob had mutton chop side burns, aviator glasses, longish curly hair, and was dressed in faded blue jeans and an old t-shirt. I was wearing a full-length wrap around skirt made from brightly coloured yellow and purple African kitenge cloth and a sleeveless t-shirt. My long, wavy, brownish-blond hair came almost down to my waist. Although we were employed and twenty-two years old, we looked more like sixteen-year-old, skinny, waif-like hippies.

On that same night, half a world away, three Japanese citizens, members of the international terror group known as the Japanese Red Army, were standing on the tarmac at Lod Airport with other disembarking passengers waiting for their luggage. The three men had come to Israel on a mission for the terrorist organization, the Popular Front for the Liberation of Palestine. When their suitcases arrived, they calmly took out machine guns and grenades and began their attack on innocent people. When they had finished, 24 people were dead and 70 wounded. Two of the terrorists were killed, and one wounded and captured.

Shock waves reverberated around the world. Very early on the morning of May 31$^{st}$, Rob and I touched down

## Chapter Forty-Two

in Nairobi. We were asked to get off the plane briefly while it was refuelled. When we re-embarked the Nairobi papers were at the entrance to the plane. "Oh my God, look at this," Rob said. "Can you believe it?" He was shaking the Daily Nation two inches in front of my nose. The headline was written in dripping red ink: 'Lod airport massacre. Israel vows reprisals.' I know I should have been thinking about all those poor unsuspecting souls in Israel, but I am ashamed to say that my first thought was for our own safety. "We're supposed to fly into Cairo. Do you think that will be dangerous?" I asked Rob.

"They are enemies, Egypt and Israel, but it should be okay," Rob answered. "We have no choice anyway, so we might as well sit back and relax. Those poor people. I just can't even imagine. Who would suspect Japanese guys? Hard to take in."

For the remainder of our flight to Cairo I couldn't sleep. So many questions kept sending me into fits of panic. I was afraid to bother Rob because I understood that he must be terribly shaken too. He had always been, and still is, extremely concerned for the fate of others. As to our own fate, he would be utterly optimistic, so I would get no sympathy in that area. It was better just to worry quietly and try not to get overly stressed. We would need all of our wits about us when we finally reached Cairo. Who knew what we might have to face there?

The trauma started even before we reached the ground. On our descent into Cairo lights started flashing and a guy from the cockpit (Oh my God, was he the pilot?) came rushing down the isle of the aircraft. He calmly ripped up the carpet, descended what looked like stairs into the bowls of the plane, and returned about ten minutes later. No explanation was given, but I suspected that he had been manually lowering the landing gear. "Oh my God," I

## Chapter Forty-Two

muttered to Rob. "I thought you said that Egypt Air had a good safety record. I don't believe this."

"Me either," Rob said. "But this is an ancient Soviet plane. Egypt Air do have a good record though. I checked."

Our landing was remarkably smooth. I felt a wave of calm wash over me. We came down the stairs onto the tarmac and all hell broke loose. The long walkway to the airport building was lined with armoured vehicles. On both sides of where we had to walk there were policemen and soldiers, looking stern, clutching machine guns. As we proceeded to airport control my palms were sweating and my heart beat at an insane rate. I glared at Rob, but softened when I realized that he was a white as a sheet. Just before entering the building, we were roughly searched from head to foot.

When we got to passport control, officious men in black uniforms screamed at us in Arabic. I had no idea what they wanted, but they kept gesturing in mad ways to indicate something. We were not in line and stood in a confused group. "Take out your passport," Rob said frantically. We, and all the other passengers, threw our passports on a table. That seemed to placate the officials. I expected them to check our identities and return our documents, but no.

"Rob, what are they doing?" I asked. "Aren't they supposed to give our passports back?"

"Apparently they're confiscating everyone's documents," Rob said uncertainly.

After they had snapped up anything that would have identified us and had gone through our luggage with extreme care, we were herded into an elevator. "Oh God where are they taking us?" I asked.

## Chapter Forty-Two

"How am I supposed to know?" Rob answered. His face had turned from white to red.

"Keep your cool," I pleaded with him. "They won't be impressed if you lose your temper and I don't want to end up in jail. This is all your fault so the least you can do is behave well," I hissed.

On the second floor we were shown to a basic hotel room. "Wow," Rob commented. "I guess this is an airport hotel. Look on the bright side. I doubt they'll charge us for our room."

Rob's optimism, after his initial anger, pissed me off. We were behind bars—bars for heaven's sake! There were bars on the windows, bars on the doors and bars at the end of the hall. What if there was a fire? We were effectively in jail and totally at the whim of the Egyptian authorities. Who knew what they had in mind for us? At least the place was air-conditioned, because it was filthy hot outside. Our room was tiny, claustrophobic, with one small window looking out onto an inner courtyard. We had no idea where we were in the airport. The toilet smelled of old urine. A basic shower consisting of a tap high up in the wall and a drain in the floor allowed us to clean up. The hot water running over my body cheered me up. Both of us were so exhausted after our showers that, despite the rock-hard bed, we slept soundly. At least the sheets were clean. Rob and I were woken early by a loud knock on the door. A man in a *galibea* (long white robe) with a turban on his head stood there with a tray of tea and biscuits. "Bed tea?" he asked.

"Thanks," said Rob. "Please just put it on the table by the bed." We hadn't been allowed to change any money, so a tip was out of the question. Our scheduled two-day stay in Cairo was non-negotiable, and now we were locked up at the airport. "I wonder what'll happen next?"

## Chapter Forty-Two

Rob questioned optimistically with an expectant grin on his face.

"Really Rob, as long as we get out of here safely, I don't care," I answered.

An hour or so later there was another knock on the door. "Please come," the man from earlier gestured.

"Oh God, come where?" I whispered to Rob.

We followed and ended up in a huge high-ceilinged room that looked like an airport hangar. There were round tables and men in long robes scurrying everywhere. "Breakfast, I think," Rob said. "I'm starved."

"How can you think of food at a time like this?" The food, when it came, was different from what we were used to. There were brown beans with oil and spices , and hard little rolls. Grainy, aromatic, very strong coffee was served in small cups with saucers.

We plunked ourselves down at table with a young British couple. "Bad timing, I think," said the guy. "The locals are pretty nervous, it seems. The Arabs are being blamed for the shoot up in Lod airport and, of course, everyone assumes the Egyptians had something to do with it. I'll be glad to see the end of this place. We'd hoped to see the pyramids, but now I just want out."

"Yuck, what's this?" asked his partner, a blond haired, blued-eyed Brit. She looked disgusted.

"What do you mean?" I asked. I was happily consuming my delicious beans.

"The rolls are awful. Kind of sour and strange tasting," she remarked.

"Oh, that would be the buffalo butter," said Rob. "Apparently it's very bitter. I was warned about it. Should have told you sooner. Sorry."

*217*

## Chapter Forty-Two

As we were finishing breakfast an announcement came over a loudspeaker. "Please prepare to get on buses," the deep voice said.

An attractive, young, Egyptian woman who spoke perfect English came over to our table, smiled, and said, "Before we go would you like to change some money at the front desk? Please collect your passports as we will be on the road." At that all the passports were thrown on the counter, and we frantically scrambled to get the right ones.

"You could take any passport you wanted. Do you know what foreign passports are worth on the black market?" Rob said, looking shocked.

We were shown to two buses, enough to accommodate all the passengers from our flight. "Now we will show you Cairo," the same woman who had come to our table said over the bus PA system. She was the first Egyptian we'd encountered who had understandable English.

"Where are you taking us?" Rob asked the Cleopatra looking guide, who smelled like jasmine.

"First we will go to the perfume factory, then to the Egyptian Museum and finally to the Pyramids in Giza," she answered.

Passports and money in hand, we set out for our tour. The perfume factory sold bottles of perfume oil—"one drop in the bathtub, and you are smelling good for too long," said the proprietor of the shop. I bought jasmine perfume oil. Maybe, if I were lucky, that perfume would make me feel more exotic. The factory, with its hundreds of perfumes, smelt sickly sweet and made my head spin.

Our next stop was the Cairo Museum. Ancient treasures, including Tutankhamen's death mask and jewels, were spread out in total disarray. There were rooms and rooms full of ancient artifacts just lying around, mostly on the floor. It was a primitive setup, but

## Chapter Forty-Two

that did not take away from the magic of the place. "Do you believe this?" Rob asked. "I wish I had days and days to look around." Instead, we were ushered back onto the bus in less than an hour. We headed out to the great pyramids of Giza. The ride seemed to take forever, and I had never experienced such awful traffic. We sat, and sat, inhaling car fumes and waiting to reach our destination. Finally, on the horizon loomed the tip of the largest pyramid, Cheops. It rose out of the flat desert far in the distance. When we arrived, our bus parked directly at the feet of the Sphinx, a stone's throw away from the three ancient wonders of the world. I couldn't wait to get closer, so I dashed off the bus and ran towards the pyramids with Rob directly behind me.

"This is amazing, don't you think?" he shouted after me, looking completely captivated. As we were making our way across the desert to the base of the pyramids, a man in a grubby, billowing white robe stood in our path.

"Free camel ride," he said. I happily accepted his offer and he helped me to mount the beast. Rob looked a bit worried by my hasty action. The fact that the camel was hissing nastily didn't help one bit.

"They seem like ugly, mean beasts," Rob shouted up to me. "What's it like up there?"

"Did you ever think we would get a chance to ride a camel around the pyramids?" I asked him.

"There are many things I have dreamed of doing," he answered "but that wasn't one of them. I hate riding animals. I feel so out of control, and anyway they make me sneeze."

I rode for about 15 minutes until it was time to think about getting back on the bus. Rob ran after the camel looking distressed, and I felt a moment of guilt. However, I was having far too much fun to over-think the situation.

## Chapter Forty-Two

Finally, the tour guide picked up the loudspeaker and announced that we would be leaving the pyramids in five minutes. "Please," I asked the camel driver, "we have to go. I need to get down now."

"First you pay," he responded.

"Wait a minute," said Rob. "I thought you said it was free."

"Free to get on. Pay to get off," announced the camel owner.

"How much then, we need to get back to the bus?" I said trying to sound authoritative.

"Ten pounds Egyptian."

"What, are you kidding? That's a lot of money. Not fair." Rob shouted.

"You want lady back or not," answered the camel driver. "She young, blond. You want I keep her for myself or sell her," the guy said boldly.

"Not sure I changed enough money."

"Rob, just give the man the money. The bus is loading, and we need to get on." Rob reluctantly handed over the bills and the camel man helped me to get down, while the camel snarled, turned toward me and bared it large yellow teeth.

"Horrible creatures," Rob muttered as we ran toward the bus. I wondered if he meant the man or the camel. We returned to the airport hotel (jail) and spent the rest of our Cairo visit sleeping, talking to other unsuspecting tourists and eating questionable food. We flew out of Cairo two days after we had arrived, breathing a sigh of enormous relief. "I never want to come here again even if I live to be a hundred," I said.

# Chapter Forty-Three
## New York Detour (1972)

"Oh God. I'm so glad to be on our way," I said as the plane took off from Cairo. We were so late leaving that our connection through London to Toronto was a lost cause. In England, we were re-routed through New York. "Last leg. Thank goodness we survived that. Before we know it, we will be landing in Toronto. I sure hope our parents know how late we'll be."

"Ya, but I'm not too thrilled to be redirected through the States," Rob said looking worried.

"Come on Rob, after what we've been through how could anything get worse? The States are the civilized world. It's okay," I answered, feeling extremely happy to be on our way to North America. "Are you as excited as I am? I can't wait to see everyone. I've been so homesick."

"I guess," said Rob. "I would rather be flying direct. This kinda sucks. All that Vietnam war crap. There are some pretty right-wing idiots in the US. and they make me nervous. We are coming from socialist Tanzania. I just hope they don't give us a hard time."

"Oh God Rob you worry way too much about the craziest things. In Dar you think everything is hunky-dory and when you get to civilization you freak out. What's with you anyway? We're almost home."

"Home is Canada, not New York."

"Relax. It's a long trip," I said, settling into my seat.

We reached New York and the first hint of disaster was the burning ship in the harbour right next to the Statue of Liberty. We circled a few times and actually flew in for a closer look. "Ships burn in the States? Why don't they do something?" I demanded.

## Chapter Forty-Three

"Bad things happen here too," Rob replied." It's not like life is easy for everyone. There's still lots of racism, and they hate hippies. Look at how we're dressed, and we're arriving from a commie African country."

He was right, of course. We looked like hippies and draft dodgers from the Vietnam War, with Rob's side burns, longish hair and aviator glasses, and my African khanga (ankle length, wrap around skirt) with pineapples, and the Tanzanian flag featured on my rear end. Naively, I had believed that we were home free.

We landed and proceeded through customs clutching our two carry-ons, a four-foot tall, Makonde carving (people tree) and a delicate, blue glass hookah. "What is that?" asked the surly customs officer, pointing to the beautiful Makonde. "Where are you coming from?"

"We're arriving from Tanzania, East Africa, and that is a traditional carving we are taking back as a present." Rob answered. He sounded grown up and authoritative. I was proud of him, but I was still worried.

"How much is it worth? You will have to declare it and pay a duty charge."

"First of all, we are in transit to Toronto, and secondly it's worth less than the limit allowed in Canada," Rob countered.

"Sorry," said the official. "That carving will have to be sawed in half to make sure there are no drugs inside."

"Please," I pleaded. "Look, we've been away from home for a year working as volunteers in Tanzania with CUSO. That's the same as your Peace Corp. I really want to give this to my mom and dad. They've missed us so much, and I know they'll love the carving. We've carried it all the way from East Africa. We weren't even sure we would get out of Cairo alive (that was a bit of an

## Chapter Forty-Three

exaggeration) and now you're telling me that you're going to cut my parents' present in half. Please!"

"Besides," said Rob. We don't take drugs and, even if we did, we're not stupid enough to carry them through Cairo. That would be worth our lives. That carving has nothing in it. There must be another way."

"Okay," said the customs official, softening a bit. "I will ask my supervisor if we can x-ray the carving, but that may take some time. Something has to be done."

"Whatever it takes. I hope it's quick though. We missed our connection through London to Toronto, which is why we're here, and our parents have been waiting for hours. We have no way to get in touch with them, and they must be frantic by now."

We went back to the waiting area. Both of us were fed up, exhausted. We dozed. After what seemed like a long time an airport worker approached us and declared the carving to be drug free. We were upgraded to business class on Air Canada (there were no other seats left) and we flew out of New York in the middle of the night.

"Wow," said Rob. "We're so lucky. Weird that they didn't even ask about the hookah. We're almost home, and we get to arrive in style—business class, no less. This is great."

You have to be kidding, I thought. We came close to disaster in Cairo, missed our flight, had to fly through New York, saw a burning ship, dealt with an officious idiot, almost had to cut our carving in half—how was that great? At that moment I just wanted to be home and in the circle of my own family. Maybe they would understand how I felt.

On the flight to Toronto, I drank too much wine, ate too much rich food and slept not a wink. I was exhausted but excited. I spent ages in the washroom combing my

## Chapter Forty-Three

hair and applying makeup, nervous about seeing my family for the first time in a year. I joined Rob as the plane prepared to land. "While you were in the toilet, we flew over Niagara Falls, and it was all lit up to welcome us home." he teased and looked at me. "Wow, you look great. You're fit, have a great tan and your hair has turned from brown to gold."

"Thanks love. You look pretty good yourself. Hope we don't have any problems at immigration."

Our trip through Canadian customs was uneventful. The official at the desk was delighted to meet us. She had a cousin who had served with CUSO in the Caribbean. Our carry-on Makonde and hookah were seen as normal acquisitions of a young couple returning from Africa. "Welcome home," she said beaming.

"God," said Rob. "I love my country. It's so good to be home."

# Chapter Forty-Four
## Canadian Interlude (1972)

I was home for a visit in Canada. For an entire year, each waking moment, I had longed for this. I had fantasized about our family reunion, about how perfect my life in Canada would be when we were finished with this African dream. Now that I was here, I felt out of step, removed from the landscape of my heart. What had I done? It was like looking through the lens of a camera, observing, one step separated from family, friends, and my country.

I wanted everyone to see me and treat me exactly as I was before I went away. I wanted to be that same, before person. Stop the clock. Rewind. Stop treating me like a guest. I am your daughter, your sister, your friend. Remember!

My little four-year-old brother took one look at Rob and me and said, "Why aren't you black? I thought you would get black over there. Go back. I want you to be black."

My mom, who is still the calmest, sweetest person I know, looked horrified. "Davy," she said, "That's not how it works. People don't just get black. They're born that way. Look though, Rob and Julie have a tan. They're browner than when they left. The sun does that. You get tanned, but you don't turn black."

"Give me a hug Dave, I missed you so much," I said, trying not to cry. He wasn't a baby anymore but a little boy, a little boy I barely recognized. How was he supposed to love us the way he did before we left? At least he remembered our names, but he didn't seem very happy to see us. He had probably felt deserted, and no

## Chapter Forty-Four

wonder. We left him. He certainly wasn't about to let me pick him up.

When I originally boarded the plane to fly away for two years, I'm not sure that I understood the penalty that I would pay for my absence. Nothing would ever be the same again. Life in Canada had moved on without us. No one was interested in the stories we told. Our friends were wrapped up in new houses, babies, and careers. Initially, we'd left everyone. Now the tables were turned. We were the ones left behind.

I felt close to Rob. I was clingy and didn't want to let him out of my sight. Our shared experience and challenges in Africa had cemented our relationship. For the first time I realized that neither Rob nor I would ever want the same things as our family and friends. A house with a white picket fence, a job as a teacher or an accountant. Two kids and a life that is safe and predictable was not something either one of us aspired to.

I had naively believed that our two-year trip away was a one-off. After Africa, we would come home and get normal, but I knew on this first visit back, after only one year, that we would be altered forever. We no longer belonged. We still loved our families and our friends, maybe more than when we went away. That was a given. We had moved on while those we left behind had stayed the same.

We went with our family to Ontario Place. The movie, 'Ontariario', at the Imax theatre, made me cry. I felt so much love for my province and my country. The fact that we were going back to Africa didn't take away from my loyalty to Canada. Even now, years and years later, after a life overseas, nine postings representing our country, I still feel that emotion, that gratitude to have been born here in this wonderful county of ours. Canadians are the luckiest

## Chapter Forty-Four

people on earth. Being away made me understand that in a more profound way.

At our family cottage in Huntsville the loons sang us their haunting and familiar song. Out in the canoe one day, just the two of us, we saw a mother loon with two babies on her back. The strings of my heart pulled tighter, and I wondered why I wanted to go back to Dar.

Three deer in my parents' yard at the lake looked in our bedroom window at first light on our last morning. They seemed to be staring at us, asking why we wanted to leave this piece of heaven for Africa.

"Do you want to go back?" I asked Rob.

"Of course," Rob muttered, half asleep. "Don't you? Back there, in Dar, when you thought we would be forced to return to Canada, you were the one who was so upset. Now we have a place to live I want to go back and finish what I started. I've never even given it a second thought. I didn't think you had either."

"I want to return too," I said. "I was just wondering how you felt. I think it will be easier this time. We only have a year left. We're halfway through. We have housing, good jobs, friends, and adventures to look forward to. It'll be good."

The summer passed far too quickly. It was time to go. Everyone trooped to the airport in Toronto. Our goodbyes this time were calm. We'd be home again in one more year. I cried but not for long. It beat the first time when I made myself ill by sobbing for the entire journey to Africa. This was definitely much easier.

Our trip home proved uneventful. We arrived in Dar and were able to take a taxi directly to our new flat in Kinondoni. I walked through the door to our home, breathed a sigh of relief and immediately began to make mental plans to redecorate. The next year would be

## Chapter Forty-Four

predictable and exciting. My homesickness disappeared in a flash and I looked forward to getting back to my classroom.

CUSO had dropped off a care kit with sheets, pillows, and kitchen essentials. The flat was fully-furnished, so we were able to move right in. "Crap," said Rob. "There are no mosquito nets over our beds and this place is swarming with insects. What are we going to do? What if we get malaria?"

"Go to bed love," I answered. "I feel numb, I'm so tired. There's nothing we can do anyway. CUSO is closed!"

Our bedroom had two single beds that we pulled together. The mattresses were hard, but we were jet-lagged and hadn't had any sleep for 24 hours, so nothing could keep us awake. When we woke up in the morning Rob and I were covered in red welts and bodies of dead mosquitoes littered the beds. "I'm sure we'll be fine," I said. "We're taking chloroquine to prevent malaria."

"Ya," answered Rob, "but one of my friends was doing that too, and he almost died of malaria."

"Oh, for God's sake Rob! You worry about the stupidest things and don't worry about stuff that is really terrifying. We'll be okay."

I was wrong!

## Chapter Forty-Five
### Torn Apart (2003)

Jen has come to visit us in Ethiopia. It's Easter and our baby granddaughter, Jen's daughter Kaia, is eight months old. It's the first time that Rob has met Kaia. Jen, Mo and Kaia were supposed to come at Christmas for a visit, but Mo had cancelled that trip at the last moment, for no apparent reason. Now, in April, he has sent his family to Addis without him.

Kai is beautiful—smiling, reaching out, babbling, and active. We have a baby walker, a circle of plastic with wheels that she sits in and can manoeuvre around our home. She flies at top speed terrifying our puppy, Griff, who jumps out of her way. It's wonderful to have our family together, but I can feel Jen's distress. "What's wrong love?" I ask my daughter.

"Mo is distant with me. He promised to come to Ethiopia again but backed out a week before we left. Mom, I think he's taking drugs, and he's drunk constantly. I don't know what to do. He's out all the time—day and night - he avoids the baby and me. We barely see him, and when we do, he's weird and a bit scary. I feel like I don't know him anymore, or maybe I never did. I should have listened to you guys."

"Oh God, I'm so glad you're here safe with us. You know we'll support you no matter what. You're not going home until this is sorted out."

"Hey," Jen says. "I have no intention of leaving Mo. I have to go back to Ottawa. I have a baby to think about and the last thing I want to be is a single mom. I still love him. I will help my husband to get better."

## Chapter Forty-Five

On Easter morning we baptize Kaia at the Lutheran seminary, at dawn, on the edge of a valley on the outskirts of Addis Ababa. As the sun rises over the horizon the priest tilts our Kaia down toward the font and anoints her head with water. The scene is reminiscent of the dawn of time—primitive, lush, divine, clean, clear, with bird song and the scent of eucalyptus trees permeating the atmosphere.

The next day I find Jen, bent over, sobbing in the den. "Oh God, what's wrong?" I ask.

"Look," Jen answers and points to an email from Mo. "I am leaving you. I can't go on. I know your parents will take care of you," the message says. Nothing more. That's it. Mo has left my daughter by email. He is also willing to abdicate responsibility for Kaia who is only eight months old. How dare he?"

"Mommy," Jen whimpers. "What did I do wrong?"

When Rob finds out he is beyond furious. "I'm going to kill him," he screams—not exactly characteristic of my husband and Jen's Dad. I've never heard him utter such things. He's a gentle, caring man, but this is his child, his little girl, and he would do anything to defend her and our baby grandchild.

"What am I going to do?" Jen asks tears streaming down her cheeks.

"You're better off without him," I answer.

"I love him Mom. I thought he loved me back. I never thought it would come to this."

"Well, one thing's for sure. You are not going home in a week. You need to stay here with us and work this out." Rob says, and I totally agree.

Now looking back, I realize that time was the beginning of our love affair with our little granddaughter. We became her second parents. Jen stayed until we

## Chapter Forty-Five

returned together from our posting to Ethiopia. I hate Mo for what he did to Jen, but at the same time I value the time that we spent with our daughter and Kaia.

Ethiopia was kind to all of us. Jen wrote a children's book called "The Ethiopian Cinderella". She substituted at the international school where I worked. Our family travelled the length of that beautiful country. Kaia bonded with our kids, her aunt and uncles. It was a magical time.

It was also a healing time for Jenny. With time and the love of her family she began to look back at the facts and to realize that Mo had been a mistake. "He didn't ever tell his parents about me, did he?" she asked us.

"Well," answered Rob. "We invited his family to the wedding and not one of them showed up. From the little bit that Mo told us, it seemed clear his parents were extremely intolerant. Maybe Mo knew that you would never have been accepted by his family. Maybe he loved you but realized he couldn't protect you, especially if you didn't produce a son. I'll bet he never told them about you. Maybe he was afraid."

"Guys," Jen pleaded. "I would have converted to the Muslim faith, but he never asked that of me. I don't get it. And he has such a beautiful daughter. How could he leave her?"

"Hey lovey," I said, "not all Muslims are alike. Not all Christians are either. You know that. There's always prejudice out there, no matter what culture or religion. You grew up overseas in international schools where different colours, cultures, and religions were the norm. I'm sorry we never conveyed the difficulty you might face being accepted into a rigid Muslim family in Canada.

"As far as I'm concerned," Rob added, "nothing changes the fact that we are all much better off without Mo. If he won't stand by you and Kaia now, he never will.

## Chapter Forty-Five

His religion is not relevant. He's a jerk, an idiot in any culture and has no idea what he's missing." When I looked at Jen's face, I could see that she was still heartbroken. No one could take away the pain and disappointment of the abandonment she was facing.

# Chapter Forty-Six
## Living and Dying (1972)

Our return to Dar, after our short visit in Canada, for our second year as volunteers with CUSO, was jubilant. Our new home was perfect. Dark hardwood shone on the floors. A little garden just outside our living room window was filled with poinsettia trees—vivid red and emerald green. Bougainvillea bushes, red, pink, orange, and white twisted and turned enveloping the fence outside our front door. The splash of vibrant colour everywhere mixed with the bird and insect sounds, the scent of frangipani flowers and fresh, moist, tropical air—paradise, at last.

Paradise had its limitations. Because we had no screens insects, especially mosquitoes, swarmed into our home. We tried burning pics and that did work, to a point. It was far too hot to close the windows. We'd ordered a mosquito net to hang over the bed, but it still hadn't arrived.

Each morning we woke to the sound of our resident rooster. The sun shone in through the windows and the air smelt like the rain that had fallen in the night. We were happy. We had our own little flat. Life was good. We had a few more days before work started, time to sort out our apartment, put our pictures up and enjoy our new place. Heaven. We cuddled and kissed and made breakfast. The toast, scrambled eggs and Tanzanian coffee made in our own small kitchen smelled heavenly.

Our Pakistani neighbour upstairs gave us yogourt starter, so every evening I would bring a pot of milk to an almost-boil, add the starter to two cups of hot milk and stir. Then I would place the mixture in our gas oven overnight where the pilot light made a perfect temperature

## Chapter Forty-Six

for yogourt to solidify. By morning, we had delicious cups of perfect homemade yogourt.

It was so good to be home after our time in Canada. The rest of this African adventure was ours for the making. Our parents were consoled, and realized that this was our dream. On our brief summer vacation to Ontario, they'd stopped fretting and had begun to see this time of our lives as something we had to do, something we would look back on with joy for the rest of our lives.

Life is fickle. It is at the best of times that the worst things happen just to remind us that our fate is always unpredictable. Two weeks after our return to Dar I started to feel ill. My head throbbed, and my skin was sensitive and prickly. Rob reached over to stroke my arm. I recoiled.

"Are you okay?" he asked. "What's wrong? Are you mad at me?"

"Don't touch me. My skin hurts. My head is pounding. I feel terrible."

Rob looked worried and put his hand on my forehead. "Oh my God. You're burning up. Your fever is super high. We'd better go to the Aga Khan Hospital."

Dizzy, disoriented and scared, I had trouble hanging onto Rob while perched on the back of the motorcycle. Our African home came with the possibility of typhoid, yellow fever, dengue, malaria or any number of other diseases— the list was endless. Who knew what I might have picked up? My imagination took over. Maybe this was the end. When we arrived at the hospital emergency department, they immediately admitted me. Oh, God — not a good sign.

Many blood tests later I was sent home to wait for the outcome. By the following evening I was hallucinating and making ridiculous bargains with the devil: If I got to

## Chapter Forty-Six

live, he could have my great grandma. She was really old, and I was just starting my life. She'd insisted for years that she wanted to die, and I was ready to give her that chance. God, what kind of person bargains away a loved one's life in return for their own? Pathetic!

I promised that if I lived, I'd become a better person (not sure how trading my great grandma's life for mine fit into that equation). Thinking back on that deal still makes me feel guilty. I like to believe that in my right mind I would never have thought of such a terrible thing.

Awake and asleep, I felt spiders on my skin, imagined being trapped in deep black caves with venomous snakes. I conversed with ghosts of dead people I had known. I ranted and raved. Smells, even pleasant ones, made me gag. I trembled and shook and was either too cold or too hot. Rob sponged me down with rubbing alcohol and sat me in a bathtub of tepid water to try to keep my fever down. Nothing worked.

I was re-admitted to the hospital. I had malaria. "We're taking prophylactics. How is that possible?" Rob asked. The doctor explained that even with medication I could contract malaria.

"Will my wife get better?" Rob pleaded as his eyes teared up.

"We can't be sure," said the doctor. "But if she hadn't taken chloroquine, it would have been far more serious."

During the next two weeks I lay there in the hospital realizing, in my lucid moments, that I could die. I don't remember much of that time but Rob does. Apparently, I continued to plead with God—heaven knows what bargains I made. Somehow, I survived. I had come to Africa. I had known the risks, and I had lived.

\*\*\*

## Chapter Forty-Six

Orillia (2015)

I was one of the lucky ones, at least until my daughter died at age 37 from lung cancer. She'd never danced with disaster, never taken the kind of chances Rob and I took at a younger age, and yet she died, and we lived. Jen would never see her daughter graduate or get married, never have another child with her wonderful second husband Michel, never realize her dream of teaching overseas again. It all just seems so unfair. I wish I had the answer to the mystery of life, but I don't.

The death of our lovely daughter will always be a tragedy—a life not fully lived. Was there something in our overseas lives that lead to her death? Both Rob and I would have happily died to save her. However, we tried our best. We did not know what the future held. We gave our children exciting, experience-filled lives.

They've all turned out to be wonderful, caring people —third culture kids. The literature suggests that these kids do so well in some respects, but not in others. They are highly confident in any culture, but never fully at home in one. They think differently, speak strangely with partial accents left over from faraway places, and try their best to pretend that they are fully Canadian.

Would I have embarked on this life of adventure had I known the consequences? To prevent Jen's death, I would have done anything. However, there are also consequences of living in one place and never moving anywhere. Many Canadians fall into the "stay near home" category and young people who have never moved get cancer as well.

I am proud that we have given our children a world view, proud that they are colour-blind when it comes to race, and completely accepting of other religions. Citizens of the world, our kids do think differently. How could

## Chapter Forty-Six

they be anything but accepting of the world's rainbow of race and religion with their background? Not one of them has ever expressed negativity when it comes to their overseas experience. I like to think that part of their intelligence, empathy, and success has to do with their childhood homes.

But the truth is, I will never know what lead to Jennifer's illness and death. I could have died of malaria in 1972. Despite all the risks, Rob and I survived and prospered. That was not the case for my Jen.

Now I understand that Rob and I are not alone. So many parents, no matter what their background, deal with tragedy, whether it is the loss of a child or a child gone wrong. I suppose the question I was asking when we learned of Jen's cancer: "Why us? Why our daughter?" is a short-sighted one. The real answer lies in humility; "Why not us?"

# Chapter Forty-Seven
## Teacher's Driver (1972)

Tanzania time moves at a languid, steady pace, with the whims and ways of Africans dancing to the passing beat of a melodious drum. When I moved here from Canada, I forgot what it meant to rush, rush, rush, to constantly check my watch to see if I needed to hurry. My inner metronome no longer ticked at a nine-to-five pace. Instead of having too little time there always seemed to be enough: enough to stop and chat with vegetable seller in the market, enough to read after dinner in our Kinondoni flat, enough to enjoy the songs of crickets at night before enjoying a sweaty but fulfilling sleep. The pulse of Africa felt steadier, calmer, and more insistent on the rhythms of humanity.

My school, Bunge Primary, started at 7:30 and finished at 2:00. The hours meshed with the climate and allowed children and teachers to have a much-needed afternoon siesta. By early afternoon the heat and humidity had built to such an extent that it was impossible to do any sort of real work. Shops shut, streets cleared of traffic, and even our vocal rooster stopped crowing while Dar es Salaam slept.

One morning at school assembly, which was running the usual twenty minutes behind schedule, Head Mistress, Mbago, decided to impart her anglicized concept of time. She stood square bodied, rigid, with shoulders back, and shouted, "I have had enough of this lateness. This is the third time this week that students have come straggling in after the bell. We can't have that. Tomorrow the school gates will be locked promptly at 7:30. Anyone who finds themselves outside will have to stay there. Do you understand?"

## Chapter Forty-Seven

This little talk resulted in a monotone chorus of, "Yes Ms. Mbago," as we all tried to figure out just how we would get to the school on time. For those children who would be coming to school on public buses from far away through heavy traffic, the threat of being on the wrong side of the bars would do little good. Even if those kids left early, there was no guarantee that they would arrive on time. Like many occurrences in Africa, like it or not, fate would play a role. Or, as Mohammed, one of my Muslim students muttered, "*Insh'allah*, (God willing). I try to get here."

I, too, had a problem. Rob, at that point in our lives, had rarely been on time for anything, including our wedding. School was no exception. Africa had managed to cement his attitude towards deadlines. "Hon," he joked, "my boss congratulated me the other day on always being on time. The thing is," he laughed, "I was actually 40 minutes late, but I was still the first one at the meeting."

Since I rode on the back of our piki-piki (little motorbike) to work every morning, Rob was going to have to break with tradition and get me to the school on time. I started to nag the moment we arrived back at our flat.

"Rob, the old battleaxe is threatening to lock us out tomorrow if we are even five minutes late," I complained.

"That means half the school will be outside the gate," he laughed as he reached into the fridge for a cold beer. "Don't worry though; I'll get you there by 7:30."

"Rob, she's not kidding! Promise me." I gave him my best exasperated look. "I mean it. Can you imagine? Just make sure you're not late, okay?"

The next morning, I woke up at 4:00 AM worrying about being late. By 6:00 AM. I began to nag. By 6:45, I

## Chapter Forty-Seven

was frantic. Rob was still in bed, which was not unusual, but today it was inexcusable.

"Rob, we have to leave by 7:00 if we're going to make it on time, and you haven't even showered yet! Please. Just this once," I pleaded.

At 7:15 we roared down the lane way and into the street. Already the sun was blazing and so was I. "You promised," I said in a tone that conveyed equal parts anger and hurt. "How could you do this to me?"

"Relax love. Your headmistress is probably just bluffing. She can't pull this off. Not here. She'd have to be crazy."

Of course, the traffic across Selander Bridge was particularly heavy. Despite all the reassurances from Rob that we would make it, when we arrived the gate was locked. As we drove up my class cheered and chanted from the inside of the bars: "Teacher! Teacher! Teacher!" The kids hung on the wire fence staring out at us and grinning.

I leapt off the bike, handed Rob my helmet, and tried to appear in control.

Rob put his hand on my arm and said, "Oh God, I'm so sorry. I thought we could make it. I really did. I can't believe she's actually locked you out. She's absolutely nuts." He gave me his most apologetic, little puppy look.

"I know what to do," he declared, as he thought-paced up and down the length of the enclosure. I'll find a hole in the fence around the back where the kids play. I'm pretty sure I've seen one there. You can crawl through it. Just wait. I'll be right back. Please don't be mad."

Mortified and embarrassed, I tried breathing deeply to gain control. I was losing the battle when Mrs. Mbago appeared at the doorway and walked purposefully toward

## Chapter Forty-Seven

the gate, taking her time. She took out her keys and let me and a dozen children into the yard without a word.

Half an hour later I was writing on the blackboard when my kids started to chant, "Teacher's driver! Teacher's driver!" I looked up to see a motorcycle helmet bobbing up and down above the half wall of our classroom. A few seconds later Rob appeared at the door, his helmet still on his head, and his body wedged between two surly looking policemen who were brandishing clubs and had guns in holsters strapped around their waists. Mrs. Mbago accompanied them.

"Is this your husband?" the taller of the two policemen growled. "We caught this man crawling through a hole in the fence between Bunge Primary School and the Bank of Tanzania," the heavy-set policeman said. "We think he might have been making plans to rob the central bank."

"Look," Rob said, "This is insane! My wife," he pointed at me, "who is a teacher here, got locked out of the school because I made her late. I was just trying to find a hole for her to crawl through so that she could get back to her kids and start teaching. I am an employee of the Local Government Division just down the road and a member of the Tanu Youth League," Rob spluttered as he groped for his official papers.

The policemen turned their attention to me. "Do you know this man?" they questioned.

"Never seen him before in my life," I announced, glaring spitefully at my husband. I'm not sure if Rob's or Mrs. Mbago's distress gave me more pleasure. The policeman nodded, as if to say, their suspicions had been confirmed, and proceeded to cuff Rob and usher him out into the hallway.

Mrs. Mbago tried to block their way with her large frame, desperately trying to explain that I was just an

## Chapter Forty-Seven

angry *mzungu* who was mad at her husband for making her late. She explained that she had locked anyone who hadn't arrived at 7:30 out of the school.

"Is this true?" both men added looking pointedly at me.

"Of course, he's my husband," I relented. "I was locked out, and it was his fault."

"Teacher's driver!" my students chanted, pointing at Rob in acknowledgement.

The police turned toward Mrs. Mbago with stunned looks on their faces. "You locked this teacher out of the school because she was a few minutes late?" they inquired, looking totally confused. "Why? Are you crazy?"

## Chapter Forty-Eight
### Robberies (1972)

"My pants have been ripped off again!" Rob shouted from the garden of our Kinondoni flat, as he surveyed the clothes line.

I leaned out the window, "I doubt they even had time to dry this time."

"That's four pairs in two months. We're gonna have to hang stuff inside," Rob added, sounding resigned.

Petty theft was the hot topic for our small expat community in Dar. Who lost what, how, when and where was a constant source of conversation as well as anxiety. None of us, even poor volunteer variety *wazungu*, were exempt. White skin meant money and money, in a poor country where most people had nothing, meant that all the crazy white people were obvious targets.

All, that is, except my friend Lucille Blunt from Winnipeg. Somehow, I doubted that anyone, even the most hardened and desperate, would dare to take anything from her. Although she worked as a volunteer teacher at a secretarial school, Lucille was different from the rest of us. For one thing, she had been in the country for a long time and spoke fluent Swahili.

But it was more than that. Lucille was one tough dame. At 60 plus, she had bleached blonde hair that hung in limp strands to her square shoulders, smoke-stained teeth and a solid athletic body. Although not overly tall the woman had presence. And the voice. I think that is what impressed me most. It was lower than a man's, husky, loud and full of authority.

Lucille was my idol. She knew everything there was to know about Tanzania, would go anywhere, do anything,

## Chapter Forty-Eight

and had the biggest, shiniest, black motorcycle in the city. She was the second wife of Mohammed the Tanzanian distributor of Coca-Cola in Dar. What a woman!

"Doesn't it bug you that Mohammed has a first wife?" I asked her once.

"Hell no," she answered. "He's a damned sight nicer than those bastards I had to put up with in Canada. Now, my last husband, he's the reason I'm here. Had to run far to get away from him. What an asshole."

Lucille's stories of her sexual exploits kept me enthralled for hours. She described techniques and suggested scenarios that left me blushing but tempted to take notes. I'd only been married to Rob for a little over three years and, according to Lucille, had a lot of living and learning to do.

Our Kinondoni flats were in the same block and had identical layouts. That was where the similarity ended. On the front door and in every room of her home Lucille had hung small voodoo dolls to ward off bad luck, a common practice in Africa, but strange for a Canadian woman. Rob and I were into colourful local art, pictures of family and friends and masses of tropical plants. Where Lucille had hung surrealistic paintings with weird twisted images of tortured humanity, we had posters of African beaches and Canadian, snow-capped mountains.

Rob was not fond of Lucille, although I think she rather fancied him, at least until the theft. After that she loved him. Still, even before that fateful event we often visited, because she was my best female friend. One night when we dropped in on Lucille, she met us at the door with a red face and tear-stained cheeks. She looked uncharacteristically dishevelled, weirdly out of control.

"The bastards have stolen my motorcycle," she blurted.

## Chapter Forty-Eight

"You're joking. What? Where?" I stammered, hardly able to take in her news.

"I was at work and when I came out poof—gone. I never thought. And in broad daylight too. The bastards."

"Don't panic, they can't have gotten far," Rob assured Lucille. "There's only one motorcycle like yours in Dar. They won't be able to disguise it that quickly. Come on, no time to lose. Grab your helmet. We'll take our piki-piki." Off they went.

I returned home to wait and hope. Three hours later Rob and Lucille were back. "No luck tonight," said Rob, "but we'll try again tomorrow."

Every night for two weeks they rode around the streets, checking all the bars and nightclubs. "I was so sure we'd find her bike. It's not such a big city and that thing she rides is so obvious. That motorcycle is famous," Rob confided in me, sounding discouraged.

After a time, even my eternally optimistic husband was forced to give up the search. I got him back in the evenings, and we settled into our established routines. Lucille seemed subdued, not the same gutsy lady. I missed her spirit and fearlessness, not to mention the roar of her motorcycle and her voice at the end of the work day.

To cheer her up we suggested that the three of us should attend the *'Saba Saba'* National Day celebration. It took place every year on July 7th to celebrate the founding of Tanu (the Tanzanian Africa National Union) in 1954, which eventually lead to independence. We were walking to the entrance of the fair grounds on our way there when Rob suddenly took off running.

"What the—where's he going?" Lucille shouted above the noise of the crowd.

"I dunno. Come on," I answered as we did our best to catch up to Rob.

## Chapter Forty-Eight

What I saw next shocked me. Rob had grabbed a huge Tanzanian guy by the scruff of the neck and was screaming into his face. The man was looking wildly about and struggling to free himself from the grip of the obviously deranged foreigner. The fact that the guy hadn't thought to knock my husband out was a mystery. He appeared more than capable of it.

"Look beside them," Lucille pointed. "My bike!" The robber had not even attempted to disguise her vehicle, but the plates had been obviously altered. Lucille's famous big, black motorcycle was impossible to mistake from any other.

The next thing I knew Rob had managed to get the keys and was trying to climb onto Lucille's bike. The man was grabbing his shoulder and attempting to pull him away. The crowd had begun to react. They made a threatening circle around the two men. The cry of "*mweze, mweze*" (thief, thief) was chanted with growing volume.

I thought back to our African orientation sessions. Rule number one was that the African crowd often takes justice into its own hands. Even in the case of a car accident, your fault or someone else's, never, ever stop. Just keep on driving, if you can, to the nearest police station. Since we were surrounded and not driving, I wondered what our next plan should be. Confusion, resulting from the colour of his skin, was the only thing protecting Rob at that point. The crowd was surging, gaining momentum, closing in.

Lucille jumped into the circle and started to scream her version of the story, creating even more uncertainty. Her shouts of "*mweze, mweze* (thief, thief)" rose above everyone else's as she pointed an accusing finger at the robber. Then out of nowhere appeared two policemen in

## Chapter Forty-Eight

uniform. The crowd parted to let them enter the inner circle.

Explanations were demanded and made. Lucille pulled her ownership and official papers out of her purse. The criminal was arrested and taken off, probably to meet a punishment that far outweighed the crime. Lucille had her motorcycle back.

"We did it!" Rob shouted.

"All right!" Lucille joined in, clenched fist held high in the air. "We won."

I still wonder what became of the young man that stole the biggest, blackest, shiniest motorcycle in Dar Es Salaam.

## Chapter Forty-Nine
### Double Happiness Butterfly Sewing Machine (1972)

"What are you wearing to the High Commission party?" asked Lucille.

"Haven't the slightest idea. It's not for another two months. What are you wearing?" I asked. Lucille got up from her comfy chair and headed for her bedroom. She came back carrying a long, flowing sleeveless dress with a matching short jacket in royal blue silk. She held it up against her short, square body, and swirled around the coffee table. Her smoke-stained teeth showed as she smiled happily. Despite her 60 plus years of age, scraggly and thinning, dyed blonde hair, Lucille would make quite a show at any event. The woman had confidence, presence, charisma—some quality that defied the imagination. When she walked into a room, heads turned, people paid attention, especially male people. She was, despite all odds, an attractive woman.

"What do you think?" she asked.

"Va, va, va boom!" I said. "You'll look great. Has Mohammed seen your dress yet?""Of course," Lucille answered. "I have been sewing it for the last two weeks."

"You made it yourself?" I asked in admiration. "Amazing."

"News flash, honey. You have to make your clothes here. There are no ready-made garments that fit builds like mine. So, do you have something you can wear? It's not often that the High Commissioner invites the likes of us to his swishy parties."

Sadly, I had nothing even remotely suitable to wear. Semi-formals were the last thing I had been expecting on

## Chapter Forty-Nine

a posting to Dar. My mind started to flip around, searching for a solution. Before I knew it, Lucille had decided that I would buy a second-hand Chinese 'Double Happiness Butterfly" treadle sewing machine. We would go to the cloth market and choose some fabric. The rest would be easy.

After my visit with Lucille, I went home to our apartment and told Rob the good news. "But Julie," he reminded me, "You hate sewing. Remember. It always drives you nuts, and you get really, really bitchy. After the last dress you tried to make you vowed never to sew again. Remember how badly it turned out? You threw it in the garbage. Are you sure this is a good idea?"

"Hey, my grandma made my wedding dress. My mom sewed most of my clothes when I was a kid. How hard can it be? Sure, I tried it before, and it didn't go very well, but I'm sure this time will be easier." Rob looked very skeptical but didn't say another word. He knew I had my mind made up and there really wasn't any other solution.

My new sewing machine was foot operated, no electricity needed. It was a work of art—shiny, black, with little gold butterflies etched on the surface. Using it was another story. I practised sewing with scrap pieces of material that Lucille had given me. Manual dexterity has never been my strong suit. Coordinating my feet to power the machine while using my hands to guide the material under the needle was a major challenge. I decided to take lessons. I had two months before the big day, plenty of time to do the job properly.

I loved learning to cut out brown paper to make my own patterns. I designed my dress easily and worked out how to convert my measurements to the pattern. Everything was going to be fine. This was fun. My next step was to visit the cloth market and pick my material. I

## Chapter Forty-Nine

climbed on the back of Lucille's motorcycle and off we sped. The choice of material was limited to kitenge cloth, which came in bright colours and patterns. Subtle it wasn't. It was, in fact, more suitable for curtains than for a semi-formal gown.

"Where did you get your material?" I asked Lucille.

"I picked it up last summer in Toronto," she answered. Great, I thought. Now you tell me that there is nothing here that will work. However, I said nothing but kept bravely looking for something, anything, that might be suitable for the High Commissioner's Ball.

"This is pretty," Lucille said pointing to fabric which had a black background and bright emerald green palm trees printed all over it.

"Not exactly your royal blue silk, is it? I think I'll keep looking."

Finally, at the back of the shop, I came across some turquoise blue material printed with pink roses. It wasn't at all what I normally would have chosen, but it was, at least, passable.

"It's lovely," said Lucille.

"It'll have to do," I answered. "I guess it's not that bad."

When I got home, I held it up for Rob's approval. I knew immediately that he didn't like it from his expression. "I guess it's okay." he stammered. I chose not to push his response. It wasn't his fault that the material was marginally hideous. "It will probably look nicer once it's made into a dress," Rob said, clearly attempting to cheer me up.

I started to cut out the material. Easy. "Want a drink?" Rob asked. "It might help you to relax." After my first *konyagi* (local gin) and tonic the process speeded up. I cut and pinned and hummed. After my second drink the dress was taking on majestic proportions. I would be the bell of

## Chapter Forty-Nine

the ball. My dress would stand out and Rob would be proud to be seen with me. At 11, I fell into bed, happy. It was the weekend, so I could continue tomorrow.

When I took up the task the next morning the garish material jumped out at me. My pinning job look crooked, erratic. I picked up the would-be dress and tried to figure out the bottom from the top.. Impossible. It looked more like a crooked tent. Oh, dear. I unpinned the lot and tried to start again. After two hours, I thought I'd sorted things out. I headed to my shiny, beautiful, sewing machine. It looked spectacular and would make a great addition to any room, especially surrounded by antique furniture. Stroking the machine made me happy. Sewing with it was another story. I ran the needle over my finger at least twice and got blood stains on the material. At least the red blood matched the red roses. Sweat dripped from every pore of my body. I wasn't going to give up but by six o'clock when Rob came home from watching cricket, I was in a terrible state.

"Oh, God," said Rob. "Have you been doing this to yourself all day?"

"Shut up," I screamed. "Leave me alone." Rob headed out the door and only came home after I had gone to sleep. It was safer that way.

The next day proceeded much the same way. By four, I was fuming and crying. My fingers were dangerously pierced-through in at least ten places. At four thirty I totally lost it. I grabbed the offending garment, pins and all, ran to the bathroom and, with a flourish of relief, flushed the dress down the toilet. I smiled and made myself a cup of chamomile tea. I took out ingredients for dinner and started to happily make chicken, chips, salad and peas. No frustration there. This I could do, and wouldn't Rob be pleased. After the way I'd acted I wanted

## Chapter Forty-Nine

to make things up to him, and a nice dinner was a good way to start. All was proceeding wonderfully until I had to use the washroom. When I flushed, the toilet gurgled, choked and spewed water all over the floor. It wouldn't stop. I finally turned off the water at the main tap. So much for a quiet dinner.

When Rob got home, I met him at the door. "Have you finished sewing?" he asked timidly.

"Yep," I answered. "I promise never to do it again. I acknowledge that it makes me crazy, and I suck at sewing. That's the good news. The bad news is that the toilet is completely blocked, because I flushed my dress. I had to turn off the water. I couldn't get it to stop overflowing."

Rob didn't say a thing. He just grabbed the phone and called Com Works, our fix it guys. They came within the hour and by that evening our bathroom had been excavated. They had to dig up the toilet and surrounding area to get to the bottom of the problem. No simple toilet snake for them. It was a mess, but at least we could turn on the water and use the facilities.

I went to talk to them and asked if they were going to clean up the mess. "No," they answered, looking annoyed at me. "We know our job." Did that mean they would come back the next day and put things together, I wondered. Actually, what it meant was that they would fix the plumbing, but never stoop so low as to clean up after themselves. That was woman's work. I spent the following week reconstructing our bathroom, a task I enjoyed a little better than sewing.

That was the last thing I have ever tried to sew. I vowed to Rob and to myself never to attempt such a thing again. I still wish I had kept my 'Double Happiness, Butterfly', Chinese sewing machine. It really was

## Chapter Forty-Nine

something special—a work of art. I regret that I had to leave it in Dar.

I did go to High Commissioner's party. I borrowed a sexy, low backed, black dress from a friend and had a great time.

## Chapter Fifty
### A Dar es Salaam Evening Out (1972)

We arrived at the front door of my friend Lucille's apartment and Rob looked horrified.

"What the hell is that? It looks like a mummified body part. Why is it hanging on her door? Couldn't we just pretend that I came down with the flu and go home?"

"It's just a voodoo doll to ward off evil. Not a bad idea really," I answered trying to hide the fact that the thing gave me the creeps too.

"Do we really need to stay for dinner and how come you didn't ask me first?" Rob whined.

"Don't be so mean. Of course, we have to. She's my best friend."

"Ya," said Rob. "But she's so weird. I mean what kind of Canadian woman marries a guy who already has one wife? Is her husband gonna be there? What am I supposed to talk about: how much fun it would be to have two wives?"

"Rob, you spent days and nights searching the bars and nightclubs in Dar to find her motorcycle. What did you expect? She's just really grateful. This is her way of saying thank you."

"Okay, okay I'll go. Did you tell her I'm allergic to nuts?"

"Of course, I did, and it'll be fun. You'll see."

I looked at Rob and wondered what the evening would be like. My husband, for all his adventuresome spirit, was in other ways a pretty conservative guy, and Lucille, well, admittedly Lucille was a bit crazy and completely unpredictable.

## Chapter Fifty

I knocked and Lucille opened the door, grabbed me and kissed me on both cheeks. Rob almost fell over backwards to try to avoid a similar fate. She was dressed in a floor-length mumu made of bright yellow kitenge cloth adorned with purple pineapples. She wore a turban of the same material on her head. Mohammed, dressed in the traditional long, white *galabea*, appeared behind Lucille. He said, "Come, come."

Many of the lights were turned off and candles illuminated the place. A *Makonde* carving depicting a giant serpent devouring a shrieking woman—head first, met us in the hallway. On the wall was a print of a famous impressionist painting showing worshippers adoring idols around bonfires, their mouths opened in screams of ecstasy. In one corner there was a five-foot, shiny, ebony phallus. The room was smoky and smelled strongly of cigarettes, incense, and something else that I couldn't quite figure out. Rob coughed and rubbed his eyes. I could see him glancing at the numerous voodoo dolls that hung on all the interior doors.

"Would you like a drink or would you prefer to smoke up?" Lucille asked calmly.

"A white wine would be lovely," I answered. Rob looked dazed so I nudged him. "Rob will probably have a beer."

"Ya that would be great," Rob said trying to recover his composure. He glared at me.

We sat down and looked at one another. Mohammed was smiling so broadly that his teeth flashed white. He looked like his face might crack. He reminded me of the Cheshire cat in 'Alice in Wonderland.' I wondered how much English he could speak and saw Rob glance at his watch. It was my turn to glare at Rob.

## Chapter Fifty

"Awe, that's so cute. What is it?" I asked searching for any topic of conversation. A long brown, skinny creature jumped up beside me and sniffed my hand. Cute was a bit of an exaggeration, but I was reaching. The thing looked a lot like a stretched-out forest rat. It jumped down and slinked across the room.

"That's No No," answered Lucille. "He's a mongoose."

"Like in that story by Rudyard Kipling about the mongoose that saved the family from the python?" Rob asked, looking interested. Mohammed looked confused.

"I haven't read that one," Lucille replied, but we do worry about snakes, and he is a great pet. It was at that point that Rob shrieked and threw himself forward grabbing his groin. I should have been concerned for my husband, but my first reaction was acute embarrassment. What on earth did he think he was doing? If he thought that acting weird was going to get him out of dinner with Lucille and Mohammed, he was wrong. I looked at his face. Rob was in pain. He wasn't faking.

"What's wrong with you?" I asked, none too sympathetically.

"That stupid little beast hit me in the balls with something hard." Rob had hoisted himself back to a sitting position on the couch, but was still grabbing his private parts. I looked across the room at the mongoose and saw it staring innocently at me. On the table beside No No was a bowl of polished small stones.

"Oh damn," said Lucille. "Sorry. He does that sometimes to men he doesn't like. It's kind of cute really the way he manages it. He picks up a smooth rock from that bowl over there, puts it between his front paws, turns his back to the guy he's after and wings the thing between his legs. He never misses. In the wild that's how a

## Chapter Fifty

mongoose opens shells to eat the insides." Rob groaned. "No No loves to practice with the stones."

I looked at my husband and wondered what was going to happen next. Rob, still clutching at himself, managed a fake smile and asked for a double *konyage* (local gin) and tonic. I joined him. Somehow, we were going to have to get through the evening. "So" Rob stammered, "How's business Mohammed? I understand that you are the Coca-Cola distributor here in Dar?"

"You are very right," Mohammed answered carefully, and that was end of the conversation. Lucille and I looked at one another, and I could almost read her thoughts. This wasn't going well. Usually just the two of us talked about all kinds of things from sex, to men, to marriage, to child bearing, to clothes. None of our topics seemed appropriate. I wondered what Lucille and Mohammed discussed when they were alone together.

Finally, dinner was served, and we moved to the dining room table. Lucille had made goat curry, which was delicious, and by then we had all had more than a few drinks. However, the conversation still wasn't flowing. "So" Lucille said, and I couldn't imagine what she was going to say next. "You must wonder what it is like to be married to a guy who already has one wife."

Rob actually choked and I thumped his back. "Um, no, no. That's okay. You don't need to explain. I've been contemplating the idea of another wife all evening."

After I had elbowed Rob as hard as I could, I glanced over at Mohammed and noticed that he looked completely relaxed. Had he understood anything that was being said? "It's really none of our business and this is Tanzania after all," I piped up, hoping that would be the end of the discussion. I should have known better. This was my friend Lucille.

## Chapter Fifty

"It's great." Lucille continued.

"Good to know. I just might try it out. I met a sweet young thing at the Kilimanjaro pool last week who seemed more than willing," Rob muttered looking straight at me.

At that moment I was thinking that for a sixty-something lady Lucille was a very unusual and exciting woman. I was also thinking that I was going to kill my husband when we got home. I knew he was kidding—but still.

"Mohammed's other wife, Ruth, is a great friend of mine. Mohammed is careful to treat us both fairly and equally. It means that I have time to be on my own, to be part of an African community, and to really begin to understand the culture here," Lucille explained.

"Sounds good to me," I said.

"Me too." Rob added. Mohammed just stared and took another slug of his fifth drink while muttering something about African Muslims being different. I wasn't sure what he was referring to... second wives? Alcohol?

"How did you meet each other?" Rob asked. I sincerely hoped that the question would be safe territory.

"Mohammed delivers Coca-Cola to the secretarial school where I teach. He almost ran over me and my motorcycle one day by mistake." I glanced over and realized that it was Mohammed who now looked mortified. Clearly, he had understood that exchange.

"Not true." he said. "You hit my truck."

"Oh, oh," I thought. Another topic to be avoided. Would this evening never end? "Rob and I met each other on a bus trip to Quebec City. Rob was pretending he was on his motorcycle and enjoying the curves in the road. I thought he was weird but really cute and the rest is history."

*261*

## Chapter Fifty

"You almost ran me down Mohammed," said Lucille. Had she not heard my story? Were they really going to have a fight in front of us?

"You know," Rob said. "It really doesn't matter how we all met. We're together, right? It's all good."

"Lucille is my lady," answered Mohammed. Maybe he understood more about the English language and life than I gave him credit for.

"Let's go in the living room for dessert and coffee." Lucille invited. That, at least, seemed like a safe thing to do, and the number of drinks we'd consumed had relaxed all of us. No No, the pet mongoose, had been locked in a cage, and the conversation began to flow more naturally. We discussed travelling upcountry and recounted our favourite places. Mohammed seemed thrilled that we obviously were enjoying Tanzania, his country.

"I made something special for dessert," Lucille said as she retreated to the kitchen. Shortly after the smell of highland Tanzanian coffee wafted temptingly towards us. I wondered what Lucille was going to serve.

Mohammed, Rob and I were seated in the living room when the electricity cut out. We could still see because of the candles on the end tables. The limited pool of light excluded the creepy aspects of the surrounding room and the effect was charming. The couch frame was made of African mahogany. Cushions of all the colours of the rainbow lined the back and seats. Even Rob looked relaxed.

Lucille entered the room carrying a delicious looking pie on a tray with the coffee. When we were all served Rob grabbed his plate and took a generous bite. "Oh God," he said immediately, "You have got to be kidding. There are nuts in this pie."

## Chapter Fifty

I looked at Lucille and I could see from the horror on her face that she had forgotten that my husband had a severe allergy to all kinds of nuts. "Oh no," she gasped, "that's a pecan pie, my specialty. I'm sorry, but I forgot all about your allergy."

"Julie, did you bring the adrenalin needle?" Rob, eyes wide with fear, questioned.

I hadn't of course. I had explained to Lucille many times that Rob had a life-threatening allergy. I'd even told her stories of all the close calls we'd experienced over the years. It never occurred to me that she would forget.

"What do we do now?" Rob asked. I looked at him and realized that his face was already swollen and red. He was having trouble breathing and was dazed and confused—not able to make his usual rational decisions. I knew we had very little time to get him to the hospital.

"Mohammed, get the car," I shouted, and we ran to the door. Minutes later we were speeding along the waterfront on our way to the Aga Khan hospital. Rob was gasping for breath and had turned a pale shade of blue. At the emergency door Mohammed and I half carried him into the hospital.

The emergency staff response, thank God, was swift and excellent. The next thing I knew Rob was hooked up to an intervenous needle that was injecting adrenalin and antihistamine directly into his veins. In minutes the swelling had diminished, and his breathing was easier. Lucille was crying, Mohammed looked like he was going to throw up, and I was shaking so hard that my teeth rattled. Rob looked at all of us and laughed, "I think you guys are all in shock, but I feel fine."

We had to stay at the hospital for four hours, and by the time we got home Rob was normal but exhausted. It was all he could do to make it down the walkway to our

## Chapter Fifty

apartment and into bed. I climbed into bed beside him. "I'm so sorry," I said breaking into tears and hugging him tight.

"Oh, come on, don't cry. It wasn't such a bad evening and I had a better time than I thought I would," Rob mumbled. "And the second wife thing sounds like a great idea. I may have to explore that further."

"I love you," I answered, but it was too late. Rob was already asleep."

## Chapter Fifty-One
### Oh, Baby (1972)

Joy and Martin, our Ugandan fneighbours, in Dar es Salaam, arrived at our door and knocked furiously. They pushed aggressively into the flat and Joy said, "I'm here. It's time."

"Time for what?" I mumbled stupidly.

"The baby of course." Martin answered. "Joy's water broke four hours ago and her labour pains are getting stronger and are quite close together."

"I'm thrilled for you. That's wonderful, but why are you here? You need to get Joy to the hospital. I would offer my husband Rob's services to drive you both, but he is away on mission for the next week."

"No hospital." Joy said as she sunk to her knees and moaned in agony.

"Look," apologized Martin, "I've tried to take Joy to *Muhumbili* hospital, but she refuses to go. She says she wants to have her baby here with you."

"Her baby—here," I said. How had this happened? Yes, Joy and I had become close friends since we'd moved into our Kinondoni flat. We visited daily and talked for hours on end. The four of us played cards and shared many a glass of wine while sitting on our couch. Even with our diverse backgrounds (Canadian and Ugandan) we had so much in common. Our topics of conversation ranged from Tanzanian socialism, to local fashions, to our hopes and dreams and what the future held. We were two young, international couples on a foreign posting, dealing with culture shock and separated from our loved ones a long way from home.

## Chapter Fifty-One

Joy: how to describe Joy. At 19, she was even younger than me. Her baby bump, at the end of her pregnancy, seemed impossibly huge. I found it hard to imagine how her slim, slight frame could still be walking around. She had flawless, ebony skin, high elegant cheek bones, tight masses of shoulder-length, dark, curly hair and almond, brown eyes that seemed to look right through me. The slight scent of rose petals surrounded her. Gentle, tall, graceful, even with her pregnancy, Joy was an African princess.

Martin, Joy's handsome, charismatic, charming husband, in his twenties, had already completed an MBA in Kenya, so was able to secure a job as a treasury officer working for the East African Community in Tanzania. He had fled his homeland of Uganda with his young, pregnant wife and found a safe refuge in Dar es Salaam (Haven of Peace). Both Joy and Martin's family were wealthy and well-connected to the former Ugandan President, Obote. When he lost power to Idi Amin, everyone Joy and Martin knew and loved was targeted and in danger. The couple had no idea if their parents, families, and friends still lived.

They had an air of sadness, and no wonder. Amin was systematically killing and torturing members of their tribe. Tears would spring to Joy's deep brown eyes when she looked at the framed pictures of our parents and siblings that hung on the walls of our flat.

"Who is this?" she asked one day looking at a photo of Rob's sister Jan. "Will she visit while you're here? I wish I had my pictures," Joy added as she lifted Jan's image and brought it closer to her face. "I miss everyone so much, especially my mom. I need her here with me when I give birth. She would be so proud and happy."

## Chapter Fifty-One

Joy had a habit of stroking her large belly and resting her hand protectively over the new life inside. Beautiful glowing people, full of promise and talent, Martin and Joy were already emotionally and spiritually damaged by fear, by guilt, and by the reality of a brutal, death bringing regime under Idi Amin.

"At home," Joy explained to me, "every female in my family would be there for the birth of my first child. No one ever goes to the hospital. It's not safe. Instead, we have a midwife in attendance at the delivery. I don't even have any photos of my family to show to my baby when it's old enough. We had to sneak away from our home in the middle of the night and there was no chance to say goodbye. We are lucky to be here and to be safe, but I wish I knew if my family got away."

"Well," I said, hesitating while I searched for something, anything positive to say. "At least Martin will be with you when you give birth."

"Oh no," Joy answered. "He will not be allowed in the room."

"Wow. The only person I want in the room when I have a baby is Rob." Joy looked at me in utter astonishment.

"Your husband—Rob?" She echoed. "Men are totally useless at times like this. You should have women around you, and you should be at home."

"I guess you and I are just different, then, because I would be scared to give birth anywhere but the hospital and I would be too shy to have anyone there but Rob." I said adamantly.

Until Joy arrived at my door, I had no idea that I was about to become her surrogate family. If only I had realized what she intended, I could at least have planned ahead. As it was, we were totally ill-equipped for the

## Chapter Fifty-One

arrival of a newborn. I had never seen a new baby before, never mind dealt with the delivery of one.

Sure, I was the oldest of six kids, but my mom had delivered all of her babies in the hospital, completely sedated, unconscious. She had remained there for at least a week after their birth. I hadn't a clue what to expect or what I was supposed to do. Not even family stories were there to guide me.

"Joy says she wants to have the baby here with you and that's what we are going to do," Martin declared. Great, I thought, all I need now is a macho idiot to guide us. Martin picked Joy up and carried her to our living room couch. He gently laid her down and got the quilt from the back of the chair to cover her.

Joy smiled at me serenely and said, "Don't look so worried. The baby and I will be fine. I just want to be safe and with someone like family who cares about me. Women do this birth thing all the time in Uganda. It's natural so stop looking scared. I'm strong, healthy, and I've seen my sister give birth."

Good to know, I thought, but I'm not family—no way. I have never been present at a birth and this is nuts. The sight of blood makes me ill. Simply put, I was less than useless as a birth attendant. I bit down so hard on the side of my cheek that I could taste blood in my mouth.

"Aren't you supposed to boil water or something? Martin said, looking hopeful.

"Martin, Joy—I'm sorry to let you down, and I love you guys but the three of us can't deliver this baby alone. Your child could die if there are any complications. You have to go to the hospital, the sooner, the better."

"Please," pleaded Joy. "I know I can deliver my baby, but I need you. You're my best friend here, the only one I can count on."

## Chapter Fifty-One

"Sorry Joy but no way!"

"I am not leaving," Joy answered just before she succumbed to a long, intense contraction.

"Oh God, oh God, oh God, help," I whispered under my breath. "Martin, pick Joy up and carry her to your car. She has to go to the hospital!"

"No," Martin answered—stupid, stupid man. "Joy will have her baby the way she wants to, here with you."

"You are delusional. We need help. I wish Rob were here, so he could talk some sense into both of you. You have to listen to me. You can't just stay here. This is dangerous."

There was a loud knock on the door. Dick Turner, another Canadian University Services Overseas (CUSO)Volunteer, from an adjacent flat in our building, had arrived to borrow a cup of sugar. I hugged him and said, "Oh my God, I'm so glad you're here. Joy is having her baby and I need your help."

Had I appeared naked at the front door I don't think Dick could have looked more horrified. His mouth hung open, and his eyes glazed over. I could smell his Old Spice aftershave. "You're kidding" he croaked. "Where's Rob?"

"He's on mission. Have you any suggestions? Joy refuses to budge and go to the hospital. I have no idea how birth works. Can you help?"

Dick put his hands up in the air. "Me," he answered. "I haven't even slept with a woman yet, never mind delivered a baby. I'm an agricultural economist, not a gynecologist. I will go and see if I can find someone to help, but I am outta here."

Back in the living room Joy seemed to be reaching a new stage of labour. She had zoned out and was completely focussed on the workings of her body. There

## Chapter Fifty-One

was no point in trying to move her. It was too late. Her contractions were almost back-to-back with little rest time in between. Joy didn't scream or cry but moaned and writhed, which somehow seemed worse to me. I found myself wondering why any woman would choose to have a baby.

Just as I was contemplating heading to the kitchen to boil water, which was the only thing I knew how to do, there was another knock on the door. Dick had come back with an elderly Tanzanian woman. "I went to all the local buildings and knocked on doors," he explained. "I found Ruth. She lives in building four, and she's a retired midwife."

"Oh, thank God," I said hugging Ruth and Dick simultaneously. "I have never been so glad to see anyone in my life. I think Joy is going to have her baby soon. Come in. Thank you for being here."

Ruth immediately took possession of the living room. She had us boiling water, gathering warm blankets and covering the couch, under Ruth, with my plastic shower curtain. "Do you have clothes ready for the baby? She asked Martin, and sent him off to gather things up and to be out of the way. Maybe Ruth also had ideas about male attendance at the birth of a child. "Don't forget diapers and receiving blankets," she called as he headed for the door.

Joy sat straight up and leaned forward. "I think you're right Julie. I want to go to the hospital. I can't do this here."

Ruth, who had just examined the patient looked amused. "Joy you are about to have your baby. It's normal to be scared at this point. You're at least eight centimetres dilated, in transition, and it is far too late for you to go anywhere. The baby is head down, in the right position, and it won't be long now.

## Chapter Fifty-One

"Try to relax between contractions because soon you will need to push the baby out."

'Relax! Are you kidding?' I thought. 'My friend is in agony, and she is about to give birth in a living room. Relaxation is so far from the reality of what we are going through that the mere suggestion is ridiculous.'

"Julie," Ruth ordered, forcing me to focus. "Get behind Joy's head and shoulders and prop her up. Let her lean into you, so she can push more easily when she is ready. It won't be long now."

I did as I was told and moments later Joy said, "I think I'm going to be sick." Dick, who had bravely remained in the room, ran for a garbage pail. He got there just in time. Joy lurched, gagged and threw up again and again. I looked at Dick, who was by then a pale shade of green, and began to understand why men weren't always invited for childbirth events. Seconds later there was another knock on the door and Martin entered carrying mounds of clothes.

Joy sat up straighter and pushed back hard against me. "I need to push," she said loudly. "Now."

Ruth stroked Joy's hair back from her forehead and wiped her face with a warm washcloth. "I know," she said, "but first I want you to pant—in and out, in and out, quick breaths. Try not to push just yet. It won't be long, I promise."

Minutes later, Ruth examined Joy again. "You're ready, fully dilated. With the next contraction go ahead and push as hard as you can."

Again, and again, Joy leaned back against me as she pushed hard with each new contraction. "I can see the baby's head," Ruth shouted. "Keep pushing. You're doing a wonderful job." The baby's head slid out. Several pushes more and the shoulders were delivered. Finally, the

## Chapter Fifty-One

whole baby slipped out into Ruth's waiting hands. "A perfect little girl," Ruth declared. "Martin, would you like to cut the cord?"

Joy, Martin, and the baby started to cry. Joy held the little one in her arms for the first time. "Offer the baby your breast," Ruth said after the cord was severed and clamped. It will help to expel the afterbirth from your uterus." I heard a sucking sound and saw a look of pure joy on the faces of both parents. The placenta came away easily and everyone was looking healthy and happy, except Dick. I doubted that he would be borrowing anything from us any time soon.

Joy named her first baby, Julie, after me. Rob and I became her godparents.

# Chapter Fifty-Two
## Joy's Muskoka Visit (1985)

I am sitting in our log cabin cottage, on Buck Lake near Huntsville, Ontario, 150 Km North of Toronto, watching the fire jump and glow inside the hundred-year-old floor to ceiling, stone fireplace. Joy, our friend from Dar, gazes intently at the flames. It's weird to have her here in this northern place so many years after our time in Africa. Joy's black hair is pulled back in a frizzy ponytail and her black skin glows and shines.

Even though it's early evening and light outside, we have candles lit on the hearth and are enjoying a glass of red wine. It is as if we are trying to recreate the atmosphere from our apartment in Tanzania so many years ago, but the smell of pine wood smoke, and the sound of the lake lapping on the shore, remind us that we are in Northern Ontario.

"Are you still cold?" I ask my friend. It's warm in the room, but not tropical warm.

"A little chilly," she answers pulling the soft white wrap more tightly around her slim shoulders.

Our children, Jen (nine) and Dan (five) are still outside playing, and Rob is in the bedroom reading his new Economist magazine. Martin, Joy's husband, and her two daughters are back in Washington D.C. It has been 13 years since I helped to deliver Julie, Joy's first child and my Goddaughter, in our Kinondoni flat in Dar es Salaam. Joy and I have kept in touch—letters, phone calls—but haven't seen each other since June 1973, when Rob and I returned to Canada from Tanzania. "How's D.C.?" I ask.

"Love it! The kids have a great neighbourhood school. Julie is into sports — loves basketball. She's really tall and a super athletic. Our baby, Jazmin, is ten now and a

## Chapter Fifty-Two

bookworm. It's hard to get her to stop reading and go outside to play. Martin and I love our jobs with the World Bank. Things are great."

Joy, I think, has become more sophisticated. She seems so self-assured and has lost the air of unhappiness that I always felt when I was around her. Even the way Joy holds her head and talks to me is more assertive. She's wearing some exotic perfume which seems so out of place in this primitive log cabin. The scent reminds me of warm ocean breezes and the tropical flowers that bloomed in our far away, long ago home in Dar. Joy has grown from a fledgling princess to an African queen. Dressed in blue jeans and a blue and red flannel shirt, she still manages an elegance that fills the room. She's young, only 32, but somehow seems older.

"Do you ever go back to Uganda?" I ask cautiously. I know both Joy and Martin have lost family and friends during the bloody reign of Idi Amin.

"We've been a couple of times over the years. Amin has been gone since 1979, but the economy has never recovered. Our family, of course, had lost everything by the early 70's. Now the middle class, including some of our family and friends, the ones who are still alive, struggle to make ends meet. At least they aren't in danger anymore. I didn't think so at the time, but we are the lucky ones to have gotten out of Uganda when we did."

"It's wonderful to be here with you and Rob. I wish you lived closer. I feel like I've lost so many loved ones over the years. I show our kids pictures of you and your family, but it's not enough. You have to come visit and meet your goddaughter again. Can you believe Julie is 13 already?"

I'm feeling guilty. Rob and I have such huge extended families and tons of close friends. Both of Joy and Martin's sets of parents are dead, while ours are still

## Chapter Fifty-Two

young and alive. I've only recently lost my great-grandmother. Rob and I are both working, and it's hard to keep up. There never seems to be enough time, so it is unlikely that a trip to Washington will happen any time soon.

"You must have made friends in Washington."

"Of course," Joy answers. "Close friends. Life is good. You'd love our house in Georgetown—a big white place with pillars out the front and a lovely garden for the kids. The weather's not too bad either, although the winters are hard for me—warmer than here but still way too cold. I miss the tropics, but the fireplace in our living room helps. I spend lots of evenings curled up in front of it trying to get warm."

"I should check on the kids," I say getting up from the couch and heading for the screen porch. "Jen, Dan," I shout. "Time to come in for dinner." I look out over our land and see my little girl in her usual spot—in the middle of our frog pond. Dan, our son, dutifully dashes into the room, slams the door and heads for the washroom to clean up.

Ten minutes later Jenny is still outside. "Jen," I shout yet again. Has she not heard me? Get out of the pond. Now! You need to wash up for dinner." Reluctantly, after another five minutes, our 9-year-old daughter emerges from the mud carrying the largest bull frog I have ever seen. It's slimy, green and dripping with muck. She has the beast cupped in her hands and held closely against her chest.

"Look, Mom. Look Aunty Joy," Jen says grinning. I saved my frog's life. I took off all the blood suckers. The poor thing was covered."

On closer observation I realize that Jenny's legs and arms are dotted with small black dots. "Good girl. Now go

## Chapter Fifty-Two

put that lucky frog in the nice clean lake where it will be safe. Come back quick. You're holding up dinner and everyone's hungry, at least they were until they saw your leaches."

"Oh Mom," Jen sighs.

"Just please do what I say."

My daughter walks down to the lake, stroking her pet frog and talking all the way. When she reaches the water Jenny bends down and releases her newest friend. For a moment, as I watch, the frog sits dumb and dazed on the sand. Finally, it croaks, hops off the beach and into the water. My little girl waves goodbye, turns and comes back to the porch.

"Should I get the saltshaker?" she asks. "I left it by the pond."

"Okay, but hurry. I hate the idea of those blood suckers on your skin."

Jenny dashes off. I look at Joy. Her eyes are huge and look too big for her face. My daughter returns, and ignoring my friend's horror, I shake salt on one slimy sucker after another. The creatures shrivel up, writhe and drop off my baby's skin. They leave little red spots, some drooling small streams of blood where they have penetrated her flesh. I carefully check between Jen's toes and fingers to make sure I don't miss any of the blood suckers.

I don't tell Joy, but this routine is something I do almost every day at the lake. Jenny loves the pond more than our pristine lake and no amount of persuasion, bribery, or distraction has deterred her from saving her bully frogs (as she calls them). I've given up. My little one is filthy, smells of swamp and is covered in brown slime, but her angelic smile lights up the room.

## Chapter Fifty-Two

"What an unusual girl," Joy says when Jen has been sent to wash up. "Isn't it dangerous to let her play in all that muck? Aren't you afraid she might get bitten by a snake? What about germs?"

I laugh. "She has yet to get sick, so I've stopped stressing about germs. The dirtier she gets, the healthier she seems to be. Can you imagine her immunities? Jenny washes up before we eat. And snakes—none of them are poisonous here. She has two small garter snakes penned up in her aquarium over there. She loves to observe them, but always lets them go after a day or so. Jenny says they have to be able to go home to their families. She's really gentle when she handles any wild creatures."

After explaining all this I realize that Joy has changed. The Joy I used to know would laugh with me instead of appearing shocked. "Hey and don't you remember digging out *tumbu* fly larvae from baby Musa's bum back in Dar. I was the one grossed out then. What about those cockroach contests we had in our flat—you know, when we put coloured dots on the bug's backs, drank beer and made bets to see whose roach would get out of the circle first? A few leaches shouldn't bother you."

"That's one of the reasons I live in the States. I want to forget all about that time. I'm so grateful that I can protect my children from filth and trauma." Joy says. It's clear that she does not approve of my child-rearing strategies. "You had better not take Jenny to Africa. She's liable to find a black mamba as a pet and that would be game over. Our girls hate snakes, frogs, and bugs."

"Maybe Jen will become a biologist or something. There's no way I can change her and I wouldn't want to anyway," I try to explain.

"Well," Joy answers. "She's a lovely little girl and someday she'll grow up and change all by herself."

## Chapter Fifty-Two

"Doubt it," I say. The future has now proven that I was right. Jen remained a saviour to small animals, bugs, snakes, people, and anything living. I loved her just the way she was.

# Chapter Fifty-Three

## Freedom Comes With Knowing Who You Are
### (*East African Proverb*) (2015)

Rob and I are on a trip in the Blue Ridge Mountains, in North Carolina. The death of our daughter has left us numb, and we are trying to escape our Orillia home and all that it reminds us of. We have been retired for four years and, after a lifetime overseas, mostly in Africa, this is our first motor trip in the United States. Our kids are grown—we have no pressing obligations. This trip is meant to make us forget our grief for a time, to attempt a sense of relaxation, to learn to be alone and happy with just the two of us.

"I think I may have hit someone," Rob says as he slams on the brakes bringing the van to a sudden stop in the middle of a busy intersection.

"That's impossible; there was no impact. We would have felt something." I've been dozing in the passenger seat but am fully alert now. I look out the window and see a huge black man, probably at least 6-feet 6-inches tall and wide across the chest, sitting on the curb about 10-feet in front of our vehicle. He is clutching his bloody, torn knee to his chest and his Vespa scooter is lying on its side, in the grass, several yards behind him.

My heart is beating wildly, and I can feel the rhythm of my pulse pounding in my skull. A sensation of stabbing icicles runs through my veins. I feel dizzy, nauseous as I tumble out of our van onto the hot black pavement. Rob joins me, and we walk towards the injured man, trying to assess how badly he has been hurt. He's screaming obscenities at us, ranting, raving, calling us f***ing bastards. I understand most of the swear words, but beyond that I am not getting much of what he's saying.

## Chapter Fifty-Three

His eyes are filled with malice and loathing. He's speaking English, but with an accent so strong that I can barely understand.

We leave the man and return to the safety of our van. "I sure hope the guy is not badly hurt—poor man." Rob says as he turns to me with wide eyes, hands on the steering wheel shaking. "This is awful. His injury seems superficial, but he could still sue the pants off us. I'm sure glad we have insurance."

A lovely young woman, electric blue eyes, red hair, snow-white skin and a friendly smile comes directly up to our open window. She smells of roses and I find myself wanting to ask her what kind of perfume she's wearing. Weird how the mind works when a person is in shock.

"Y'all okay? Not from here are ya?" she drawls in a heavy southern accent. "Don't y'all worry much now. T'wasn't your fault. Saw everything, and I'll be a witness for ya. That guy," she points accusingly at the injured man on the sidewalk, who has become quieter while he is examining his torn and bloody knee—"he was driving his motorcycle illegally, weaving along-side the stopped line of traffic. When he saw your van comin t'ward him into the intersection, I guess he panicked, cause he drove his bike up over the curb and fell off. You weren't even close to hitting him. Y'all had stopped before he hit the dirt. Maybe he did that so he could get some money out-a-ya. Same kinda thing happened to me a few years back, but there were no witnesses."

I look at Rob and realize that he is bright red and breathing hard. I feel a moment of concern, but my husband smiles at the young woman and says, "Thanks for hanging around. We really appreciate it. Seems like a bit of a hostile crowd." By this point there are many spectators, most of them black. They are finger pointing,

## Chapter Fifty-Three

shouting, cursing—their hatred almost palpable. I catch the words, "white trash, white scumbags, white killers." I am horrified. This accident was not our fault and yet most everyone at the scene will say that it is. Thank God for the young woman who has agreed to be a witness.

Sirens scream above the crowd and several police cars approach from the adjoining road. I look around, and almost every black face has scurried off, leaving the victim alone to face the law. What the injured man does next shocks me so much that I feel like I'm going to vomit. He lies back, closes his eyes, folds his arms over his chest and pretends to be unconscious. Oh, God, did he hit his head? Is he just faking?

Five white police men jump out as the screaming, flashing police cars screech to a stop. "Who was driving?" Rob steps forward. The officer in charge asks, "How are y'all? Ya look pretty shook up. Y'all gonna be okay? Y'all from Canada? Sorry this had to happen—not very good hospitality. Seems a shame." The cop puts his arm around my shoulders. At this point, no one has bothered to approach the black man lying by the side of the road.

Our red-haired witness comes forward and explains her version of the event. One of the officers laughs and says, "Figures! We know this dude." They search his saddlebags but all they find is a can of pop. The cop then asks Rob to back our van out of the intersection, so the police can free up the oncoming lines of traffic. I wonder why there has been no measuring of tire tracks, no attempt to figure out what has happened here.

When the ambulance arrives, the white paramedics lift the wounded man onto a stretcher and strap him in. He's screaming, "Stop, stop. Leave me. I got no insurance." They ignore him, check for vital signs and stash him into the back of the ambulance.

## Chapter Fifty-Three

Both Rob and I are desperate to know what state the victim is in. We try to peek in, but the policeman comes, takes my elbow and directs the two of us towards our parked van. "Will he be okay?" Rob asks the paramedic, who declines to answer.

"Don't y'all worry about him now. He'll be just fine," the cop reassures us. "Y'all just get back in that vehicle of yours and enjoy the rest of your visit here."

"Don't you need my license or insurance or anything?" Rob asks.

"No need, not your fault."

I'm ashamed to feel a rushing sense of relief. We will not be sued. We have good pensions, but we couldn't afford a huge lawsuit.

"Still," Rob pushes, "Could I have your name and particulars just in case? Please take my license and insurance details. My insurance agency back home will want to be sure this was done properly."

"Sure, not necessary though, but if you insist," the policeman responds, looking impatient. He hands Rob a business card and copies down our particulars. We are dismissed.

"We're at Motel Six—we won't leave 'til ten tomorrow morning in case you want any more information," Rob calls over his shoulder as we walk away. It's clear that the police are beginning to get annoyed. We have little choice but to drive away.

"We have to stay in this town for at least one day," Rob insists. "Maybe we can find out how that guy who crashed is doing. The police might want to get in touch with us." I'm doubtful on both accounts but agree reluctantly to hang around. I realize I have no idea what has just happened. I'm left feeling like a, just-caught fish, flopping and gasping for breath in the bottom of a boat.

## Chapter Fifty-Three

After a life spent primarily in Africa, many of our friends are black—black African, black Caribbean, black Canadian. But for me and for my family, black is just a colour and has nothing much to do with anything. I do not understand the hatred I have just encountered.

I suspect that the look of loathing on those black faces has little to do with the incident that has just occurred. I'm not used to being judged by the colour of my skin. I feel confused, disoriented and angry. I am also aware that the response of the white authorities involved at the accident scene has been all wrong. That leads to a sense of guilt. What will become of that man? At the same time, I am aware that the accident was definitely not our fault.

In this foreign culture I have no idea who I am in relationship to other people. I'm lost, a pawn in this game from American history that sometimes seems to pit blacks against whites. I prefer not to be on the white team. Team humanity is much more to my liking. I find myself yearning for my international or Canadian culture where I am closer to knowing the rules and can play out my sense of what's fair. It will be a long time before I return to the States.

# Chapter Fifty-Four
## Lay Down Your Heart (2015)

Back home in Orillia I wonder who I have been kidding? Clearly racism exists in Canada too. I've been deceiving myself, living in denial. The day after we arrive home from our trip to the States, I tell my friend about the accident in Asheville on our way to the Blue Ridge Mountain Trail. "I just can't believe what happened," I say. "I'll never know if that guy was just faking. Maybe he really was unconscious for a few minutes."

Anne shocks me with her answer. "Oh God, let it go. It was his fault and he was horrible to you. Anyway, you can't tell me that you wouldn't be upset if your daughter or son married a black person," she adds.

I'm so startled, so utterly sidelined by her answer that for a moment I can't speak. I feel raw anger, anguish rushing up through my face which is burning hot. Tempted to scream, to throw things and to leave her home and never return, instead I struggle to be calm, to try to make her see the stupidity of what she has just said. I owe her that much. We've been friends since elementary school.

"You forget, darlin—my daughter Jen married an Indian guy. Our granddaughter Kaia is coloured. Did I mention that she just won the Kiwanis student of the year award at her school in Orillia? She's 13 now, and she's on the honours with distinction list as well as being a great writer and a super athlete. More than that, she's a wonderful, caring human being—so much like her mom that the resemblance takes my breath away. Do you think for one second that I love her less because of the colour of her skin? You're mad."

## Chapter Fifty-Four

"Kaia's beautiful and she's brown not black. That's different—not fair to compare," Anne says. Her face turns red, and she clasps her hands together. Had she forgotten about Kaia?

"Would you love a black dog less than a white one? Come on admit it, you love your black lab. You love him because he's a friendly, gentle, wonderful animal. Heh, maybe if you're so against the colour black you should get rid of him and get a golden retriever." I'm now so angry that I stop talking. My arguments sound stupid even to me. If I say anything more, I'll start to insult and wound Anne. I know that if I take that road, it will end our friendship forever. "I have to go. Rob will be home by now and expecting me," I lie.

I just want to get out into the fresh air and as far away from my friend as I can. Does she really feel this way? Is it possible that for all these years I have missed that she's a racist? At this point I doubt that I will ever be able to forget and forgive what she has just said. More than that, I just can't understand how Anne, who is generally an intelligent woman, a university prof for heaven's sake, can be so stupid and so wrong. She has no excuse, no reason for mistrusting people of colour.

I do understand the resentment that some black Americans have. I'm no stranger to the agony that we, as the white race, have imposed on them. I have tried to block the memory of our trip, years ago, to Bagamoya, but the stupid accident in the States and the aftermath have brought the details of that day flooding back.

It's 1972 in Tanzania. Rob and I travelled by motorcycle to Bagamoya. We packed a picnic and strapped it to the back of our *piki piki* (small motorcycle) Off we went, excited to be out of the city and seeing some of the countryside close to Dar. The warm air whipped my

## Chapter Fifty-Four

face and flung my long, brown, sun-streaked hair around my head as we sped along the potholed highway. Red, dry earth, disturbed by our passing, sent up clouds of dust that made it hard to breath. The flat landscape was interrupted by thorn bushes and the occasional giant baobab tree.

We arrived in Bagamoya and the Indian Ocean stretched out at the foot of the ancient town. Sugar sands and turquoise blue water topped with white frosting capped waves greeted us. Women were dressed in colourful kitenge cloth—one length wrapped around their tops, one twisted about their bottoms and still another used as turbans for their heads. The colours swayed and danced in the shimmering heat waves. Men wore simple, beige cotton pants and short-sleeved white shirts. Arab dhows—fat, wooden, chunky, reliable vessels—with their giant white sails, plied the waters just out from the shore. The air was fresher than in Dar, and the smell of salt, heat, sand, and frangipani calmed our senses. It was wonderful to be in the countryside after months in the big city.

We spread out our picnic lunch beneath a beach-side cashew nut tree. I lay on my back, happy and relaxed, while I gazed up into the branches overhead. "What's that?" I asked Rob. Above me was a brilliant, emerald green, thin, 6-foot rope wrapped around and around a slender tree branch not far from our heads. It shone and sparkled in the light of the bright sun and looked amazing—so pretty.

Rob gazed up and gasped. "Don't move quickly," he whispered. "What you're looking at is a deadly poisonous green mamba. Just inch your body away from under the tree, carefully and as slowly as you can manage. Don't worry about the food or the blanket. Leave everything where it is. Just let's get out of here—our lives depend on it."

## Chapter Fifty-Four

We crawled across the ground and abandoned our picnic. "There's a *duka* (small Indian store) over there, and we can buy Coke and biscuits or crisps (chips) to eat a bit later. We can't go back under that tree. Those snakes are slow moving and not terribly aggressive, but are one of the most poisonous species in East Africa. We're lucky we didn't disturb the thing. I'll be damned if I'm leaving yet though. Let's go see the sights," Rob suggested.

The Catholic Cathedral, which had been built on top of the original, open slave market, was the most impressive structure in the small town. We wandered inside. It took some time before we could see clearly in the dim light. Once our eyes adjusted, the images on the walls of what was now a small museum assaulted our senses. Pictures of slaves—children, women, men—attached to one another by lengths of thick chain, walking forward while slave masters whipped them, lined the walls.

Posters informed us that slaves were captured in the interior of Africa and brought to Bagamoya to be shipped to Arabia, South Africa, Reunion, Mauritius, Pemba, and Zanzibar. Apparently, male slaves who ended up in Zanzibar were castrated to ensure that their black genes would not affect the populations of people who would act as their masters. Slaves were often abandoned before they ever reached the coast. Tethered to a slave stick, (a long, heavy tree limb with a hole in one end that went around the slave's neck), many were left to die of starvation because the traders had run out of enough food or water. That museum in Bagamoya portrayed unimaginable cruelty and atrocities perpetrated by Arab and European slave traders.

*Bagamoya* means 'lay down your heart'. If the slaves were lucky enough to complete the long journey alive, this

## Chapter Fifty-Four

small town on the Indian Ocean would be the last time they ever saw their homes and their loved ones.

"I want to go home," I said to Rob. "This place gives me the creeps."

\*\*\*

What I didn't tell my husband, that day so long ago, in the dark, dismal Cathedral, is that I somehow felt personally responsible for the atrocities that were portrayed. I have tried hard, over the years, to bury my memory of that awful, haunting place. Now, forty years later, I realize that I haven't managed to forget. My sense of guilt has never really left me.

For my Canadian friend there is no reasonable explanation for her prejudice. I will never understand why she feels the way she does. Never. It seems that Canada is not the 'Garden of Eden' I had imagined it to be.

# Chapter Fifty-Five
## Learning to Drive in Dar (1972)

"Julie, you have to learn to drive. I'm travelling so much now, and you can't keep asking people to get you to work. You can do it—it's easy. This avoidance is ridiculous!" Rob jumped up, grabbed the motorcycle keys and headed outside. "No time like the present. Let's go."

"I can't. I'm afraid."

"But why?" Rob asked.

"My first experience learning to drive ended horribly. It was so bad that my dad never gave me another driving lesson," I answered.

\*\*\*

My thoughts flipped involuntarily back six years to that summer at the lake when my father took me out driving for the first time. I'm 16 years old and as excited as I have ever been. I'm in the driver's seat of my dad's shiny, blue Oldsmobile convertible with the top down. "Put the key in the ignition, turn it, put the gear shift in first and gently put your foot on the accelerator pedal," Dad tells me. We inch our way out of the driveway and onto the tarmac. The car jerks forward and slows down, jerks forward and slows down.

"Use more even pressure. Relax. There's hardly any traffic on this back road." Before I know it, we are cruising down the dirt road dust billowing around us. I sneeze. I know I shouldn't, but I can't help closing my eyes, if only for a second. The warm summer wind whips my face and tangles my hair. The smell of pine surrounds us as we speed up into the forest. A stop sign appears in the near distance and Dad asks me to put my foot on the

## Chapter Fifty-Five

brake pedal. The car stops gently, in the right position, and I'm filled with confidence. "Well done," Dad says smiling.

We leave the woods and enter an area of open fields. "You can go a bit faster now. Not so many turns." I look to my right and see cornfields. I'm daydreaming of a time when I will have my own car. I return my focus to the road. I'm shocked. There's a brown and white cow straight ahead of us, right in the middle of the road. "Brake, brake," dad shouts. I'm so startled that I panic and jam my foot on the accelerator instead.

The car shoots forward like a rocket. Dad propels himself to my side of the car and slams his left foot on the brake pedal. We come to an abrupt stop. Both of us hit the dashboard and sit, hurt and dazed saying nothing. The cow is two inches in front of our bumper. Dad's face is bright red, even redder than his hair. He turns and glares at me. This car is his pride and joy. I have disappointed my father. "Get out. Change sides," he says.

The cow's doleful, brown eyes look directly at me as she chews her cud. I imagine that she is wondering how I could be so stupid. You could have killed me the animal is thinking. Cars kill. I no longer want to learn to drive — not ever. My father drives us home. His silence is more damning than any words could be. My dreams are smashed, and that's the last time I have tried to learn to drive anything, never mind a motorcycle. Until now.

***

The description of my long-ago driving disaster has not impressed my husband one bit. Rob looked sympathetic, but he wasn't giving up on me. "That's awful. Bad luck. But what are you going to do now? Like I said, I don't think you have any choice. You're not 16 anymore. You have to get to work and I have to travel, so I can't drive

## Chapter Fifty-Five

you. Besides, I'm way more patient than your dad. You can do this. Piece of cake."

Reluctantly, I followed Rob out to our shiny, black Honda 125. The stupid bike was so heavy that I had trouble getting it off the kick stand. "Jump on," Rob said. Despite my shaking and sweating, I managed to ride the bike solo twice around our compound parking lot. "Way to go. See it's not so hard, is it?" Rob congratulated me.

"Great job," our neighbour Dick added, as he stood next to Rob and observed my feeble attempts to drive. "If you want, I can take you for some lessons when Rob's away. I taught my little sister how to drive. It was fun," Dick said. Had he known what was going to happen on our ill-fated lesson, I'm sure that Dick would never have volunteered his services.

Rob was gone on mission by the next day, so my neighbour and I headed out on our motorcycles. "Just follow me. We're going to go downtown, so you can get the feel of the city," he said. I dutifully drove along behind Dick. My stomach flipped over, my pants and shirt were already soaked with sweat. I felt sick. Gone was any youthful notion of competence when it came to driving. I was shaking so hard that the bike was quivering under me.

Despite my trepidation, things were going well. We had been driving for a whole half hour when it happened. We came to a halt at a stop sign and were waiting for the traffic from the left and the right to clear. I was busy watching the oncoming vehicles. When there was a space, I accelerated into the intersection. Sadly Dick, who was directly in front of me, failed to follow my example. I guess he was waiting for me.

I sped forward, not wanting to miss my opportunity, and crashed into him. Both of us fell to the ground, winded, surprised. Neither one of us was hurt. Dick

*293*

## Chapter Fifty-Five

looked at me and started to laugh. "I can't believe you just did that," he said. That's when the trouble started. We looked up and realized that a circle of hostile looking people had surrounded us and our motorcycles. We were trapped.

"What the hell," Dick said. "What's wrong with everyone? No one got hurt." I looked more closely at the angry faces and saw that people appeared to be furious with Dick, not with me.

"*Pole sana mama, pole sana,*" people were chanting.

"What are they saying?" I asked.

"I think—so␣sorry lady, so sorry'," Dick answered.

"Oh my God, I get it. They think you hit me, and now you're laughing at me. I doubt they know that we're friends. Do you know how I can say, "it's not his fault in Swahili?" I asked Dick.

"Sadly, no, and they won't believe me anyway. It's kinda hard to figure out who hit whom," Dick pointed out.

By now the crowd was circling us looking angrier and shaking their fists. Instant justice was how traffic accidents were handled in East Africa. In orientation, we were warned time and time again not to remain at the scene of an accident.

It was too late to keep driving. Our bikes were on the ground and the crowd had us blocked in. We had to do something—fast—or Dick was going to get punished by the mob. I hugged Dick. Then I pulled him closer and kissed him squarely on the mouth. His response was to jump backwards where he bumped into his bike and fell to the ground. The crowd looked totally confused and so did Dick.

I gestured to my wedding ring and pointed at him. The crowd backed up and some of the people started to grin. In Africa, if I was this man's wife, he could do anything he

## Chapter Fifty-Five

wanted with me. I was his property. He might be a mean bastard, unfeeling and ridiculous in the eyes of the crowd, but that was our business. This was a personal matter and required no further action on the part of the mob. The crowd started to drift away and soon Dick and I were alone.

"I'm so sorry Dick."

"Sorry about what?" Dick asked—"hitting me with your motorcycle or kissing me?"

"Both. Hey dude, admit it. I saved the day."

"Ya, ya," Dick said smiling, "but wait till I tell your darling husband that you kissed me against my will."

"Dick, under the circumstances, I think Rob will understand."

"Course he will. Just kidding. The crowd didn't punish me, thank God. I was pretty scared there for a bit," Dick said wiping the back of his hand across his forehead. "I still can't believe that you crashed into me. It's a funny story, although I doubt any of my friends will believe me."

"I guess that's the end of our driving lessons," I said feeling relieved but also a bit disappointed.

"Hell no. You're not getting out of this. Rob and I have decided that you will learn to drive no matter what. Just get back on your bike. We have to get home. But don't run into me again, agreed?"

"Agreed."

## Chapter Fifty-Six
### House Boy (1972)

The first indication that something had changed was the state of our shiny black motorcycle sitting in our driveway in Dar.

"Thanks for washing the bike," Rob greeted me early one Monday morning as we prepared to go to work. "When did you get a chance to wash it? Looks great. Good job".

"Hey, I'd love to take credit, but I didn't wash anything. I was with you the whole day."

"That's weird. It's sparkly clean, polished even." Rob said.

"I've no idea why our bike looks so good. I didn't clean it."

"Strange," Rob answered. The mystery of the washed motorcycle went on for a week and was beginning to creep us both out. When we arrived home after work, it would be mud splattered and by morning when we came out the bike would be polished and sparkling.

"What the hell," Rob greeted me on Friday morning. There has to be some explanation."

Sunday arrived. No work. We slept late. At 9:30 we were woken by determined knocking. I pulled my cotton housecoat around me and dashed to the door. The person in front of me was a complete stranger. "Hi," I mumbled. "Can I help you?"

"I am Juma. I work for you. I have wife and baby. We live here." Juma pointed to the empty servant quarters, across the parking lot, facing the front door of our ground level flat. "We come today."

## Chapter Fifty-Six

"Lovely to meet you," I stammered, thinking, 'what are you talking about?'

"I wash your bike every day—very dirty. You need me. I come clean, cook for you. You no servant. Now I servant of you. Son, wife come too. Live here."

"But, but," I stammered. "We're Canadian. We're perfectly capable of taking care of ourselves." Juma looked like he hadn't registered anything that I had just pronounced. The thought of servants shocked me. How could Rob and I possibly have someone do our dirty work? We had come here to help, not to be helped. My mom and dad had raised six kids, worked and maintained our home by themselves. They would be appalled. Servants would not, if I had anything to say about it, have any place in our lives. Servants spelled decadence, servitude, and ineptitude.

"This first wife and only wife Zara and son Musa," Juma insisted. "We need home."

"Oh dear?" I said, astonished.

Rob appeared behind me at the door. "What's up?" he asked.

"Well," I answered, "the mystery of the clean motorcycle is solved. Apparently, Juma here has been washing our bike for a week. He now says his family just moved into the empty servant quarters that go with our flat. He also says he wants to be our houseboy."

"Wow," said Rob. "Hi Juma. Thanks so much for washing our motorbike. We could use some help. Why not?"

Although I could think of thousands of 'why nots', I didn't have the heart to turn away the beautiful, young, eager family. Juma looked to be about 18. His skin was ebony black, and he had a cheerful, wide-toothed smile and handsome broad-faced features. His wife, Zara was

## Chapter Fifty-Six

maybe 16, but probably younger. She had high cheekbones, a chocolate brown complexion, and enormous, round, dark eyes. Zara was not exactly beautiful, but she was extremely attractive and painfully shy. She looked down at her feet and refused to make eye contact.

Musa, their ten-month-old baby, was bound to his mother's back by a brightly coloured, kitenge cloth sling. He peeked around his mom's body and gave me a two-toothed grin. My heart melted despite my resolve not to have any help. I looked at Rob and realized that he had already made up his mind. We were about to hire a servant.

"I start tomorrow, sharp," said Juma.

"Okay," answered Rob. "See you at six thirty. We have to be at work for seven thirty."

As soon as Juma returned to his home out-back, I started to have misgivings. Who was this good-looking Tanzanian teenager? "Shouldn't we have asked for references?" I asked Rob.

"Since they've already moved in, I don't see how we could kick them out. Maybe people will stop knocking at our door looking for work. Let's give it a go and see what happens," Rob answered.

I went upstairs for a chat and a cup of tea with my friends Joy and Martin. Julie, their seven-month-old, was dressed in a simple blue, cotton dress with little matching slippers on her feet. Her curly black hair was caught up on top of her head with a light blue silk ribbon. I picked the little one up, and she snuggled her face affectionately into my neck. She smelled of baby shampoo and talcum powder. My maternal instincts kicked in, and I found myself yearning for a baby of my own.

## Chapter Fifty-Six

"Guess what?" I said to my Ugandan neighbours. "We just hired a houseboy."

"It's about time," answered Joy. "Good for you. It's important to employ people here. So many need jobs and can't find them. Did you get the house boy's name from the Canadian High Commission or from CUSO (Canadian University Services Overseas)?"

"Neither. He just showed up at our door."

"Whoa," said Martin. "Not so smart. How do you know he's not a criminal? He could kill you in your sleep and steal all your possessions. Happens all the time to unsuspecting foreigners."

"Hadn't thought of that," I answered. "But I guess it's too late now."

Later, back in our flat, I mentioned my conversation with our neighbours to Rob. "Well, one thing's for sure—Juma's smart as a whip. Washing our motor bike for a week before he asked to work for us and moving his family into the empty quarters was an excellent strategy. How could we possibly say no? We owed the guy. Besides, the family seems nice to me. Juma even speaks a fair bit of English. It'll be fine. You'll see."

The next morning well before dawn we heard a persistent knock. I stumbled out of bed bleary-eyed. Juma was at our door looking dapper, professional in a starched white shirt, khaki pants and brown, leather sandals. "Bit early. Go have tea and come back after the sun comes up," I said. Juma dutifully complied.

That evening we came home to find our flat gleaming and Juma beaming from ear to ear. All of our clothes, even the clean ones, had been washed and hung on the line to dry. The only problem was that everything we had to wear (we didn't have much) was soaking wet. There was no way that our clothes would be dry for work by

## Chapter Fifty-Six

morning—too humid. "Guess we'll just have to wear the same clothes we have on today again tomorrow," Rob whispered to me.

"Great job Juma. Well done," Rob said. You can go home now." Juma looked shocked.

"I not finished. I cook now," he insisted.

"That's okay, thanks, but we love to do our own cooking. It's kind of our way of relaxing after work. But you can make breakfast tomorrow," Rob added. Juma looked uncertain but he smiled and headed home.

"He probably would have stayed for the evening if we'd wanted him to. I get the feeling that working hours for house boys are long. Hope he doesn't want to work on the weekend cause there's no way that's happening," I said. "He's really nice. I like him."

We soon got used to having Juma and his family around. We settled into a comfortable routine. I loved the sound of their drumming and singing in the evening. The smell of wood smoke from their cooking fire wafted into our window and reminded me of summer camping trips up north in Algonquin Park.

Things were going very well until Martin thundered down to our place when we arrived home from work one day. As soon as I saw his face, I knew he was very upset about something. I hoped that baby Julie and Joy were okay and that nothing terrible had happened. "Do you have any idea what your servant is doing after dark every night?" Martin asked directing his agitated gaze at Rob.

"They sing and drum, but Julie and I enjoy that. They seem to have a few friends over, but that's also fine with us. Hope they're not disturbing you guys. Juma's respectful and hardworking."

"Ya but they smoke *bhangi* (marijuana) around the fire. Can't you smell it?" Martin asked Rob.

## Chapter Fifty-Six

"Can't say as I've noticed—thought it was just woodsmoke. What Juma does in his spare time is up to him. Heck, I drink Tusker beer and *Konyagi* (local gin) on occasion."

"But that's different. *Bhangi* is illegal," Martin spluttered.

"Maybe, but Juma's a great worker, and he certainly has never smoked inside our flat."

I listened to Rob and Martin's conversation but remained silent. In Africa, it wasn't a woman's place to comment on matters like this. Rob needed to appear to be the boss, or he would lose face.

The fact that Juma was smoking marijuana didn't shock me at all. There were numerous *bhangi* stalls at the open vegetable market where I shopped. My friend, Cathy, who worked at the Dar Technical College, had commented that her students didn't drink alcohol but smoked up openly at recess and lunch breaks. I was surprised that marijuana was even illegal in Tanzania.

Martin backed off. "Well, I guess if you don't mind—just thought you'd like to know."

"Come in for a beer," Rob said. "I doubt Juma will be picked up any time soon for doing what half the country does."

## Chapter Fifty-Seven
### *Tumbu* Fly (1972)

Juma continued to be an exemplary house boy. I hated that stupid name—house boy. Somehow it seemed to diminish the bright, ambitious, helpful, young man who worked for us. Zara, lovely, shy Zara, would walk about the yard with baby Musa on her back. Her quiet dignity and perfect posture lent a regal air to the young woman.

Baby Musa never cried. He was constantly smiling. Thinking back to my own baby brother, who at a similar age cried all the time, I wondered if the African style of child minding wasn't more effective. It amazed me that Zara could nurse her child by simply shifting Musa in his sling, from back to front. He would cuddle in and attach himself to his mother's breast. Zara accomplished this task while starting the fire, cooking dinner or washing clothing. It all seemed so practical.

I did wonder how the baby would ever learn to crawl or walk. He seemed to be constantly attached to his mom by the kitenge cloth wrap. Although Zara rarely spoke, she now made regular eye contact. Her wide smile and warm, friendly eyes expressed more than mere words.

Rob and I arrived home from work one afternoon to find Zara standing in the middle of the driveway. As we drove up, she raced over to us, hands flying, eyes wide. "Bwana, Mam, Musa sick. You see." Zara followed us into our flat and removed the baby from his kitenge-cloth carrier. She sat crossed legged on the kitchen floor beside her son and proceeded to remove his cloth diaper. Musa grinned up at me. He didn't seem sick at all. Relief flooded through my body.

## Chapter Fifty-Seven

But what we saw on the baby's round little bottom shocked me. Not wanting to upset Zara or Musa, I took a deep breath and tried to respond calmly. Rob's face had visibly paled, and his hands were dripping sweat. Three huge, red, nasty looking boils almost covered one side of the baby's bum. On closer inspection, the boils appeared to be moving, pulsating. There was definitely something squirming and wiggling in each volcanic, red bump. Yellow puss oozed out of the craters at the top of the sores.

I suppressed the urge to gag. Rob moved in for a closer look and reached out his hand to touch the boils. Musa howled in response and Rob's hand shot back to his side. "How long has he had these sores?" Rob asked. Zara looked startled by the question and clearly had not understood a word.

"Where's Juma?" I asked.

Again, silence—no response. "There's no use asking anything," Rob said looking at me. "Go get Joy. She speaks Swahili. She's also from East Africa, so maybe she'll know what's wrong with Musa. At least she'll be able to ask questions."

Fortunately, Joy was home. "Joy," I said, "leave baby Julie upstairs with Martin. Musa has these ghastly looking boils on his bottom, and they're moving—totally gross. Whatever he has might be contagious."

Joy didn't react the way I had predicted. She smiled serenely and said, "I think I know the problem. Relax, you look terrible."

When we arrived back at our flat, both Rob and Zara looked expectantly up at us. Joy flopped down, cross-legged, on the concrete, kitchen floor beside Musa and Zara. She examined the sores and spoke in rapid, incomprehensible Swahili. Zara's panic-stricken

## Chapter Fifty-Seven

expression lifted. Her serene demeanour fell back into place.

"Do you have Vaseline?" Joy asked. We produced some and Joy calmly smeared it on the three sores. "That'll kill the larvae—can't breathe. I'll be able to pull them out with tweezers in about two days' time."

"Yuck Joy! What are you talking about? Kill what? Shouldn't we take Musa to the hospital?" Rob asked.

"Course not," Joy answered. "My baby has had the same problem. I know what to do from my own mom. The *tumbu* fly lays eggs on damp cloth like Musa's diapers, hanging on the clothes line. I have our servant iron everything that comes in contact with baby Julie's skin to kill the *tumbu* fly's eggs, but it's easy to miss a spot. If an egg isn't killed by the hot iron, it penetrates the skin. After two or three days the larvae hatch out beneath the surface and begin to eat the baby's flesh. It grows and prospers. A *tumbu* fly boil occurs."

"That is the grossest thing I have ever heard. Yuck, yuck and double yuck," I said staring at Musa's fat little bum.

"If the larvae had matured it would've eaten its way to the surface, so the mature insect could fly away. It's a terribly irritating and painful process for the victim, but not serious. When baby Julie had this, we discovered the problem early. Musa's larvae are more advanced, but the fly clearly isn't an adult yet. We can deal with this. No problem. In two days or so, the white larvae will surface. They can't breathe if we keep the sore covered with Vaseline. We'll be able to pull them out with tweezers."

"Are you sure? I asked, appalled. "I still think we should take Musa to the doctor."

"Course it'll work. It's really common in East Africa. Don't worry. No need to waste money on a doctor."

## Chapter Fifty-Seven

Two days later, we all congregated at Juma and Zara's quarters. Zara removed the baby's diaper. The three boils were oozing even more puss and each had come to a head. "That's the larvae surfacing," Joy explained. She clamped her tweezers on the white tip of the boil and carefully and slowly pulled. "I have to take my time," Joy explained. "If the larvae split and pieces are left inside it can cause a bad infection."

"A white slug-like worm about a centimetre long slid out of Musa's bottom. The larvae from the third and final boil had begun to develop wings. You could see the shadow of the fly that would have eventually evolved had we not interrupted the process.

When Joy had completely extracted the three larvae, Musa was left with red lumps. There was a large hole at the centre of each sore. We all breathed a collective sigh of relief. Zara hugged Joy and spoke words of gratitude in Swahili. Although we couldn't understand, we got the gist of the conversation. The two women seemed to have bonded.

A week later, we drove our motorbike up the driveway and saw Julie and Musa playing together on the grass in front of the servants' quarters. Joy and Zara remained good friends for the rest of our posting. So much for social status.

## Chapter Fifty-Eight
### Beating the Toad (2004)

I'm about to close the curtains in our front window in Bangladesh when I see him. It's dusk. The light fades fast here in Dhaka, not like the lingering sunsets of a Canadian landscape. I don't recognize the young Bangladeshi man standing in our front yard. As I watch, he crouches down in the grass with his back to me.

"Jen," I call softly. My daughter is putting her two-year-old, Kaia, to sleep in the front bedroom. Although I'm reluctant to disturb her, I'm frightened by the presence of this strange person in our front courtyard and Rob, my husband, is away on a mission, out of the country. My two younger kids are in their rooms, reading or doing their homework, and I don't want to alarm them.

"Little ones asleep, at last. What's up?" Jen asks as she emerges from the dark room, her longish red, blonde hair forming a circle of crazy curls around her head. She's wearing a turquoise and pink shalwar kameez, the local dress, which consists of a knee-length dress with a slit up both sides and harem pants. Her tall, slim form looks exotic as she glides across the room to join me at the window.

"Look. See that guy out there? He's wearing a guard uniform, but I've never seen him before. Ahmed or Mehedi, our usual Canadian High Commission guards, should be on duty tonight, and not for another half hour. Kinda weird, don't ya think?"

"Ya, and why is he squatting down like that? What if that dude has tied up our regular guard and left him in the guard house? And Mom, he looks like he's performing some voodoo spell."

## Chapter Fifty-Eight

By now I'm regretting having alerted Jenny to the situation. Her imagination is ridiculous. What was I thinking? "Oh Jen. Stop it. That's just silly," I tell her, but it's too late.

"Voodoo happens all the time here. Wish Dad were home. He'd know what to do. He always seems to be away when we really need him. Never mind, we can deal with this. Go get your *galabeya*—you know, that long flowing gown from West Africa, the one with the butterfly sleeves. I'll wear mine too. We can go out there and cast a counter spell."

"Has anyone ever told you that you're wasting your time as a teacher. You should be writing fantasy novels," I tell my daughter, although I understand that she will carry out her plan, with or without me, so I go and change my clothes.

Together we swoop out into the yard, arms flapping. Jen circle dances around the shocked young man twirling windmill style with her arms stretched out on either side of her body. She chants some eerie, meditation mantra in a high clear voice that brings goosebumps to my skin. Jen looks like an apparition—beautiful but terrifying—a kind of avenging angel.

I walk up to the poor bugger who has jumped to his feet. He's trembling, and his face is dripping sweat. The whites of his eyes shine in his dark face. I can smell his fear.

"Jen, stop it," I beg. "The guys clearly petrified. He's liable to have a heart attack if you keep this up."

"What are you doing crouching in our yard? What have you done with our guard?" Jen shouts at him.

"I replacement guard. He sick. I sit down to beat the toad."

"Toad," I say bewildered.

## Chapter Fifty-Eight

"See, I told you Mom. Toads are part of voodoo ceremonies here."

"Oh, for God's sake Jen. Look at the guy. He's obviously harmless. He's gonna faint. Leave him alone and come back into the house."

"Okay," Jen agrees, but she checks the guard hut first just in case there are any dead bodies. "Nothing here," she calls and we both go inside. Jen locks and bolts all the windows and doors. "I guess we're safe here, but I still wonder what he was up to."

Next morning, I call my friend Tanisha, who is Bangladeshi-Canadian, and explain about the man in the yard.

"He said he was beating the toad," I tell her.

As soon as I stop talking, she erupts into hysterical laughter. "Oh my God, you just made my day. He was just peeing, you doof. Beating the toad is just a euphemism like pee and poo. Poor guy."

"But he was crouching," I stammer, bewildered.

"Talk about cultural insensitivity," Tanisha giggles. "Have you not noticed that men here squat to pee? He was probably a replacement guard and too nervous to ask you if he could use the toilet. I'm guessing the High Commission didn't trust him with the key."

"Guys squat to take a leak—you're kidding. Why?"

"I don't know," Tanisha answers. "Why do men stand up to pee in Canada, always miss, and never put the damn seat down? I'm betting you or the Canadian High Commission will never see that guard again. He's off somewhere getting anti-voodoo treatment."

Tanisha was right. The guy vanished. After that, our own guards treated us with extreme respect, but looked at us strangely.

## Chapter Fifty-Eight

No chance that they, or anyone else, would presume to rob this crazy house, or beat the toad in our neighbourhood. We, the voodoo queens, were safe. Nuts, but safe.

# Chapter Fifty-Nine
## No-Fly Zone (1972)

I still look back on that day in Dar and wonder about my sanity. Nothing that Saturday morning was unusual. Rob and I slept in. The scent of Tanzanian highland coffee wafted through the apartment as we ate our scrambled eggs and toast. Even though it was only ten o'clock the day was bright and hot already. I had settled in for a lazy day of reading and writing.

"It's your turn to go to the *duka*," Rob reminded me. "We're out of eggs and milk powder."

Reluctantly I got up from the cozy couch, made my way outside and jumped on our *piki piki*. When I arrived at the little Asian grocery store at the corner, I was met by what I thought at first was a beggar dressed in rags with a smile as bright as the sun. I immediately felt the force of his charm. This guy was not to be pitied. He clearly had spirit.

"You take, I happy," he said blocking my way into the *duka*. Now this was different. I was reaching into my money belt for some shillings to give him when I realized he wasn't just asking me for money. No. He had something for me to buy.

"*Jambo*" I said, as he reached into a covered woven basket that lay on the pavement beside him. I should have just given the guy some money and gone into the store, but I was curious. Oh, God, I thought as he bent down and seemed to be struggling with a live creature. Could it be that he had a snake in there? I stepped quickly back, just in case.

What the young man finally produced was a large, live bird. On closer examination I saw that he had trapped

## Chapter Fifty-Nine

one very terrified Egyptian goose and had bound the poor thing tightly with twine so that it couldn't escape. The bird's eyes looked at me with intelligence as well as terror. No dumb bird that one.

"You buy," said the man. "Cook, eat." I have no idea what possessed me but without a word I took an overly generous wad of shillings out of my money belt and handed them to the guy. He took off immediately before I had the chance to reconsider. It was about then that I began to have serious doubts. The bird, which closely resembled a smaller version of a Canada goose, was not a friendly fellow and although tied up was perfectly capable of biting me viciously.

All I wanted to do was to get Lucy (I'd already named my goose) safely home where I could cut the ties and allow her to fly free. If I'd left the goose, even for a few minutes to find scissors in the store, she was going to end up in someone's cooking pot.

By now, a curious crowd had gathered around me and my goose. Fortunately, the basket was sitting empty on the ground beside Lucy, who was writhing on the pavement.

Somehow, I managed to get the bird back inside. My next challenge was to get home. I was a terrible and nervous motorcycle driver at the best of times, so carrying a basket with a thrashing goose inside was not an easy task.

When I arrived at the flat, Rob met me at the door. "I was worried," he said. "That took a long time. What's in the basket? Where are the milk and eggs?"

"I'll have to go back later. I had a little problem," I answered, lifting the top off the basket.

"What the hell!" Rob said peering at Lucy. "You're kidding right. What are we supposed to do with that?"

## Chapter Fifty-Nine

"Just get the scissors, and we'll cut her free. Don't worry she'll fly away. Her name is Lucy, by the way."

"How do you know it's a girl?"

As we were trying to free the goose, she was fighting and biting with all her heart and soul. The results of our struggle were serrated hands and wrists. "What were you thinking? This is nuts," Rob protested. "Geese are scary—don't you remember the Canada geese on Toronto Island?"

"Sorry," I mumbled. I mean, what was I supposed to say? This had not been my brightest move. We finally managed to free the goose. She proceeded to thank us by hissing theatrically, backing away and pooping. We watched expectantly. "Why isn't she flying," I asked Rob.

"On no! You're kidding. Her wings don't work. Please dear God tell me they're not clipped. She'll be with us forever. Now what are we supposed to do?" Rob looked almost as pissed-off as the goose.

"Juma, help," I shrieked. Our houseboy came running. When he saw Lucy, he looked totally baffled. What were Bwana and Mam doing with an angry goose in the garden?

"Juma, why goose not fly?" I asked stupidly.

His look suggested a comment of "How the hell should I know?" Being polite he just stared and said nothing as Lucy continued to wobble around hissing and looking threatening—still no flying.

I went upstairs to ask Martin and Joy if they had any ideas of how to handle a wild goose. They suggested we contact their vet who arrived the next day in a run-down Volkswagen Beetle. "The goose has an injured wing," the vet declared. "It needs muscle medicine."

Muscle medicine seemed a bit loosey-goosey to me, but we decided to take the vet's advice. For days after Rob, Juma, and I spent hours trapping Lucy, opening her

## Chapter Fifty-Nine

beak and squirting drops down her throat. We all still have the scars to prove it.

After a month of feeding Lucy grain and medication she began to get to know us. No longer did she hiss and back away. Now she ran to see us whenever we were outside. She would practice using her wings and was healing.

Lucy spent hours playing with our resident children, and before we knew it, she would allow them to pat her, although she never let them pick her up.

Lucy became, as it turned out, a friendly creature with real personality. If I sat down outside on the lawn chair, she would lay at my feet and quack softly. She begged for grain constantly and could be heard quacking Rob hello when he got home from work. She was beautiful, too with her distinct brown, white and black markings.

"I worry about Lucy," I told Rob as we watched her strutting proudly around the apartment compound. "What if someone traps and eats her? She's become such a great pet."

"Doubt that's gonna happen," answered my husband. "Have you not noticed how she is with strangers? Lucy is the best guard animal I've ever seen. She's also going to be able to fly away soon. The medicine is working."

The next time someone came to visit I watched Lucy, and sure enough she became formidable. The guard of our compound had to escort the guest to the apartment building.

Lucy rushed at the stranger, flapping her wings, quacking madly and nipping at their heels. She was terrifying, especially in the African context. No one had a guard goose. Geese were meant to be dinner, not vicious pets.

## Chapter Fifty-Nine

A goose in the garden signified a curse, a weird event, something not to be trusted. No one ever robbed any of the tenants of Kinondoni flats during Lucy's occupancy. Who needed a boring, old dog that could be drugged with tainted meat? Lucy was the perfect guard.

Still no flying, though.

# Chapter Sixty
## Mr. Goose (1972)

I didn't notice, at first, that Lucy had stopped greeting us when we returned home after work. I wasn't worried because I could hear her constant, happy honking all day and all night. Rob remarked on her change of habits first. "What's with Lucy? She's still taking grain out of her bowl, but I haven't seen her in a day or two. What's gotten into her?"

Rob and I went out into the garden to unravel the Lucy mystery. We walked up and down a few times, but didn't see her. "Could it be that she has learned to fly and is just coming home on occasion for dinner? I asked Rob. Just as we were about to go back into the flat, we heard soft honking coming from a sheltered area at the back of the garden. Tall grass and small bushes obscured our view, so we walked in closer to find our goose.

There was Lucy huddled down in the ground cover with another goose. "Lucy," said Rob. "Want to introduce us to your friend?"

"So adorable. He must be male though, cause he's bigger and his markings are different. He's a handsome boy," I said as we cautiously moved in for a closer look. Mr. Goose hissed at us and backed away. "Well, I guess we called it—Lucy is definitely female."

Lucy stared at her mate in amazement. "Wo", she seemed to be saying. "This is my family. What's with you?"

Her calm acceptance of us did nothing to reassure the gander. He ran at us, so we headed for the shelter of our apartment. Just as we reached our door, we turned around just in time to see Mr. Goose fly away.

## Chapter Sixty

"Later that day we went out in the yard. The new goose had returned and was strutting around, head held high. "Screw you, go away," his attitude said. Lucy followed dutifully after him, but turned and looked innocently back at us. Over the next few months Mr. Goose flew off regularly. He was sometimes gone for more than a day, but he always returned.

One Saturday morning just at sunrise we were woken up by hysterical honking. We raced out into the yard and were greeted by Lucy frantically circling four baby goslings. "Oh look, how sweet. But they're so little," I said.

"Luce," Rob asked. "How long has this been going on? We didn't even know you'd laid eggs. Where is that lazy husband of yours? He should be protecting you and your babies, not off flying around." Lucy answered by honking repeatedly. We looked up in the sky and saw a hawk circling dangerously overhead.

"Poor goose, she's clearly terrified. That hawk will pick off those goslings in seconds, as soon as we go back into the apartment. Now what are we supposed to do?" Rob asked.

"We can't leave her."

"Maybe not today, but Julie, we both have jobs. On Monday we have to go to work."

We spent the weekend on lawn chairs, under sun umbrellas, taking turns watching over our four babies. In the evening Lucy lead her offspring back to the nest, and we were finally able to go inside.

Monday morning at dawn we heard mad quacking again. However, this time it was only Mr. Goose returning home from his wild weekend away. We left for work hoping that the goslings would survive our absence.

## Chapter Sixty

Despite our fears and the ever-present hawks, the babies prospered. Lucy was a wonderful mother, and I like to think that Rob and I helped too. We spent as much time out in the garden as we could. Mr. Goose never got used to us but became less threatening. The goslings grew steadily and soon were about six inches tall. Now they were begging for grain along with their mother.

We named them after four of the dwarves in my favourite fairy tale, 'Snow White'—Sleepy, Bashful, Happy and Grumpy. Each gosling had a distinct personality, but they were all lovely little creatures. 'Happy' was my favourite. Much like Lucy, with similar markings, Happy was friendly, confident, easy going and loved to eat grain.

Rob had a preference for Grumpy because he was bigger, more aggressive and honked constantly for grain or attention—we were never sure quite what he wanted. "He must be male," Rob speculated. "He's obviously practising to be a type-A business goose. That goose is going places."

The little geese were such good pets, but we had a problem. All of them were taking after their mama. No one —and I mean no one who they were not familiar with —could get near our compound, never mind come in for a visit. Our neighbours began to complain. One goose was one thing, six geese quite another.

Things started to heat up when the goslings became teenagers and then adults. They began to have attitude and would get aggressive, even with the residents. They just wanted to be fed, but still ... "Rob," Martin said one day, twisting his hands together and looking mortified. "I hate to be the one to break the bad news, but you have to do something about all those geese. No one will visit our family anymore. Our friends are too proud to admit their

## Chapter Sixty

fear, but they're spooked by your geese. It's just not natural, and those birds are scary and mean when they don't know people. They're pooping everywhere. They're dirty."

"I know, said Rob sadly. "I think, once they learn to fly, they'll just take off."

"What are we going to do? I love those little guys. We can't hurt them and there is no bird sanctuary or animal shelter in Dar. I checked," I told Rob.

We continued to ignore the protests of our neighbours. One day we woke up and heard no honking. It was a bit like waking up and not seeing the daylight, we had become so used to the sound. Grabbing our housecoats, we raced outside to see what the problem might be. No geese! None—not even Lucy. Mystified, we searched the entire yard. We hadn't solved the problem when we had to go to work.

That evening when we got home—still no geese. I wanted to believe that they flew away. Rob and I, as well as a few of our neighbours, missed them terribly. The other possibility was too horrible to contemplate.

About a week later we heard honking at dawn. Lucy had come home. She stayed for the day, but in the evening, as we watched, she honked goodbye and flew away for the last time. I like to think that all of the geese formed families of their own and lived long and healthy lives. I'll never know for sure what happened to them. At least I knew Lucy was safe.

## Chapter Sixty-One
### Catastrophe (2007)

Cats—you gotta love them and I do—really! However, spoiler alert. This chapter is not kind to cats, so beware. If you are a cat lover you might want to stop reading right now.

After our posting in Bangladesh, Rob is called back to headquarters in Ottawa. Jen and Kaia are living in the countryside south-west of Ottawa, renting the downstairs part of a big home. They have lots of windows, a fire place, an enormous yard that borders on forest in all directions—the boonies. Because they're so isolated I worry that they're lonely, so I visit on an almost daily basis. It's spring and the woods are beautiful, with new budding trees, blue snow flowers, yellow forsythia bushes. Blue jays, cardinals, and goldfinches have come out to play after the long winter, and they screech their joy in the sunshine. After our last posting, I have only managed to find a part-time teaching job in Ottawa, so I have time to spend with my daughter and granddaughter. Kaia is in kindergarten and so cute that I can hardly stand it. Jen is not just my daughter. She is my friend.

Rob and I have a mutt from Ethiopia—a horrible, mean but beautiful retriever mix named Griff. He has bitten my kids and many of our friends. We should have put this animal down a long time ago, but my husband loves him. It would kill Rob to destroy his pup. Instead, we are very careful with Griff at all times. The dog has some redeeming features. He loves several people—Rob, of course, as well as me, Jen, Kaia and Andrew, our youngest. He hates everyone else.

## Chapter Sixty-One

"Jen, is it okay if I bring Griff to your house? It'll be great to let him run in the forest. He can't get into much trouble. Kaia will want to see him."

"Great mom. Bring him along."

As I'm driving for our visit, I have a rare premonition about Griff. Something bad is gonna happen. I'm the least prophetic person in the world, so I dismiss my doubts. What could possibly go wrong? When I arrive, Kaia's all ready for school, waiting with her mom for the school bus at the end of the lane. "Grandma's here Mom. Can I stay home from school and play with Griff? I want to visit too."

"Sorry sweetie but you have to go to school. Grandma and Griff will be here when you come home, and we'll have lunch together. Off you go," Jen insists.

Kaia drags her feet up the bus steps. Griff gets away from me and bounds onto the bus with thirty little kids. I pole vault up the three stairs, land beside the driver, grab Griff's collar and haul him out. "Beautiful dog," the driver calls after me.

"Oh, if you only knew," I respond with visions of little children being eaten by my beast dancing through my head. The driver looks confused. When Griff is back on the ground Jen and I giggle. "Can you imagine?" I say and Jen grins.

"We need a very large cup of Earl Grey tea," my daughter tells me, and we head back down the lane to her place. We're both feeling relieved and amused. We don't pay any attention to Griff—never a wise decision. He's running in the forest. Gary, Jen's landlord, is at work, and we are alone.

After about an hour I realize I haven't seen my beast out the window for quite a long time. "Let's go outside and check on the dog."

## Chapter Sixty-One

Griff is at the back door with a tiny dead tabby cat in his jaws. He drops the cat at Jen's feet and smiles up at her expecting to be praised. "Oh my God—he's killed a cat," Jen moans. "Gary loves cats. Poor kitty. This is terrible. Bad dog Griff!"

"Please dear God, tell me that's not Gary's cat," I plead.

"No," Jen answers. "It's a stray cat that Kaia and I have been feeding. Still so sad. It was such a cute kitty. Kaia can't know about this. Nor can Gary. He would kick me out of our home if he found out. The man adores cats—any cats. He's going to kill me because I allowed your nasty dog to be loose on his property,"

"How was I supposed to know that Griff would find a forest cat?" I answer. "I thought there was no trouble he could get into out here in the middle of nowhere."

"We have to do something," Jen says. "Go get a green garbage bag. We need to hide the evidence. We're going to bury the cat."

We put pussy into the bag, seal it carefully with a wire tie and dig a shallow, but huge hole close to the edge of the forest. It's not too far from the back porch that Jen shares with Gary, her landlord. We don't have time to be thorough. Gary is self-employed and sometimes drops in during working hours. He could show up any second. We lower the cat gently into the ground. Jen has brought a bouquet of spring daffodils, which she places on top of the kitty. We shovel earth, which smells like spring, back into the hole.

Jen leads us in prayers with tears dripping down her cheeks. She sprinkles water over the grave site. I don't dare to ask her why—must be some pagan ritual. I keep Griff on the leash, and he looks up at me. No pats, no, thank you, no doggy-treats—what a mean bitch you are—he tells me with his eyes. When the service is over, we tie

## Chapter Sixty-One

Griff up and go back into Jen's home to drink copious amounts of tea.

A week later I'm back at Jen's house. Gary is home and the three of us are sitting on the back porch drinking Indian chai and talking. It's quiet except for bird songs and the wind in the bushes. Peaceful—until the explosion—a huge firecracker sound coming from the place where we buried the cat. Dirt and dead daffodils fly in every direction. "Oh my God," says Gary, "What the hell was that?"

I look at Jen. She looks at me. We simultaneously blush. We know what we've done. Jen is first to regain her composure. She smiles serenely and says, "Must be an underground gas eruption. Sometimes that happens. It's not dangerous, just a natural phenomenon. Plant material rots and creates gas and then poof. Haven't you ever experienced this before?" she asks Gary.

Gary looks sheepish. "Course I have," he answers, and we go on drinking chai.

Much later when Gary has gone into his half of the house Jen says, "How stupid of us. We buried that cat in a sealed bag. I guess as the body decomposed it created lots of gas and poof an explosion. Poor cat. At least Gary bought my story. Glad Kaia wasn't here. She would have asked a lot more questions. She would have figured out what really happened.

# Chapter Sixty-Two
## Beadle Hotel (1972)

The rule with CUSO volunteers in East Africa was that if you were agreeable, other volunteers were welcome to stay in your home. They had to pay one dollar a day for electricity and other charges relating to the running of your place. They also had to contribute to the food. Rob and I were happy to accommodate visitors.

My husband was, is, and always will be, extremely friendly and extroverted. Before I knew it our flat had become a welcome centre, a hotel for visiting volunteers, not just from Tanzania, but from East Africa. We seemed to be a magnet for young hippies who were travelling in the region. Fred, our CUSO field staff officer, would send everyone he met our way. Clearly, he didn't want people staying at his place.

I arrived at our flat one evening before Rob, to find a young, gay couple cooking in my kitchen. At least they had their own food. "Oh hi. Hope you don't mind. Fred sent us here. He said you loved visitors. We're here for a conference on the rights of women. I'm Jane and this is Sybil."

Jane was probably six feet tall—blonde, attractive, athletic and masculine looking. Sybil, her partner, was red haired and drop dead gorgeous—light blue, translucent eyes, perfect pale skin, high cheek bones and a figure to die for. I found myself thankful that Sybil preferred the female sex. Otherwise, I would be jealous if she were in the same room as Rob. No one could fail to be charmed by her looks and youth.

"What's your husband like?" asked Sybil. Strange question coming from a guest, I thought.

## Chapter Sixty-Two

"He's great," I said. "Actually, he's the reason you're here. He loves people and welcomes everyone to our home. Naturally, I'm fine with that, but it is his idea to do this, not mine."

"Really?" added Jane. I wondered why she sounded so surprised. "But do you honestly have equal rights?" she asked. "I bet your husband forced you to come to Africa. I also suspect that you do most of the cooking and cleaning."

"Coming to Africa was originally my idea. I've wanted this since I was ten years old. Rob adopted my dream. As to cleaning—we have a house boy who does all of that. His name is Juma—you'll meet him. Juma would cook and shop too, but Rob didn't want to give that up. Rob cooks to relax, and he's too picky to let anyone buy the ingredients for his culinary endeavours. I confess that I don't do much around the house anymore. I do make delicious yogurt for breakfast every day."

"Wow," said the striking Sybil. "You're really unusual for a straight couple."

It was at this point in our conversation that Gary and Fern, two young people from Toronto who were travelling through East Africa, showed up.

"Hi," Fern said. "The CUSO field staff officer sent us here. We know we have to pay a dollar a day. We'll also contribute to food and any other expenses you might have. It's so kind of you to allow visitors in your home."

"Come on in. Meet Jane and Sybil. They just arrived. They're here for a conference in Dar. The only problem is that we have one spare bedroom with a double bed, but you're welcome to pitch up in the living room. I have to warn you that there are no screens on the windows—gets pretty buggy in here. The pics help though. We burn them every evening, and they seem to deter mosquitoes."

## Chapter Sixty-Two

"We're gay," pronounced Jane. "We were here first so if you have any objections too bad."

"Wo," said Gary. "No worries. We're Jewish. Any problems with that?"

I sensed conflict, which I hate, so excused myself pleading exhaustion from my long teaching day. I retreated to my bedroom to read Somerset Maugham's 'Of Human Bondage'. "Make yourselves at home," I called heading out of the living room. I read a few pages and fell fast asleep.

When I woke up an hour or so later, I could smell marijuana and hear screaming. "Chauvinist pigs," Sybil shouted, "that's what men are."

"Wait a minute," answered Fern. "That's so unfair. Gary is a kind, gentle, caring human being. You can't generalize like that. Not all men are chauvinistic. I lost some of my family in Nazi Germany, but I'm smart enough to know that not all Germans are responsible. My best friend is German and she's wonderful. Her father was put in a Nazi war camp for objecting to Hitler. Her husband's Jewish. This argument is just stupid. Please stop attacking my husband because he's male."

"You have to admit that women always get the short end of the stick," Jane said.

"Talk about puns," Gary laughed. "I like to think my lovely wife gets the long end of my stick."

It was at that point that I got up and returned to the living room. Just as I arrived, Rob came through the door. "Hi," he said innocently. Did he not see the red faces of our guests? Could he not sense the tension? "Welcome to the Beadle Hotel. I see our illustrious leader, Fred has been busy. Funny how he never has anyone staying with him. It's fine though—I mean you're being here. Welcome. Hi wifey," Rob joked, winking at me. I held my

## Chapter Sixty-Two

breath. He'd never called me that. Such bad timing. What was he thinking?

Predictably, Jane and Sybil freaked. "What did you just call your wife?" asked Jane.

"How dare you?" added Sybil.

"Excuse me," answered Rob. "It's a joke between us, a term of endearment."

"Bull garbage," I thought, "but nice try Rob—term of endearment—please!"

"Julie calls me hubby all the time." I had never done such a thing (hubby for heaven's sake—what idiot says that). I had certainly called Rob much worse things like idiot, moron, jerk—you get the picture. I had to admire Rob's attempt to defuse the argument.

"You're lying," returned Jane.

"Actually," said Rob. "Why would I bother to lie to you? Who are you anyway? Am I wrong in assuming that you are both here in our home because we were kind enough to offer our hospitality? Kind of strange for you to criticize us! You're free to leave any time. But just for your info we're not anti-gay. Your choice of partners is your business. Just try not to judge us for our choices, especially when you're here as our guests."

The two women looked sheepish. "Sorry, I guess you're right," Sybil said. "It's just that we're at this conference fighting for the rights of women. We got carried away, but there really are inequalities out there between the sexes, especially in Africa."

"Look, I don't disagree," said Rob. "You're welcome here but let's not attack each other. We can work on the issue of sexual stereotyping together—men and women. I admire the fight for female rights and I get that you need to pick your allies carefully. However, not all men are your enemies and not all men are chauvinists."

## Chapter Sixty-Two

We heard a knock on the door. "Wow," I said. "Looks like the inn will be full tonight. I wonder who that is?" Joy stood on our doorstep with baby Julie in her arms.

"Come on in," Rob called. "The more, the merrier."

"Can I borrow a cup of sugar?" Joy asked. "I'm making a Canadian style cake from your recipe as a special surprise for Martin. Hi," Joy greeted our four guests.

"Meet Sybil, Jane, Gary, and Fern" Oops, I thought, maybe I should have put Fern's name in front of Gary's. I looked around furtively. No one seemed to have taken offence.

"Do you have beds for everyone?" Joy asked.

"Actually no," Rob answered. "One couple will have to pitch up on the living room floor."

"Two of you can sleep upstairs in our flat," Joy invited. The baby still sleeps in her crib in our room, so we have a guest room with a double bed.

Oh my God, help us, I thought. Joy and Martin were a traditional African couple. Joy did all the work around the house and was exclusively in charge of baby rearing. Martin did zippo. Our gay couple would eat them up, tear them apart. "That's really nice of you, but we volunteer types are pretty crazy and loud. We'd better all stay here," I said firmly.

Of course, Joy didn't listen. "No, really. We'd love to have visitors. It's not fair that you guys should have all the fun. Why don't the two ladies come upstairs. They can help me make the cake—it's my first time. I looked at the gay couple, and they were beaming.

"Wow, we'd love that," said Sybil. "Are you having an African dish? All we ever get is Canadian food, even here in Africa."

"Of course," answered Joy. "We're having *'nyama ndzi'*, a stew made with beef and cooking bananas. It's a

## Chapter Sixty-Two

typical, East African dish. Thanks to Julie we're having cake for dessert—she taught me how to make it. We have lots of food."

"Sounds wonderful. We're in," said Sybil. "Thanks so much Joy."

"Why don't you bring all of your food down here, we will add ours and have a feast. Later the ladies can sleep upstairs in your flat."

"Great idea," said Joy.

An hour later everyone, including Martin, Joy's husband, arrived back at our place. Just as we were sitting down to dinner there was yet another knock on the door and in came John, a young, Tanzanian, Jesuit priest from the Chagga Tribe—near Mount Kilimanjaro. "Hi," said John. "Great to meet you. My friend Godfrey, who works with Rob—you know Godfrey right?—said you welcome visitors, so here I am. Godfrey thinks you're great. Which one of you is Rob, by the way.? I'm so excited to be here because I want to discuss the role of the church in Africa."

"That would be me, I'm Rob," my husband said stepping forward and offering his hand. "Great to meet you too. We have a few other visitors with us—this is Fern, Gary, Sybil, Jane and our upstairs neighbours Joy, Martin and their baby, Julie. You, of course, are welcome to stay with us. Godfrey has spoken so highly of you. We do have a bit of a problem though. We only have one spare bedroom. You're gonna have to pitch up in the living room and there are no screens on the windows."

"No problem," said John. "I brought my tent and sleeping gear. I'll just set up here if that's okay with you."

Oh no, I thought. I'm betting that the Catholic Church doesn't condone gay marriage or living common law. I also wondered how this young man felt about smoking pot

## Chapter Sixty-Two

and drinking alcohol. This whole situation was getting a bit out of hand.

We had nine people in our flat (ten including baby Julie, who was fast asleep in my bedroom). We ate goat curry with rice, Joy's *nyama ndizi* dish and chocolate cake for dessert.

I was nervous at first. All these individuals with different ideas, cultures, and backgrounds together in our small place. To add to the drama, the power went off, as it often did, around nine o'clock. We lit tons of candles and kept the piks burning to ward off the mosquitoes. Our young priest drank a bit too much. Our pot smokers got very mellow, sleepy. The amazing thing was that we all had a fabulous time. In theory, we solved the problems of the world. The only real difficulty was that some of us had to get up early the next morning to go to work.

Gone were all our stupid differences. We were just nine, young, international types with a lot in common. We had a great evening, an evening I will never forget.

# Chapter Sixty-Three
## Staying, or Leaving (1973)

I'm not sure when it came to me. The realization that I wasn't ready to leave Africa in the next few months hit me with no warning. I had been longing for home, but suddenly could not imagine going there. Africa had spun its web around my soul. I was sure that I needed more time. I might never get the chance to come back to this magical continent.

It was just when I had decided that I wanted to extend our posting that Rob came home with his big news. "Guess what," he said. "I've been offered a job as the economist and financial planner on the CIDA (Canadian International Development Agency) Bee Keeping Project in Arusha. The pay and benefits are great. Housing and a car are provided. Not only that, our good friends John and Sandra are also thinking of going. John was offered the job as biologist, so we would be with friends. What do you think?"

I threw my arms around Rob's neck. "This is so perfect. We're so lucky."

"That's a surprise. I thought you didn't want to stay. I know how much you've missed home. I admit, I'm relieved that you're on board, but I'm not sure about this job. Let's go to Arusha and take a look. We can stay with the guy whose house and job we'll inherit. Should be a good break, if nothing else.

After our visit to Arusha, I had written my letter home ten times and still it just didn't seem right. I asked myself again and again—how could I consider staying for another two to three years? My family was looking forward to our return, and here I was thinking about having a baby in Arusha.

## Chapter Sixty-Three

*Dear Dad and Mom,*

*Rob has been offered a job in Arusha. I don't know if I will be able to teach, but it doesn't matter because I intend to have a baby. Rob's salary would be beyond our wildest imagination, so I don't have to work. Arusha is a paradise. We have visited the project up in the hills—all green and cool with lush vegetation shining in the tropical sunshine on the side of a mountain with a gorgeous view over the plains. The colours—how to describe the vibrancy and freshness of that place, and the smells—divine. If I had to imagine a garden of Eden, this would be it. In the morning when I woke up the sounds of the birds were so loud and melodic—hypnotic really—that I couldn't sleep. I just wanted to get up and meet the new day. Who can sleep when the world is so alive and inviting?*

*I want nothing more than to attach myself to this magical place and breed. The people we are replacing have a little girl named Miel (honey). She is two years old with blonde curls and a dimple in one cheek. Miel is all giggly and squirmy. No wonder she's happy. The day of our visit she spent the entire time making mud cakes that she decorated with flowers and leaves. The child wore nothing but a pale blue floppy sun hat (her blonde curls cascaded out the sides) and a simple pink cotton dress which, of course, was covered with dirt by the time we left. The little one sleeps in a pink room with frilly white curtains at the window. What a wonderful place to bring up a child—no snowsuits, complete freedom and a perfect climate.*

*In our garden to be there are so many fruit trees—a spreading leafy mango tree, ten banana trees, and five tall, gawky papaya trees. There is also a huge avocado*

## Chapter Sixty-Three

tree with dark green leaves that looms over the back garden producing food and tons of shade. I can't wait for you to visit. There are three bedrooms in this delightful bungalow and plenty of space. It even has a fireplace in the living room and a huge wrap around porch—so perfect. You'll love it. Now you have to visit—no more excuses.

Please don't be mad. We will come back after this job. I really miss everyone so much, but I may never get this opportunity again. I love Africa, and I'm just not ready to leave. I also want my family to experience this incredible continent.

Love, Julie

I have read the letter over for the umpteenth time. I can imagine my dad's response—"How can you possibly think of living anywhere but Canada? You're wasting your life. We accepted that you would be gone for two years, but this is just wrong. Come home. Don't you miss us? Stop this nonsense. This is Rob's doing, isn't it? Your future is here—not in some faraway place where you will never belong. The thought of you having a baby in an underdeveloped country makes me ill. What if there are complications? They don't have the same facilities that we do. You can't possibly think of putting your own child at risk. Just give up these silly plans and come home!"

In the end I never did send my letter. Rob solved that dilemma. He came in the door a week after our visit to Arusha, looking serious. I was sitting at the desk in the living room writing a new improved version of my letter home. "Please don't bother to write," Rob said. "I've decided not to accept the job with CIDA."

My heart sank. "You're kidding. This is an opportunity of a lifetime. Just think—we could be so happy in that

## Chapter Sixty-Three

home and the garden is to die for. I want a baby and Arusha is the perfect place to start our family. Please say you haven't turned them down already."

"Not yet. I wanted to explain to you first. I'm just not sure I'm cut out to be a glorified accountant. I've taken a really close look at the job, and it just isn't me. I'd hate working with numbers all day. I'm more of a people person."

"You'll be fine. I know you will be," I begged.

"Look, we've already been gone for almost two years. If we stay on, we'll have been out of Canada for four or five years by the time we get home. We'll lose touch. We both need to go back to school and get some real qualifications, the sooner, the better, while we still can. The next time I work in a developing country I want to be able to offer some real skills, do something that matters. The longer we wait, the harder it'll be. I haven't told you yet, but I've applied to take my Masters of Business Administration at University of Toronto or at Queens in Kingston."

"Wow, listen to yourself. Since when is our future only your decision? I want to stay in Africa. You know that. You just got offered a job in paradise. You can always go to school, but a job like this comes up once in a lifetime. Please just take the job. I want this so badly."

"Sorry love," Rob answered, "Your dream, not mine. I've done my time in Tanzania. It's time to go home and grow up. I need more qualifications to do the job I've just been offered, and I'm smart enough to see that. I refuse to fake it. I'd be in way over my head. Not to mention that it is not the sort of job I see myself ever doing."

As we argued African singing and drumming wafted in through the window with the scent of wood smoke. I knew then that the beat of that rhythm, those deep chanting

## Chapter Sixty-Three

voices, the smell of fires, dust, and night blooming jasmine would never leave me. I would forever yearn for this land, these people. Even though I would never be of this place, it had become my new reality. The thought of snowy, grey weather, white landscapes and skeletal trees left me with a feeling of dread.

"I want to stay," I stated stubbornly. "Please don't force us to go home. You love it here too. Just two more years. We can save money—we won't have to take student loans. We'll have a baby, enjoy our lives."

"Julie, the job was offered to me not you. I'm turning it down. I suggest you start applying to teacher's college, like we discussed before all this came up. We had our nerve coming here with no skills to offer, and I won't make that mistake again. For the record—there's lots of time to have a baby—and I'm not sure I'm ready to be a dad yet."

In that moment, so long ago, I felt angry, hurt and deeply disappointed. I also felt like Rob was making our life decisions by himself without considering what I needed to be happy. The fact that his argument made perfect sense didn't make me feel any better.

# Chapter Sixty-Four
## Nairobi, Kenya (1973)

Our decision to leave Africa was made, the job in Arusha declined. It was time to move on, to figure out what the next year, back in Canada would hold for us. We went to Nairobi in March 1973 so that Rob could write entrance exams for a Masters of Business Administration. He'd applied to various universities in Ontario, and they all required a pre-Master's exam. Rob had gone on ahead of me by motorcycle. I'd stayed to complete the rest of my teaching term. Alone, I took the bus from Dar to Nairobi in order to join him for the final bit of his Nairobi trip. By that time, I could no longer cling to the belief that he would change his mind. Rob was Canada-bound and so was I, whether I liked it or not.

The bus scene was something I was used to, so the crates of chickens, the bound and bleating goats, the people in all states of dress and undress—on top of the bus and in it, didn't faze me much—just another day in Africa. I clutched my backpack to me and dragged myself up the stairs falling into a window seat as close to the front as I could get. Shortly after, a very fat, matronly, Tanzanian woman threw herself down beside me, grunting and sweating. "*Jambo Mama*" she said turning my way and shifting her weight so that a quarter of her body was in my half of the seat.

"*Jambo, habari gani,*" I mumbled in response as I was squashed up against the window—pinned in my place. Sucking on a peppermint to try to ward off the scent of body odour and wet animals, I took out my book, 'Of Human Bondage,' and started to read. This was going to be a long trip. The woman, who said her name was Ruth,

## Chapter Sixty-Four

ignored my desire for privacy and began to speak to me in rapid Swahili. Understanding only a fraction of what she was saying, all I could do was nod and smile. My face ached from the effort, but I didn't want to appear rude.

Ruth dozed off about an hour into the journey with her head on my shoulder. Not daring to move a muscle, I closed my eyes and managed to fall asleep. I woke up as the bus pulled to a stop and all the passengers filed out to use the restroom and get a bite to eat at the Pitstop Restaurant. I followed and made my way to the women's toilet.

By now it was dark outside. A lonely lightbulb hanging from the ceiling lit the tiny cubicle. There was a hole in the floor to squat over (I was used to that). There were feces everywhere and the stench was overwhelming. It was impossible to make it to the toilet without stepping in poop. Definitely the dirtiest toilet I'd ever seen—gross! Instead of going in I decided that the bush would be a far better option.

The rest stop was surrounded by parked transport trucks—at least 20 of them. The jungle was across a major highway, so I decided to squat in the shadow of a truck that was parked as far away from the restaurant as I could get. Surely, no one would notice me. Had I forgotten that I was the only white foreigner for miles around?

I pulled up my skirt, bent my knees and squatted. Just as I had slipped my underwear down the lights of the truck I was sheltering under came on, and the vehicle began to inch backwards. I jumped up, white bum exposed and leapt back away from danger. I immediately heard laughter and knee slapping as a crowd of onlookers gathered around me. My seatmate, Ruth, walked sedately over to me and shot some rude Swahili at the gawking crowd. She took my hand and lead me behind the

## Chapter Sixty-Four

restaurant where I finally got to pee. Why hadn't I thought of that? Did no one use real restrooms?

Ruth babbled away in incomprehensible Swahili, looking amused and enormously pleased with herself. When I was finished, she hooked her arm around mine and lead me to the restaurant where she motioned to a barrel of rainwater where I was able to rinse my hands. "Sit," Ruth commanded using the first English word I'd heard from her. "Eat."

I selected two fat, greasy samosas which were filled with spicy, hamburger meat and a large cup of tea with copious quantities of sweetened carnation milk. Delicious! At least I wasn't going to starve, unless, of course, I got food poisoning.

When we got back on the bus, there was still giggling and pointing from the other passengers. I joined them in their laughter and settled back into my seat. A couple of hours later we reached the Tanzanian-Kenyan border. We were herded off the bus, our passports were confiscated, and we were frisked. We stood at the border for two hours waiting. Finally, we were handed our documents and allowed to resume our voyage.

When we arrived in Nairobi, Rob and our friend Thorn Walden were there to greet me. We went straight back to Thorn's apartment above Westgate Mall. Thorn had made a lovely dinner. We started with avocados stuffed with egg salad. We'd never eaten avocados before, although they grew in our garden. "Wow, these are great," Rob said. "Something to add to our vegetable intake. Usually we eat cabbage boiled, cabbage curried, cabbage pickled, cabbage, cabbage and more cabbage. What a discovery."

"You're kidding! You haven't eaten avocados? Glad I introduced them to you. Wait till you try mangos for

## Chapter Sixty-Four

dessert. I bet you haven't had them either. They've just come into season."

"We haven't. Can't wait." I answered.

The following day, after Rob completed his exam, we wandered around downtown Nairobi. I was dressed in a Tanzanian wrap-around kanga skirt and a sleeveless tie-dyed t-shirt, while women in this big city were wearing heels, smart skirts or pants and matching jackets—so sophisticated. With my long ponytail, flip-flop sandals, and hippy outfit I felt like a country bumpkin. Still, we enjoyed the big city. "Wo," said Rob. "They have bacon and cheese in the grocery store. Do you think we could take some back with us across the border?"

We went to a play—'West Side Story' and drank exotic cocktails at a funky bar. We danced to West African music. We wandered the streets till all hours of the night with no thought to our personal safety. Nairobi was safe in those days—not like now. Now the world is a different place—a place where a talented, dedicated, young diplomat can die of a terrorist attack in an upscale shopping mall.

***

Orillia (2013)

Two weeks after our daughter's passing, we received a condolence letter from Julie Desloges, a former colleague of Rob's. Her younger sister, Annemarie, was a 29-year-old career diplomat, serving with the Canadian Embassy in Nairobi, Kenya, when she was gunned down in the Westgate shopping mall attack by the Horn of Africa terrorist group Al Shabab. It was the 21st of September 2013. She was off duty and shopping with her husband. By the end of the incident there were 67 deaths and 175 wounded. It was hard to believe that in 1973 we had spent

## Chapter Sixty-Four

a few days in the very place where the terrorists would choose to attack so many years later. Had the world really changed so much that an innocuous mall in Kenya was now a dangerous location?

Julie's email to us after Jen's death read,

> *Dear Rob and Julie,*
>
> *As I am writing to you, I realize there is not much I can say. I offer my deepest condolences for your tragic loss knowing that this will not help or bring any comfort. Having recently, two months ago today, very suddenly lost my sister Annemarie, I can only tell you that I understand. When I received letters, I just kept repeating, why, why are you sending me condolences, it doesn't make sense ... And it still doesn't. I know the combination of utter disbelief, extreme pain, feeling completely lost and infinitely sad seems unbearable and sometimes, creeps up on me. I almost forget that I can survive it. This is when it is important to turn to those who are left, who still need us, as we need them. People want to help, and although we might not feel like it ... they offer. Accepting does actually help a little. I do hope that you will be able to find some comfort in friends and family. And please know that we are thinking of you in these terrible times.*
>
> *Sincerely,*
> *Julie Desloges*

## Chapter Sixty-Four

Annemarie's position in the immigration section of the embassy meant that part of her job was to relocate hundreds of people from war torn regions so that they could have fulfilling, safe lives in Canada. Her whole family were career diplomats, all of them in positions dedicated to the betterment of the human race.

Somehow, because of our common background, that email connected our tragedy with that of the Desloges family and their lovely daughter Annemarie. Terrible things happen to good people. No one can understand why. There is no explanation, no making it right or better.

Annemarie and our daughter both grew up overseas. At one point our family moved into the same house in Jamaica that the Desloges family had left on their return to Ottawa. Was Jen's death somehow linked to her growing up in the Third World? Would Annemarie have been working in Kenya if her parents had not followed their overseas path?

Sympathy from those who haven't lost anything doesn't help me as much as it should. My anger gets in the way. I find myself thinking, "it didn't freaking happen to you. How the hell do you know how we're feeling? Your loved ones are still alive." The wise email from Julie Desloges struck a chord. I could feel her reaching out to us even though it must have been so painful to do so. I am grateful for her kindness and courage and sorrier for her loss than I can articulate.

# Chapter Sixty-Five
## Saying Hello, Saying Goodbye (2015)

Rob and I have taken our granddaughter Kaia, who is now 13, to Jen's grave site. This is a pilgrimage that we often do when Kaia, who now lives in Ottawa, comes back to Orillia. We go out on the mid-summer roadside and pick armfuls of wildflowers: daisies, black-eyed Susans, Queen Anne's lace, wild orange day lilies, butter cups, devil's paint brush, purple and white clover—the same flowers we picked for Jen's second wedding to Michel, our wonderful son-in-law, Kaia's new dad and the love of Jennifer's life.

Kaia sets the huge bouquet in front of her mom's gravestone and sits cross-legged on the ground above where Jen is buried. Rob and I wander off to give her a bit of privacy as she bows her head in prayer. I want to comfort her, but I don't know how. Later we will take her out for English tea and scones at the White Lion Tea House, a ritual we had performed with her mother after her cancer diagnosis. Can tea really make things better? —Jen thought it could.

Our granddaughter will stay at her mom's grave quietly praying for at least an hour. Kaia is remarkably well-adjusted and was recently awarded the "Principles Award for Student Leadership" at her grade eight graduation. She excels at school, in music, dance and sports, but more than any of these things she is a lovely, caring, and kind young woman, much like her mom.

These trips to the grave site conjure up memories of Jen's funeral and burial. Just days before her death, we had been driving in country. We came across a quaint, old Anglican Church, St. Georges, Fair Valley, on top of a hill, that was framed by huge sugar maple trees and farmers' fields with lowing black and white cows. "I want to be buried here," Jen told us.

None of us said much then, but our unexpressed fear was that being Bahai might preclude a burial in this beautiful, Anglican grave site. Our minister was open-minded and had connections with that particular church, so was able to get permission for the inclusion of a Bahai grave. At least Jen got that wish granted.

I think I was in shock after Jen's death. My memories are foggy. I remember that in the Bahai tradition the burial site had to be within an hour of where she lived. I remember, a few days before the burial and just after the death, an intimate family service was held. The casket was open, and we went, one at a time, into a small room at the funeral parlour to view the body. Somehow, I did not feel that Jen was there anymore. She had fled her earthly form and her spirit was flying free, far away from all of our grief.

I remember being worried for Kaia and Michel, whose job it was to wash the body and wrap it in a shroud of white cloth. After that the casket was closed. Prayers were said—Bahai prayers that seemed beautiful, gentle and soothing. Jen would have loved the service. Everyone was devastated—so many tears, sobbing.

Jen died on November 6th around 2 in the afternoon. I stayed with the body, in the hospital, while Michel and Rob went to Kaia's elementary school to give her the terrible news and to bring her to see her mother's body. The service in the funeral home took place two days later on November 8th.

The burial happened on November 11th, Remembrance Day: Our brothers, sisters, mother, Michel's relatives, a few very close friends came—an intimate gathering. We circled around the grave site and held hands as the casket

## Chapter Sixty-Five

was lowered into the ground. We prayed and threw flowers into the hole. Our lovely minister, Martha, took the service—not one of those rituals where the priest says all the wrong things and seems to have no idea of the deceased. Martha, in her gentle, caring way, made the day as bearable as it could be. Her words gave me some solace and echo still in my heart.

It was raining—a cold, nasty, windy day—that seemed to suit the occasion. I hate November. I hate the need for Remembrance Day. I thought of all the parents who had lost children in wartime, of all the children who were left behind without fathers or mothers, of all the women and men who lost their spouses during those awful years. I wondered how those families survived in those difficult times. I wondered how my family would survive.

# Chapter Sixty-Six
## The To-Do List (1973)

After we returned to Dar from Nairobi, Rob and I danced around each other, avoiding the conversation we needed to have. I felt he owed me an apology—he had just gutted my dream of living in paradise in Arusha and having our first baby. He was forcing me to go back to Canada. I was sullen, silent.

"For God's sake Julie, lighten up," Rob said to me as I skulked around our apartment in a black mood. "You've been like this for days. If you continue in this state, you're going to put a damper on any enjoyment we have left here. That's stupid. We should be planning trips—we both have time off coming up. Let's take advantage of that."

"I'm trying to understand why we have to go home," I shot back. "I just feel sad."

"I know," Rob answered. "And I'm sorry, but we've been through the reasons, and I'm not going to change my mind. Why don't we plan a trip to Zanzibar? That's been on our 'to-do list' since we got here. Maybe we can convince Gary and Fern (our house guests) to come along."

Was Rob thinking we might have a better time if we invited friends to distract his bitchy wife? I had to admit that his idea of a trip with friends was exciting. Maybe it was time to start to savour every minute of our remaining time in Africa. I clearly wasn't going to win this argument. "Okay, okay," I relented. "Sounds like a good idea."

Gary and Fern had been our guests for several weeks. Before they arrived at Beadle Hotel (our home) we'd never met them. They were a young couple from Toronto who were travelling throughout East Africa.

As their stay with us lengthened, it became clear that the four of us were kindred spirits. Gary had long, curly, red hair and a short, even redder, beard. He was slight, wiry, full of energy and willing to try just about anything. His crazy, donkey laugh was contagious.

Gary's wife, Ferny, had chocolate brown, Afro curls that spilled down around her shoulders, fair skin and green cat's eyes. With a winning smile and a sweet, sensitive personality, she was always ready to talk and to listen. The four of us would stay up late discussing the fate of the Africa.

Our guests were great to live with. Every night when we came home from work our dinner was prepared. Gary and Fern would shop in the morning and cook in the afternoon. All we had to do was mix *konyagi* (local gin) with tonic for the four of us, sit down at our dining room table, turn off the lights, light the candles and listen to Joni Mitchell. Somehow days lead to weeks, and we never got tired of our new friends. They also had bought an old Volkswagen Beetle, and were happy to travel with us.

Gary and Fern agreed that Zanzibar was a great idea—something they had on their to-do list. "We can drive to the airport in our car, leave it in the sheltered parking and take a flight from Dar to Zanzibar," Gary suggested.

With an adventure to look forward to my mood improved. When we got to the domestic airport there was a small, funny looking plane on the runway. With wings on top, it resembled a strange bug. "Oh God, that's the plane!" Ferny stammered. "Can we all fit? Are you sure it's safe?"

"Ya," Rob answered. "That's a Canadian-made Twin Otter. Those planes have a great safety record. They almost never fall out of the sky. Don't look so worried."

"Good to know," Gary laughed. "My first safe flight in Africa. This should be fun."

Fun it was not. The thing bumped and swayed. At one point it dropped down, leaving my stomach in the air, only to soar straight up into the blue several seconds later. It was like being on a roller coaster ride—a ride some of the people on board were not enjoying. Passengers were gasping and groaning.

When we reached Zanzibar, I was green. Thank God it was only a forty-minute ride. The smells of the port assaulted me—cloves, salt spray, and urine. I looked around frantically for a bathroom but, of course, there was nothing. I gagged but managed to hold it together.

"You look terrible," Ferny said, looking concerned, after we had landed. "You gonna be okay?" I stood on the hot, black tarmac trying desperately not to throw up. When I finally was well enough to look around, I was surprised to see that my three companions were completely relaxed and excited to have arrived in Zanzibar.

"Great flight eh. Told you it would be fun and safe," Rob shouted over the roar of the propellers, as the little plane revved up to return to Dar. We started to walk to the tiny airport terminal.

"Mam, sir," a young woman said stopping us. "Must cover, must cover."

"What's the problem?" Gary asked.

"Shoulders not allowed," she said looking at Fern and I, who were wearing sleeveless t-shirts. We rummaged around in our suitcases and found shawls to drape over our exposed limbs. We were then allowed to enter Zanzibar.

My first impression, after I started to feel better, was how close the ocean was to the town. The beach met the pavement and ocean spray filled the air. There were majestic, dignified dhows with their tall white sails and wooden, bathtub bottoms plying the Indian Ocean. People were dressed more conservatively here. Many women were completely covered in black abayas. Men had skull caps on their heads and long white gowns that reflected the sun. They looked far more comfortable in their chosen attire than the wives at their sides.

I hugged my shawl around my shoulders. People glared at us—no smiles. Clearly this place was far more conservative than my Dar home. The air smelled like fish and salt. We made our way to our hotel in Stone Town through a maze of narrow, winding passages, with children following us chanting "*wazungu, wazungu.*" (crazy white people).

The decaying, crumbling buildings still held a hint of their magnificent past—a mixture of colonial grandeur and Arabic, Swahili roots. "If only I had the money to restore these places. I can just imagine opening a B&B here," I said. Rob groaned.

We spent that evening at the night market on the waterfront. The sun dove into the blue, white tipped ocean, painting the sky with vibrant red, purple, pink and grey streaks. I found myself crying. "Please," I whimpered to Rob. "Do we need to leave this place? I want to stay in East Africa."

We were with friends and Rob, embarrassed by my emotional display, took my hands in his, looked me in the eyes and said, "Not now. We've discussed this already, and I'm sure we will again. Let it go."

I had no choice so I shut up. We ate shell fish at the street stalls, peeling the prawns and savouring cardamon flavoured rice. We drank Tusker beer until our brains were fuzzy. I would come back. I knew it. Africa was in my blood.

Our first stop next day was the old slave market which was now the site of the Anglican cathedral. We read on a plaque that Zanzibar was the centre of the East African slave and ivory trade in the 18th and 19th centuries when forty-five thousand slaves were shipped from Zanzibar to Brazil, India, and Arab countries. The only evidence of the island's horrific past was one dark, dingy chamber, about the size of a one car garage, where slaves, awaiting auction, had been kept for months at a time. Many did not survive their ordeal. The ones that didn't die were sold, shipped into servitude, far away, to strange lands, having lost their families, friends, and homes.

Rusty shackles and chains were still attached to the stone walls, a testament to human suffering, a harrowing reminder of a not-so-distant past. The ghosts of Zanzibar left me longing for my home in Dar. As beautiful as this island was, I had no desire to live here—too conservative, too reminiscent of a past that left me with a burden of guilt.

The next stop on our tour was the *Maruhubi* Palace about four kilometres north of Zanzibar town. Built in 1882 for Sultan Barghash, it had housed one hundred women, one wife and ninety-nine concubines (official mistresses). Ghosts of those former beautiful ladies (that was what he would have chosen) called out to me. It was eerie. I imagined vying for the formidable sultan's time, befriending the rest of the harem and bathing in bath houses—parts of which could still be seen. Much of the building had been destroyed by a fire in 1899, but giant pillars and ponds with water lilies still remained.

I wondered what the lives of the woman in the harem would have been like? They were sequestered in small, individual rooms. Despite the lack of freedom, I suspect that they found some luxury and enjoyment in everyday living, unlike their neighbours, the slaves. Did they laugh? Did they dance? Were they jealous of one another? Did they spend hours preening and making up their faces, doing their hair to attract the great one's attention, or were they sullen and resentful of the power he held over them?

And then there were the ghosts of long ago, now extinct, island elephants. Once, Zanzibar had an abundant elephant population and the brass spikes on the ebony doors to ward off the giant beasts still exist to this day. The Zanzibari doors, ornately carved, individual art works with arched tops and floral designs reflected passages from the Qua-ran—fish (representing the wish for many children), date trees (representing abundance and blessings) and lotus flowers (representing regeneration, youth, and beauty). A remarkable number of these doors still remained—at least 600.

Slaves, concubines, elephants were all still there in my imagination. Mingled with the scent of cloves, cinnamon, allspice—such exotic, intoxicating fragrances—was the feeling of danger, repression, and sorrow. Although I wanted to stay in Tanzania, this island was not for me. Here I felt limited, restricted, a bit afraid. I was fascinated, charmed, intrigued, but ready to go back home to my mainland home.

We headed to the airport on Sunday afternoon for the return trip. When we arrived with our tickets firmly clasped in our hands, we were told calmly that we'd been bumped from the flight because four local politicians wanted to get on our plane. They clearly were more important than us, so we would have to wait, but not to worry, we would be allowed to leave the next day.

"Hey," Rob said spluttering. "You can't do that. We booked our tickets weeks ago. We have jobs that we have to get back to. People are counting on us. I work for the prime minister's office." Rob whipped out his identity card.

"Oh," said the powers that be. "In that case we will see what we can do." It took some time, but the same official came back and said, pointing to Rob and me, "You can board but your friends (pointing to Gary and Fern) will have to wait till tomorrow."

Gary and Fern were happy to stay another day, so it was settled. When we got on the plane it was half empty. I still wonder what was going on that day so long ago. The feeling of ghosts, corruption, unlimited power, and mystery lingered.

Maybe it was better that we were going back to Canada to study, mature and figure things out. Did I really feel comfortable enough to have a baby in this far away land? Had I become complacent in believing that I belonged in East Africa?

# Chapter Sixty-Seven
## Refugees (2016)

Sitting in my Orillia home I'm feeling particularly sorry for myself today. It's November again, three years since our eldest daughter died. The sun hasn't shone in weeks. The greyness has permeated my soul. I feel utterly dejected—lost. At the same time, I'm aware that I need to move on. It's not like we're the only ones who have experienced loss.

Ironic that Jen was buried on November 11th, Remembrance Day. I'm compelled to focus not just on my own grief. I think about the First and Second World Wars. I think about Nazi Germany and the camps. Whole families just gone—no one even to remember them. I've spent most of my life in the Third World—so many babies don't survive their first year. I've been a witness to that. I know my grief is not unique. I feel ashamed. I feel like I should get on with my life, honour my child but also live for her. Make her proud.

My telephone rings. It's early, just before seven—probably another stupid telemarketer. I answer the phone abruptly, ready to hang up. "What do you want?" I say too loudly into the mouthpiece. Rude.

"Julie, I hope I didn't wake you. It's Sriwan. I need to talk."

"Oh God Sriwan, I thought you were a telemarketer. I didn't mean to sound so abrupt. How are you? What time is it in Paris?"

I hear a muffled sob on the other end of the line. "What's happened?" I ask. The terrorist attacks in Paris occurred mere days ago and, of course, my friend is in the middle of the whole thing. I have checked via email to see

## Chapter Sixty-Seven

that Sriwan and her family are safe, but I can't imagine the psychological impact that she must be experiencing. Her 23-year-old son could have been at the concert where many of those lives were lost. He wasn't there, but still ...

"What is happening to the world? All those innocent people," Sriwan says over the phone. "Paris has been brought to its knees. Paris! Unbelievable. So evil, so unfair. I just don't understand."

I don't know what to say. I hear my friend crying on the other end of the phone line and there is nothing I can do to help. In all the many years of knowing her I have never heard Sriwan cry. Her stoic, Thai ways lend themselves to a quiet strength, a steely, self-possessed shyness and a warmth of being that embraces anyone in her presence. I've only seen her in the role of comforter, and now she needs comforting, and I am not there. Half a world away, I'm still mourning the loss of my daughter and have little time for the grief of my friend. I am trying to find words, any words that will help her.

Before I can say anything Sriwan starts to talk. "We waited a year to see our son," she says. "He'd only been here two days when the attacks happened. He could've been at that concert Julie. He loves that band, but he was still jet-lagged, so he didn't go. Thank God! But the Marine Corps in the States called him back to work immediately, so he left yesterday."

"I'm so sorry," I say stupidly. "Are you okay?"

"It's not just that. We just got back from Lesbos in Greece. We were worried about vacationing there because of all their problems, but our friends really wanted us to come, so we decided to go for two weeks. We were having a wonderful time with two friends from our Peace Corps days. The sun was shining the whole time. The weather was perfect, and the ocean was almost as

## Chapter Sixty-Seven

beautiful as it is in Thailand. We were eating cold seafood and drinking chilled white wine under an umbrella on a sand beach when it happened."

As she talks, I can picture my friend in her Paris apartment. She's one of the most beautiful people I know, both physically and mentally. Mark, her wonderful, American husband calls her, *Dukda*, which in Thai means little doll. Sriwan is tiny, exquisite, like an exotic orchard. Even though she's at least fifty, she still turns heads in a city of lovely women.

"So far your trip to Greece sounds wonderful. Must have helped you to not miss Thailand so much," I say across the distance from Canada to Paris.

"It was perfect at first—until six rubber dinghies, each holding about thirty refugees, swept up on our beach. The tide was coming in and the waves crashing on the shore were tipping the boats over. There were children, babies, old people and a few pregnant women. The water was washing over everyone. I was afraid that some of them wouldn't make it."

I am clenching my fists so hard that my hands go numb. I want to reach across the miles and hug my friend, teleport myself to her apartment. "Oh God, Sriwan. How horrible. You must have felt so helpless."

"We left our lunch and waded into the water to help out but there were so many desperate people. We had no blankets, no warm, dry clothes—nothing to give them after they got out of the water. They were all shivering and in terrible shape. Some of the elderly could no longer stand up. We did what we could, but it just wasn't enough. I'm not even sure they all survived."

"What happened next?" I ask horrified, clutching the phone.

## Chapter Sixty-Seven

"The boats were abandoned, and the people just started to walk the 75 kilometres to the nearest processing centre. Mark says none of them want to stay in Greece. They are on their way to other parts of Europe to settle, but few countries will let them in. So tragic. After we'd done what we could, which wasn't much, we went back to our hotel."

"Oh Sriwan, how awful," I tell my friend as the winter sun rises sending rays of light into our front picture window.

"It gets worse," Sriwan tells me. "As we were heading to the airport to go home the next day there was a line of refugees, as far as the eye could see, along the route we were taking. About ten minutes into our trip, we saw a cripple crawling along the road. Our host, the driver of the car, asked if we minded giving the poor, old man a ride. We stopped to help the guy into the car. I moved to the front because Mark was afraid the man would be uncomfortable sitting beside a woman."

"The old man, with a younger male companion to help him, got into the back. I rolled down the front window to get some air and a woman in a burka pushed her little girl through the window and ran away. The little one was crying her eyes out. I tried to comfort the child, but she was inconsolable."

"Oh my God, Sriwan. She gave you her baby?"

"Not a baby. I think the child was about three. The men in the back seat of the van were pointing at the child and trying to tell us something. I like to think they were related to the little girl and would make sure she got back to her mother. I'll never really know. Who gives their child to a foreign stranger? That mom must have been so desperate."

"Probably the child wasn't big enough to walk 75 kilometres, but was too big to carry. The mother didn't

*360*

## Chapter Sixty-Seven

really have any choice," I answer, fighting my own tears and wondering how on earth to console my friend. There really are no words, nothing I can do to make the world a kinder place.

Sriwan interrupts my thoughts, "When we got to the refugee reception centre, we let our passengers out. That little child clung to me and screamed the whole time. I had to pry her off. I had no choice but to leave her there. No one would let her get on the plane with us. Mark had to get back for the 'Climate Change Summit' in Paris. You know how involved he is in that. All those world leaders and so much responsibility for him. I hated leaving without knowing what was going to happen."

"Sriwan, I wish there were something I could say to help but we both know there isn't. I hate that you had to live through that. I wish I was with you now, in Paris. Let's just hope the child will be reunited with her mother."

After I hang up the phone, I sit in my living room and realize, despite my terrible loss, I am still one of the lucky ones—lucky to have been born in Canada and lucky to have had four beautiful children who grew up without hunger or fear. My daughter died at 37, but up until that time she lived a full and wonderful life. Not everyone gets that privilege.

# Chapter Sixty-Eight
## A New Song (2016)

I am at my Orillia church in my usual spot, singing in the choir, front row beside my friend Anna. Somehow today is different. I feel my body relaxing, and I can breathe normally. My usual constricted throat, the inevitable descent into tears, is not happening. The words of the bible readings resonate with me and the hymns transport my soul to another level of being—a meditative state.

"Be not afraid, my love is stronger than your fear. Be not afraid for I promise to be always near." Could the words of the hymn we are singing be true? I do feel the presence of something bigger, stronger, more all-knowing around me.

Most of the time I can't hear my daughter. I can see her picture always in my mind's eye. I would like to be sure that her spirit lives on, and today I can almost believe that Jen is near me. There is one thing about Jennifer that I can no longer deny. She would want us to live our lives without anger and grief. She had such courage and faith and I know I have failed to follow her example.

The universe and I have been discordant until this moment. Since Jen died, I have not been singing my life in tune. Anger and grief have prevented me from understanding that there is beauty all around me. There have been some brief exceptions to my refusal to live in peace with myself. I have continued to find joy in my grandchildren—nothing can get in the way of that feeling.

The other day five-year-old Ben was at our home. He found Jen's old drums and began to play, totally in rhythm, with the reggae music on the stereo. He has his Aunty Jen's spirit for sure. Then there is my little

## Chapter Sixty-Eight

pterodactyl, shrieking grandson Max who, at two, is so active and full of mischief that it takes every ounce of my energy to be in the same room with him. No sadness there.

Jenny's daughter Kaia, at 14, is so much like her mom at the same age. She is kind, caring, smart, slim, athletic and empathetic. Wise beyond her years, Rob and I often refer to her as 13 going on 30. She excels in everything she does and is a remarkable young woman.

I still can't help catching my breath and feeling such sadness when I confront the fact that Jen will never see her Kaia graduate, or get married. She will never meet her own grandchildren. Jen worked so hard as a mother to create the kind of person that Kaia is ending up to be, and yet she will never enjoy the results of her labour. It feels so unfair.

I still can't feel Jen's presence, although I am trying, Instead I'm aware of a gentle goodness, a soft, bird feather quality in the air around me, a warm acceptance that has not been available to me since my daughter passed.

The anger that I have felt for these last three years is beginning to dissipate. There is still the knowing that life will never be the same. There is still the sad thought that Jenny should have had a much longer life.

However, for the first time I am focussed on what my daughter would want for us. She would want us to be happy, to do our best to make the world a better place, to love our family as she loved them, and to make sure that everyone is okay, especially her daughter, Kaia, and her husband Michel.

Grief has stripped me of the ability to assess the needs of those I love. It's time to get on board again and start to live—time to give back and help others.

I am trying to believe that Jen is here in spirit. Doesn't say much for my faith, does it? I continue to pray for the

*Chapter Sixty-Eight*

safety and well-being of my family, although I'm not sure it will do any good. The truth is that Jen believed in the power of prayer, and it didn't help her—or did it? Is she really in a better place—looking down on us?

# Chapter Sixty-Nine
## Lent—40 Days in the Wilderness (2016)

I'm not sure when I finally get that Rob and I are going to make it as a couple—probably at our first Florida State Park during our 40 days of Lent in the wilderness, camping in a tent. All of our friends think we're crazy. This is reminiscent of the opinions of others when we decided to go to Tanzania. "A tent—you're sleeping in a tent?" is the most common refrain. "Come visit us instead. We have a comfortable bed. You're too old for this kind of nonsense." Our shared, bloody-minded, stubborn intent to embark on this adventure feels good to both of us.

Our three adult kids, who know us better, aren't surprised or particularly impressed—just their mom and dad going on another life defining, or is it life defying, journey. "Is this some kind of religious thing? Cause it's Lent," my son, Dan, asks. "Hope you don't suffer too much out there. Seriously though, be careful—take turns driving and stop if you get tired."

Ironically, Rob and I haven't planned our journey to coincide with the religious celebration 40 days before Easter—although I doubt anyone who knows us believes it was a coincidence. They joke that it's a bit extreme to give up our bed for Lent. Couldn't we give up chocolate or alcohol—something a bit less dramatic?

The truth is that we are sick and tired of winter and a plane trip is out of the question because we have a 14-year-old golden-retriever, Griff, who has to come with us. We would leave him in a kennel but the last time we tried he bit the owner and went on a hunger strike—lost 10 - pounds. We're also on a budget, and we want to be out of

## Chapter Sixty-Nine

winter for as long as possible, so Florida and tenting seems a logical option.

We arrive in Alafia State Park in central Florida late, at 5:45 pm. The light is rapidly fading as we throw up our tent, drag our travel-weary bodies around our site and manage to get our blow-up mattress, bedding, and lights organized by the time darkness falls. Our cheater fire log (there is a limit to this roughing it in the bush thing) starts immediately, and we add the wood we bought at the park gate.

"Think this calls for a celebration," Rob says as he pours us both a glass of champagne. We sit back on our comfy, camp chairs, listen to the frog orchestra and relax. It's cold—much colder than we had expected—so we get our winter coats and toques out of the van. The air is sweet and fresh, the moon is full, life is good, and we are happy, happier than we have been for a very long time.

It is so bright outside that after our champagne we decide to take a stroll with Griff. We turn off the flashlight and wander past the toilet complex and out onto a secluded path that runs alongside the forest. Our shadows loom in front of us. It is utterly and eerily silent. "Oh nature," Rob says. "Glad we're doing this?"

"I am, but maybe we should go back now. We've walked a long way, and we don't have a cell phone. What if we get into trouble?" I answer.

"Relax hon," Rob tells me. "This isn't as secluded as it feels." Rob and Griff walk ahead, taking the lead. We're striding along at a rapid pace when Rob stops abruptly, directly in front of me. I crash into him.

"Ouch! Why'd you do that?"

"Didn't you see that?" he whispers, frozen in front of me. I look at my dog and notice that the hair on the back of his neck is standing straight up. Griff hasn't barked

## Chapter Sixty-Nine

though, or made one sound. He stands frozen on the path, sidled up to Rob.

"I saw an animal just ahead of us. It looked like a big cat, about the size of our retriever."

"Okay, dude. I'm out of here." I turn and head back to our campsite. Now I'm in the lead and moving fast. Rob raises no objections. We practically run home.

"Probably just an innocent deer," Rob reassures me.

When we return to the campsite it's dark but still only nine o'clock, too early to go to sleep. We go into the tent, turn on the light and hunker down into our zipped-together sleeping bags. We read until we're tired, and then huddle together for warmth. It's freaking freezing! We haven't slept wound around one another like this since we shared a single bed at university. I feel connected to Rob. My anger and resentment melt away. This person I am glued to tonight is my partner of a lifetime, and I love him.

I realize that one of my problems has been that Rob reminds me of my daughter, Jen, so much that it hurts. The lateness, the desire to save people and animals, the sensitivity to everyone and everything in the world, the constant need to reach out to others, the sweaty palms when disaster strikes, the anxiety, even the smile and the dimples—it's all there.

But now, instead of rejecting Rob, I embrace him. I have said before that it doesn't matter what happens to us —wrong. I can't lose my best friend, the person I've loved for as long as I can remember. I'm not mad at him anymore. I'm no longer mad at myself either. We did our best. Jen was a wonderful person She lived fully and contributed more in her short time on earth than most people manage in a long lifetime. It's not our fault that she got cancer and died too young. My guilt and anger are gradually melting.

## Chapter Sixty-Nine

I can finally acknowledge that it's not God's fault either. I imagine that the powers that be are frustrated by cancer too. In retrospect, I doubt that a divine presence has any more ability to prevent disease or disaster than I do. History has taught us that.

Next morning the very young park ranger—good-looking, informative—pulls up to our site for a chat. Rob is off to the washroom complex to shave and have a hot shower, so I'm alone. "Have you any questions?" he asks politely.

"Ya, I do. We walked last night and saw an animal, brown, cat-like, about the size of our dog. Any idea what that might have been?"

"Well, my best guess is a Florida panther. We've had a few sightings in the last week. You're lucky to have seen one. We go for years without spotting them."

"A panther," I gasp, astonished. "Here!"

"Sure thing. This park adjoins to two others—miles of wilderness. Don't worry though. Panthers are way more afraid of you than you are of them."

Highly unlikely, I think, but I just nod stupidly in agreement.

"The feral pigs, now, they're really dangerous, but they almost never enter the campsite area. Just make sure you lock up all of your food. There are also plenty of deer here. They're harmless. Maybe that's what you saw."

I vow to be careful with our garbage and food— very careful!

# Chapter Seventy

## Halfway to Heaven (2017)

Grief is a kind of insanity. One minute the very thought of my daughter brings me to my knees. The next I want to jump up, dance about, proclaim what a wonderful girl (woman) she was. I want to tell the world my story as it relates to Jenny. I need to celebrate her life and get over my spirit death. I want others to walk this path of loss with me. To learn. Maybe I can help. Sharing my heartache is difficult, but it also makes me feel that I'm not alone.

I'm at our cottage on Christian Island, Beausoleil First Nation. It is now slightly over four years since we discovered that Jen was dying—June 21st National Aboriginal Day. We go into the village to see the celebrations. There are native dancers, a bouncy castle for the kids, fresh fried white fish and french fries for lunch. Native arts and crafts are for sale. I buy a pair of deer skin moccasins embroidered with yellow beaded flowers.

I miss my daughter so much today that I feel slightly ill. It was probably a mistake to come here where everyone is happy. I can see Jen on this day during that last year of her life, only months before she died. She's laughing, joining in on all the ceremonies, dancing, drumming, listening with rapt attention to the native storytellers. She loved this island and called it her soul's home.

So many of my most poignant memories of Jen as an adult are here. I can see her swimming like a fish in the cold, clear waters of Georgian Bay, or making sand castles in the dunes with her young daughter Kaia. She loved the storms that rolled in over Big Sand Bay and would stand out in the rain and wind to watch them. When Jennifer was married, instead of giving out pieces of cake, she

## Chapter Seventy

gave everyone little white pine saplings in baggies. Her brother Dan planted dozens of the trees on our island property. Only five have survived, but they are now finally about a foot and a half tall.

Jen believed that she was part native. Her dad, Rob, was adopted at birth in Timmins. The family saga maintained that he was Metis, adopted by parents of British heritage. The last name on Rob's birth certificate (Cadeau) was the Metis spelling and strongly suggested a native heritage.

People would randomly stop Jen, not only on the reserve, but also in Ottawa and ask her if she were Nish (Anishinaabe). Given that she had blue eyes and fair skin I never understood their questions. But this thrilled her. She wanted desperately to be part of a native heritage. She begged her dad to find out about his birth family.

Rob resisted. I saw his point. He loved his adoptive parents and didn't want to do anything that would hurt them. He also was not interested in finding a mother, native or not, who had left him as a newborn. Also, Rob does not look native, nor do any of our children. They are fair skinned and have blue-green eyes. I never understood Jen's notion that she had native roots. Nothing could deter her in that belief.

In fairness to Jen, there must have been something in her demeanour that made complete strangers call her Nish. Perhaps it was her love of nature or her ability to drum and dance with the best of them—perhaps it was Jen's disregard for material possessions or for time. Who knows? Maybe it was her uncanny psychic ability.

The fact that she seemed to be able to see the future made me crazy. "Mom, Dad," she proclaimed in 1997. "You guys are going to live in Paris. I dreamt it."

## Chapter Seventy

"Oh God, please stop! That is absolute nonsense." I remember answering. "Your dad is with CIDA (Canadian International Development Agency). The only postings he'll be getting are to the Third World. Why on earth would he go to Paris?—so not happening."

"You're wrong. You're going. You'll see." Jen persisted.

We did see. About a year later Rob was in Ottawa doing a job he hated. It didn't look like he was going to escape it any time soon, so he applied to the World Bank in Washington, the African Development Bank in Tunis and the Organization for Economic Development (OECD) in Paris. The Paris job was offered first, so as of April 1st, 1998, my husband took a leave of absence from CIDA and immediately set about finding a funky, Paris apartment in the 6th arrondissement. I followed him in September with our two youngest children. We spent the next two years there. Jen was right!

There was another time when Jen reached across time and space—while we were continents removed—to feel the pain of her sibling. Our youngest son Andrew and Jen always had a special bond. She was sixteen when he was born, and a second mother to him. "Mom," Jenny screamed across the phone line from Ottawa (where she was a student) to Manila (where we were posted). "What's wrong with Andrew? I know something terrible has happened."

Although I had picked up the telephone, I wasn't able to answer my daughter. I handed the phone to my husband standing beside me. I was too busy stemming the flow of blood from baby Andrew's almost severed finger.

"Jen," Rob said into the phone. "We're on the way to the hospital. Andrew got his finger slammed in the bedroom door. He's badly cut. It doesn't look good, but

## Chapter Seventy

we'll call you as soon as we can. We're hoping they can save his finger."

That story, thank God, ended well. The doctor was able to perform a miracle. Andrew was left with a scar but has the full use of his hand.

"How did Jen know that Andrew was hurt? That girl is not of this earth," Rob said.

"Halfway to heaven," I jokingly proclaimed.

There were so many other instances when Jen foretold the future. After a time, we all just got used to her ability. We learned to listen to her predictions and act accordingly. She always maintained that it was her native heritage that gave her that superpower.

After our daughter's death, Rob, worried about the health of our other kids, got genetic testing. He wanted to know if he was a carrier for any particular types of cancer or other serious diseases. He got a clean bill of health. The lung cancer that Jen had is not hereditary.

In an ironic twist of fate, that same testing revealed his ancestry. Rob is British, French, Irish with a touch of Scandinavian thrown in, and has no Native blood. My ancestry is British—we've always known that. I'm so glad that Jen did not learn this before she died. She would have been so disappointed not to have had Native heritage.

# Chapter Seventy-One
## Saying Goodbye (1973)

Head up, chin forward—stride on. We were going home. I had to make plans and get prepared—no choice. Goodbye, Africa. Hello Canada. Visions of sparkling snowflakes and jumping, orange flames from a cozy fireplace danced through my brain. I dreamed about crisp, red Mackintosh apples, hot dogs and real Canadian bacon with maple syrup on waffles.

No more nagging and pleading. Too late. Both of us had been accepted to Queen's University in Kingston – Rob to do his MBA and me to do my Bachelors of Education. Our motorcycle trip across Europe, from England to Russia and back, was to be our next big adventure.

As to a baby—that could still happen. My womb ached to reproduce. I stalked babies, begging to hold them and babbling sweet whispers into their fat, adorable faces as I took in their milky, baby powder scent. "Hon," I said one night as I wound my arms around Rob's neck, "We've been married for almost four years now. Shouldn't we be trying for a baby?"

Rob pulled away from my embrace and looked dismayed. "If you get pregnant, we couldn't go to school. I'd end up in some dead-end job, and you might never work again. Forget your plans to go back to Africa. Think —car salesman in Toronto for me. God only knows what you'd do. That's not my dream. When you're being reasonable, it's not yours either. We're not ready for kids —no way, not yet. I do want kids, just not now."

Rob and I began to distance ourselves from our friends and our home in Africa. There were tears, and promises.

## Chapter Seventy-One

There were goodbye parties and late-night conversations about staying in touch, but friends were moving on and preparing for us to be gone. We were the deserters.

I went to the Bank of Tanzania to take out my savings in travellers' cheques. The teller looked at me in disbelief, "You can't just take this money," he said, squaring his shoulders and standing taller.

"Why not? I'm leaving the country soon," I explained.

"You need permission from your husband. He has to sign for the money."

My face blazed red. Sweat beaded on my forehead. I took a deep breath. "What! You're kidding, right?"

"No ma'am. Sorry. Come back with your husband and I'd be happy to help you."

That was it. Done. Pissed off. Finished. Why was the world such an unfair place? I left the bank fuming and headed home. I wasn't going to get anywhere with reason or argument. I needed Rob's signature. It seemed I needed Rob's okay for everything I wanted. This wasn't just about my bank account.

Rob met me at the door. "What's up?" he asked surveying my body language. He looked worried.

"It seems I need your signature to get my money."

"Sorry. That's awful. Things will be better in Canada. Women have way more rights there."

The day of our departure arrived. We'd left everything to the last minute. The apartment was full of our stuff. Nothing was packed except our suitcases containing only what we needed for our trip through Europe. Books, papers, dishes, extra clothes, food in the fridge—all still there.

Our plane wasn't leaving until just after 11 at night, but we had been invited to go to Lucille's for a quick dinner,

## Chapter Seventy-One

so there wasn't much time left. We slept in and rolled out of bed about ten that morning. "Rob, what are we gonna do? We're not ready to leave," I said, stating the obvious. "Maybe we'll have to postpone our trip."

"There's plenty of time. No worries."

I laughed. "You sound like an Aussie. No worries. Please worry—we need to get this done."

"I have to go and get the electricity cut off. Gotta run," Rob said, grabbing his helmet.

"You're kidding. You haven't organized that yet?"

"Won't take long. You worry too much." Rob slammed the door and headed out. I looked around in dismay and started to put things in boxes. I had to start somewhere.

Two hours later, at 12 o'clock Rob came sashaying through the front door. "Meet Ahmed. He's from Tanesco (Tanzanian Electrical Supply Company). Sorry I took so long. I stood for hours in line to get a technician then brought him here on the back of the bike. Apparently, Ahmed has to read our meter and then cut off the power supply. After that I have to go back to the office again and pay. Once I finish there, I'll go to Internal Revenue and get my tax clearance," Rob explained.

"Nice to meet you, Ahmed." Rob was lucky we had company, because had we been alone, I would have had a meltdown. Had he not thought about all these pre-departure procedures? What a joke. There was no way on earth that we were going to finish and get on a plane. Impossible!

Rob eventually returned home around five with all the paper work completed. It was amazing that he'd managed what he had to do in such a short time. "Okay," Rob said. "Let's get packing."

## Chapter Seventy-One

"Have you forgotten that we're going to Lucille's for an early dinner? We'll be on time at least. She said around five."

"No way. We need to pack."

"We have to go—too late to cop out now. She'll have everything prepared."

"I hate going there. You know that. Can't believe you got us into this again."

"I promised and you agreed. It won't take long, and we won't have to prepare dinner. That'll save time."

When we got to Lucille's there was a giant tree spider, a foot across, sitting just above the door-frame, busily spinning its web. "God, I hate spiders. Is this some kind of bad omen? Lucille's place gives me the creeps so let's hurry up and get this over with," Rob said as he knocked on the door.

Lucille had spread out a buffet of cold chicken, bread rolls and salads. As a special treat she'd produced a huge box of Laura Secord chocolates to celebrate our last evening in Dar. I hugged her and felt tears welling up. Don't cry, don't cry, I thought. Despite my attempts at restraint, I found myself sobbing in her arms. Damn it!

"Stop that," Lucille begged. "We'll see each other again. I promise to come to Canada for a visit."

"Where on earth did you get those chocolates?" Rob asked. "Haven't seen anything like that locally."

"One of the ladies I work with brought them back from Canada for me. I wanted to save them for a special occasion and this certainly qualifies. I'm gonna really miss you guys."

"Sadly, we don't have much time," Rob said after a quick dinner. We still have to clean up the apartment and organize some things. Hate to eat and run, but no choice,"

## Chapter Seventy-One

Rob stood and popped a cherry filled dark chocolate ball into his mouth. "Yum, delicious! Thanks for inviting us."

"At least sit down for another five minutes and have a cup of coffee," Lucille pleaded. We did as we were told, and I was busy talking to my friend when I realized that Rob was uncharacteristically quiet. I turned to look at him and almost threw up on the spot. Oh God, please no! Not again! My stomach did another flip-flop before I could speak.

"Rob! There were nuts in those chocolates, weren't there? Your lips are already swelling, and your face is as red as a beet. Oh God, you are having trouble getting your breath.

"Still breathing—but definitely a nut. Sorry Lucille—off to the hospital—not your fault. Should've known better." I hugged Lucille and ran for our motorcycle. We headed straight for the Aga Khan Hospital.

The attack was not the worst Rob had experienced over the years, so he was still conscious when we got to emerge. The doctors already knew him, so he was admitted immediately. Within minutes, he was hooked up to an Adrenalin drip and the swelling around his face had shrunk. "I have to leave now," Rob told his attending physician when his condition had almost returned to normal.

"We have to keep you under observation for at least four hours," the doctor answered.

Rob explained that we needed to catch a plane by 11:00 PM. I suspect that in most countries we would have been out of luck, but the doctor understood our predicament and let us go. By the time we roared back home it was eight o'clock. We had a half hour to get ready for the

## Chapter Seventy-One

CUSO director who would take over our motorcycle and drive us to the airport.

"Now what do we do?" I asked. "No way we're gonna finish. No time and we have hours of work left to pack all our stuff and clean the apartment."

"All the big stuff is done. Motorcycle's sold. Tickets bought. Ride to the airport organized. All the paper work is complete, so they'll let us out of the country. It makes life easier in the long run. We won't have to arrange to ship anything back to Canada by sea. Juma will be happy —all that stuff—I'm sure they'll be able to put it to good use."

"But Rob. All our books and papers, our dishes, our art work."

"Sorry love. We shouldn't have gone to Lucille's."

A car honked outside. We grabbed our suitcases, carefully checked for passports, tickets, travellers' checks and headed out. As we drove down Ocean Drive, I still found it difficult to believe that we were leaving. Would we ever return? My eyes caressed the ocean at low tide; the mud flats offshore—their shiny backs exposed to the full moon, the white swirl of the waves as they rolled in and out, the tall, straight palms swaying on the beach.

"Look at that view. Reminds me of Van Gogh's 'Starry Night.' Do the stars look the same in Canada?" I asked.

"Nope, they're reversed. Still beautiful though," Rob answered.

To my right, across a low wall of entwined bougainvillea—red, pink, yellow, mauve, white flowers—lay the modest, presidential palace illuminated by spotlights. I wondered what my students, Obote's child and nephew, Jack and John, were doing. I pictured them in bed in Nyerere's guest wing where they'd been living since

## Chapter Seventy-One

fleeing Idi Amin's reign of terror in Uganda. I hoped that they would go on to be good people, leaders who did not torture, intimidate or kill to rule others. I hoped that the infamous dictator, Idi Amin, still in power in Uganda, would not silence them before they could help their country.

We continued along Ocean Drive past the fish market with its wooden huts and stinky smells. "Won't miss that," Rob said holding his nose. After the scent shifted to wood smoke mixed with night blooming jasmine, I closed my eyes and tried to imagine arriving home, finding somewhere to live, studying at Queen's and driving to the cottage for weekends—so different from the life I'd lead for the past two years.

"Look," said Rob. "There's the Tanzania Library Service Apartment where Ruth lives. Remember our moon gazing parties on the roof?"

"Sure do. Such fun, eh," I answered, looking closely at Rob to check if he was completely better after his nut-attack. His face had returned to a healthy colour and his lips had shrunk back to their normal size. "Thank God you're okay. Kinda puts things into perspective, doesn't it? How am I supposed to stay mad at you for making us leave when you persist in almost dying? Not fair."

Rob grinned sheepishly and squeezed my hand as we drove past the Kinondoni ferry, the ferry that had taken us to a pristine beach to go snorkelling and beachcombing during our first weeks in Dar. I imagined the feel of the sand and the salt water on my skin. I could still see the rainbow of fish that dwelt beneath the waves.

"Penny for your thoughts," Rob said, looking closely at me. "You're not still mad, are you?"

## Chapter Seventy-One

"Not so much mad as disappointed. I'd painted a picture of this idyllic life, with a baby, living in the garden of Eden. Bit stupid, I guess, but there it is. I'm going to miss this place."

Rob draped his arm protectively around my shoulder. "We will have babies. We'll come back."

We turned up Independence Avenue past the Askari (soldier) monument, past the *Twiga* (giraffe) Hotel where we'd spent our first night in Dar, and finally past the CUSO office and *Mnazi Moja* (one palm tree) round about.

On Airport Road *dukas* (little roadside stores run by Asians), with their open fronts and swinging gas lanterns, stood out against the backdrop of the black jungle behind them. Through the openings I could see Sony tape recorders, Panasonic radios and colourful *urafiki* (friendship) textiles. Those *dukas* sold everything from cereal to nails and in between. I wondered if the shopkeepers would have to flee the country if the anti-Ismaili sentiment continued to grow. Please, dear God—do not let this country I love, turn into the nightmare that is Uganda.

The heat was melting us in the non-air-conditioned car. I didn't care. The sweat pouring from my body made me feel alive. Too soon the snow of winter, the cold wind, and ice on my doorstep would be my reality. As we moved away from the city the sound of drums beating entered the car. The darkness deepened.

At the airport nothing had changed. As we walked across the pavement, I noticed the same weeds poking through giant cracks in the tarmac. The smells of jet fuel, body odour and heat filled the air. The kaleidoscope of brightly coloured kitenge cloth, worn by Tanzanian

## Chapter Seventy-One

women, swirled and swished as we entered the departure area. People stared at us, the only whites around.

But the change in Rob and me was immeasurable—not obvious, but life altering. This magical continent had forced us to become adults in a mere two years—adults with a different world view. We had received so much, made so many errors and had given back so little.

"You know," I said to Rob after we were settled in our seats on the airplane, "For the record—you're right. I believe that when we come back to Africa, we'll have actual skills to share. We have so much to learn. This is the right step. Just promise me that we'll return someday."

"We will. I promise," Rob answered.

# Chapter Seventy-Two
## 'I Will Make Beauty of This' (2023)

I am sitting in my living room looking out my bay window at the Jennifer tree. I remember planting the tree in the spring, when we learned that our daughter was ill. "Get a red maple," she advised. "They're great because in the fall they're so colourful, so full of life—brilliant red."

You never know when disaster will strike. You could be sleeping in your bed or making breakfast in your cozy kitchen, or, in our case, on a long-anticipated holiday to our former posting in the ancient kingdom of Ethiopia. Misfortune lurks; it creeps; it waits, and then when you least expect it, disaster strikes. Our family disaster came in the form of Adina Carcinoma, a type of lung cancer.

Jenny had been coughing, just a dry persistent cough, but it had gone on for almost a year. We had begged her to get medical attention, but she was too busy finishing her Bachelor of Education. My husband and I left on our trip to Ethiopia in the last days of Jen's studies in early March.

Soon after our departure our daughter began to cough up blood, and went immediately to our local hospital. Tests confirmed that she had massive tumours on both her lungs.

By the time we managed to fly home, the verdict was in. The doctors gave Jen seven to nine months without treatment and twelve to fifteen months with chemo and radiation. Had she been abducted by aliens or died in a road accident, we would have been less surprised. Her thyroid had been removed years before, so that her struggles with Grave's was a thing of the past. She was, to our knowledge, a completely healthy, athletic, slim, young woman who radiated fitness and good habits. No alcohol, drugs, or smoking for her.

## Chapter Seventy-two

Initially all of us, including Jen, were in denial. She would beat the odds. She was too healthy and young to succumb to the prognosis. She would be the exception.

Jenny, despite trying everything including chemo, radiation, acupuncture and massive doses of vitamin C, made it from late March to early November before she died of an aneurysm resulting from a secondary tumour in her brain. Her death was painless and sudden. The day before she passed, she was still riding her bicycle, stunning in her perky, after-chemo wig. No one would have ever guessed how ill she was.

Now years later, on November 11th, Remembrance Day, the Jennifer tree is stripped of leaves. It stands shivering in the wind and the cold, looking entirely sad and dead. But I know, come next spring, it will bloom again. This tree gives me hope. Nothing ever really ends. The miracle of life goes on.

I have learned in my journey that grief is unpredictable. I used to believe that I would progress linearly through all the stages of grief until I reached acceptance. Wrong! It's not a line, but rather, a circle—a carousel of emotions that range from denial, to anger, to guilt, to depression, to acceptance, and around and around and around again. And yet, life persists.

Lately I have been going through Jen's writing. I always knew how prophetic and spiritual my daughter was. My wise, wise Jennifer in her last words, has ultimately given me the strength to go on, to believe in miracles.

Well before she knew she was dying, Jen shared a remarkable quote on Facebook for all the world to see. "Few souls ever wrote about rending the veils of illusion asunder to uncover love more gut wrenchingly than Rumi

## Chapter Seventy-two

—one of the most outstanding, romantic, spiritual poets of all time."

> "Your body is away from me
> But there is a window open
> from my heart to yours.
> From this window, like the moon
> I keep sending news secretly."
>
> *Rumi*

After her diagnosis, while undergoing treatment and hoping for a cure, Jen wrote,

> "I have been stripped down past my clothes to my bones and marrow, to curvy scans of my body that show everything, as they expose my very soul to strangers and to God. I have been forced into this submission against my will. I will make beauty of this. I will expose the weakness of this flesh, my flesh, and learn of a painful purpose, a deeper meaning. I will let those I love see how I really feel. I will let them see me vulnerable, and yet know all the limits and barriers to love are released and wild, and as mysterious as stars of light in the darkness. Everything in my vision dims to encompass the undying, unending limits of love."

## Chapter Seventy-two

I am working hard to have half the faith my daughter managed, and her words are helping me. The truth is that I will never get over the grief I feel—nor do I wish to. That would mean forgetting. That I never want to do. Jen's death touched all of us who loved her. Knowing Jen, loving her, has become part of our ongoing reality.

She will shine forth from her daughter, her husband, her family, her close friends in a way that makes us all better people. Her memory will live on for as long as we are alive, and then beyond in the stories that will be told. She will endure.

Jen used to carry the book, 'The Prophet', by Gibran with her. It is now with Gibran's words that I finish writing this book. Jen would love that.

> *"For what is it to die but to stand*
> *naked in the wind and to*
> *melt into the sun?*
> *And what is it to cease breathing*
> *but to free the breath from*
> *its restless tides, that it may*
> *rise and expand and seek*
> *God unencumbered?*
> *Only when you drink from the river*
> *of silence shall you indeed*
> *sing and when you have*
> *reached the mountain top*
> *then shall begin to climb.*
> *And when the earth shall claim*
> *your limbs, then shall you*
> *truly dance."*
> *(Kahlil Gibran, The Prophet)*

www.ingramcontent.com/pod-product-compliance
Lightning Source LLC
Chambersburg PA
CBHW060550230426
43670CB00011B/1757